The
Space of
Literature

The
Space of
Literature

Maurice Blanchot

Translated, with an Introduction, by Ann Smock

University of
Nebraska Press
Lincoln,
London
1982

L'Espace littéraire
© Éditions Gallimard, 1955
Introduction © 1982, by the University of Nebraska Press
All rights reserved
Manufactured in the United States of America
The paper in this book meets the guidelines for
permanance and durability of the Committee on
Production Guidelines for Book Longevity
of the Council on Library Resources.

Library of Congress Cataloging in Publication Data

Blanchot, Maurice.
The space of literature.

Includes bibliographical references.
1. Literature – Philosophy.   2. Creation
(Literary, artistic, etc.)   I. Title.
PN45.B42413   801   82-2062
ISBN 0-8032-1166-X   AACR2

A book, even a fragmentary one, has a center which attracts it. This center is not fixed, but is displaced by the pressure of the book and circumstances of its composition. Yet it is also a fixed center which, if it is genuine, displaces itself, while remaining the same and becoming always more central, more hidden, more uncertain and more imperious. He who writes the book writes it out of desire for this center and out of ignorance. The feeling of having touched it can very well be only the illusion of having reached it. When the book in question is one whose purpose is to elucidate, there is a kind of methodological good faith in stating toward what point it seems to be directed: here, toward the pages entitled "Orpheus' Gaze."

Contents

Translator's
Introduction

Why is it that, notwithstanding all the other means of investigating and ordering the world which mankind has developed, and in spite of all the reservations great poets have expressed about their own endeavor, we are still interested in literature? What *is* literature, and what is implied about our learning in general and about its history, if it must be said at this late date that something we call literature has never stopped fascinating us? Maurice Blanchot asks this question with such infinite patience — with so much care and precision — that it has come to preoccupy a whole generation of French critics and social commentators. Hence Blanchot's imposing reputation.

The list of postwar writers in France who have responded to his emphasis on the question of literature and its implications for all our questions is long and impressive. Their names are associated with the most provocative intellectual developments of recent times: not only have Jean-Paul Sartre, Georges Poulet, and Jean Starobinski written about Blanchot, not only Emmanuel Levinas, Georges Bataille, Michel Leiris, and Pierre Klossowski, but also Michel Foucault, Jacques Derrida, Jean-Luc Nancy, and Philippe Lacoue-Labarthe.[1] One way of indicating Blanchot's enormous importance in French thought during the last half century is by reference to Jeffrey Mehlman's commentary in the pages of *Modern*

[1] A lengthy bibliography of Blanchot's works and of studies about him by others may be consulted in *Sub-stance*, no. 14 (1976), an issue entirely devoted to his writing. Here, I simply draw the reader's attention to essays by Georges Poulet, Jean Starobinski, Emmanuel Levinas, Michel Foucault, and Roger Laporte, among others, which appeared in *Critique*, no. 229 (June 1966). Jean-Paul Sartre's commentary, "*Aminadab*; ou, du fantastique considéré comme un langage," appears in *Situations I* (Paris: Gallimard, 1947). Roger Laporte's and Bernard Noël's *Deux lectures de Maurice Blanchot* (Montpellier: Fata Morgana, 1973), should also be mentioned. Emmanuel Levinas's book, *Sur Maurice Blanchot*

Language Notes.[2] When Mehlman, certainly one of the most informed and lively interpreters of modern French letters to an American readership, undertakes to bring this very modernity radically into doubt, he begins with a reading of Blanchot's earliest publications: as though Blanchot's work were a key—*the* point to tackle. The present translation of *L'Espace littéraire*, a book from the middle of Blanchot's career which elaborates many of the issues central to his entire work, should serve to help Americans understand what is at stake in an ongoing assessment of contemporary French thought.

It would be wrong, however, to imply that Blanchot's writing has escaped until now the attention of serious readers in this country. In fact, his work has influenced a good deal of recent American criticism whose object is to question the critical enterprise itself and its relation to the nature of writing. Blanchot provides a model of literary study because, as Geoffrey Hartman says, his criticism always goes from the work under discussion to the problematic nature of literature. "He illumines, therefore, the literary activity in general as well as in this or that

---

(Montpellier: Fata Morgana, 1975), is of particular interest; Pierre Klossowski wrote an essay of that same title which is printed in *Un Si Funeste Désir* (Paris: Gallimard, 1963). For Jacques Derrida's reading of Blanchot, the reader may wish to see "Living On," in *Deconstruction and Criticism* (New Haven, Conn.: Yale University Press, 1979). Finally, I note a volume to which Jean-Luc Nancy and Philippe Lacoue-Labarthe, among others, contributed, *Misère de la littérature* (Paris: Christian Bourgois, 1978). Here, the essays cannot be said to be *on* Blanchot. A short piece written by him, "Il n'est d'explosion . . . ," opens the book, and by implication, the "literary space" to which the authors of the following texts feel they belong.

[2] Jeffrey Mehlman, "Blanchot at *Combat*: Of Literature and Terror," *Modern Language Notes*, French Issue, 95 (1980): 808–29. Mehlman's essay draws attention to Blanchot's political writings during the 1930s. Indeed, between 1930 and 1940, Blanchot was an active contributor to right-wing journals in France (see Jean-Louis Loubet del Bayle, *Les Nonconformistes des années* 30, Paris: le Seuil, 1969). The war ended this particular—and, in light of his subsequent reputation, surprising—engagement, but not his attention to political issues. Blanchot's literary reflections after the war led him to take, notably in 1958 and in 1968, a different sort of position entirely: a leftist one. He was, for example, one of the initiators of the manifesto called *Le Manifeste des* 121, supporting the right of Frenchmen to refuse to serve in the army during the Algerian War (see the volume intitled *Le Droit à l'insoumission* [Paris: Maspéro, 1961], which assembles, around the manifesto itself, numerous texts attesting to the political debate it elicited). The relation between Blanchot's initial political views and his later ones, and the connection between these views and his critical and literary work, are very important and complicated problems which Mehlman begins to elucidate. No doubt they have significant implications for contemporary French thought in general. They require, in my view, a great deal of further consideration. I cite Mehlman's text, not as the definitive word in this matter, but primarily in order to suggest how much is generally recognized to hang upon Blanchot's writing: the very character of critical reflection in France today.

text."[3] Paul de Man included in *Blindness and Insight* an important chapter on Blanchot's reading of Mallarmé in which he examines central sections of *L'Espace littéraire*.[4] Edward Said, to give another example, refers in *Beginnings* to Blanchot's reflections on the "origin" of literature, and he too cites *L'Espace littéraire*.[5]

In order to suggest the unusual character of Blanchot's appeal and the unsettling force of his writing, we ought to include here another statement of Hartman's: "Blanchot's work offers no point of approach whatsoever"; or even this remark of Poulet's, which I translate somewhat freely: "Blanchot is an even greater waste of time than Proust."[6] For, surely, the significance of a book like *L'Espace littéraire* lies in its constant association of literature's purest and most authentic grandeur with just such expressions as "wasted time." It presents the literary work as that which permits no approach other than wasted steps; it uninterruptedly expresses the incomparable passion which literature commands.

Its purpose, even its mission — for this is a term Blanchot somewhat startlingly employs — is to interrupt the purposeful steps we are always taking toward deeper understanding and a surer grasp upon things. It wants to make us hear, and become unable to ignore, the stifled call of a language spoken by no one, which affords no grasp upon anything. For this distress, this utter insecurity, is, Blanchot states, "the source of all authenticity."

In dreams, Blanchot says, one sometimes thinks one knows one is dreaming, but only dreams this. In the same way, the reader of *L'Espace littéraire* imagines that, alongside Blanchot, he is in search of certain answers. He is aware, he thinks, of the difficulties, the dangerous confusions, and therefore he is not at their mercy, but more than likely to see the light eventually or, in other words, to awaken. He has yet, however, to begin the dream; he has yet to see that he is in the dark.

---

[3]Geoffrey Hartman, "Maurice Blanchot: Philosopher-Novelist," *Beyond Formalism* (New Haven, Conn: Yale University Press, 1970).

[4]Paul de Man, "Impersonality in the Criticism of Maurice Blanchot," *Blindness and Insight* (Oxford: Oxford University Press, 1971). This essay appeared first in French in *Critique*, no. 229 [June 1966], as "La Circularité de l'interprétation dans l'oeuvre critique de Maurice Blanchot."

[5]Edward Said, *Beginnings* (Baltimore: Johns Hopkins University Press, 1975).

[6]Hartman, *Beyond Formalism*, p. 93. Georges Poulet: "aussi, beaucoup plus radicalement encore que Proust, Maurice Blanchot apparaît-il comme l'homme du

By the end, the reader is able to make out some important questions: What moves a writer to write? What is the origin of his undertaking, and how does this origin determine the nature of his creativity? What is the role of the reader? How is the work's meaning communicated? How do reading and writing relate to other human endeavors? How are literary, philosophical, social and political history intertwined? Certainly, one does pursue these difficult questions in the pages of *L'Espace littéraire*. One pursues them, moreover, through what are without doubt some of the most perceptive and engaging discussions in existence on Mallarmé, on Kafka, on Rilke, and on Hölderlin. This gratifying process, however, leads to where one thought it began: to the difficulties, the questions, as though they—the very obstacles along the way, marking and measuring the approach (*"l'approche de l'espace littéraire"*)—had been the answers already, wonderfully transparent, though now they arise opaque and strange, and as though one were just now, when long departed deep within *L'Espace littéraire*, ready to begin approaching it.

Such paradoxes are characteristic of Blanchot's work. They present to the reader difficulties of an unusual sort: difficulties which it is difficult to confront, to encounter, problems it is hard to know one is having. Hence the uncanny ease which one also experiences. I first discovered Blanchot's critical work in a university course on fantastic literature. Ever since, it has seemed to me that complaints about his abstruse qualities express readers' premonition of the eeriest limpidity, their foreboding sense of the incredible lightness of the task before them. The muscles they have limbered up in readiness will not be necessary. To be sure, Blanchot's books take for granted a considerable erudition on the reader's part; he ranges familiarly over world literature and philosophy. But they are not aimed at experts or connoisseurs, just at readers. And reading is the simplest thing, he says. It requires no talent, no gifts, no special knowledge, no singular strength at all. But weakness, uncertainty—yes, in abundance.

It calls upon uncertainty, I was suggesting, about uncertainty itself: uncertainty about limits such as those that distinguish the dark and the light, the obscurities of the work itself and its elucidation, the inside and the outside of the text—literature and criticism. Still,

---

'temps perdu'" ("Thus, much more radically even than Proust, Maurice Blanchot appears as a man of 'lost time'" ("Maurice Blanchot, critique et romancier," *Critique*, no. 229 [June 1966]).

L'Espace littéraire retains plenty of the outward signs of straightforward discussion. Among its paradoxes, moreover, there are, not infrequently, aphorisms, pleasing in their definitive tone: "Art is primarily the consciousness of unhappiness, not its consolation," for example. Or: "The central point of the work of art is the work as origin, the point which cannot be reached, yet the only one which is worth reaching." In fact, *L'Espace littéraire* is practically the last book in which Blanchot allowed himself such resoundingly definite postulates. It was published by Gallimard in 1955 after a number of fictions (for example, *Thomas l'obscur, L'Arrêt de mort, Le Très-Haut*) and several critical works (notably *Faux Pas, Lautréamont et Sade, La Part du feu*).[7] Thereafter, the relation between critical discussion and its object becomes ever more problematic and the distinction between Blanchot's own critical texts and his fictional narratives less pertinent. From *L'Attente l'oubli* (Paris: Gallimard, 1962) to *La Folie du jour* (Montpellier: Fata Morgana, 1973) and *L'Ecriture du désastre* (Paris: Gallimard, 1980), it is increasingly doubtful not only whether literature is something about which one can adequately speak but also whether there is any such thing as the literature about which we do, in any case, speak. In other words, it is ever harder to be sure that questions such as "What is literature?" or even "Is literature?" are not themselves already, or merely, literature. Is it into literature at last, or finally out of its shadowy domain, that *Le Pas au-delà* (Paris: Gallimard, 1973) would step? It is not possible to say; it is possible only to retrace the step which, repetitively marking their separation, renders within and without indistinguishable. The reader of *L'Espace littéraire* will be in a good position to understand why this is the case, even if he must remain inconsolable.

In *L'Espace littéraire*, as in Blanchot's work generally, there is a continually implicit, and often explicit, reference to German philosophy: especially to Hegel, to Heidegger — whose meditation, through the works of Hölderlin, upon the essence of poetry is particularly significant

---

[7]All the works cited here, with the exception of *Lautréamont et Sade* (Paris: Editions de Minuit, 1949), were published in Paris by Gallimard: *Thomas l'Obscur* in 1941, *L'Arrêt de mort* and *Le Très-Haut* in 1948, *Faux Pas* in 1943, *La Part du feu* in 1949.

Both *Thomas l'Obscur* and *L'Arrêt de mort* have been translated into English. Robert Lamberton is the translator of *Thomas l'Obscur (Thomas the Obscure* [New York: D. Lewis, 1973])—or, more precisely, of the "new version" of this narrative published by Blanchot in 1950, nine years after the first edition. Lydia Davis translated *L'Arrêt de mort (Death Sentence* [Tarrytown, N.Y.: Station Hill Press, 1978]). These are, so far, the only books by Blanchot, besides the present volume, available in their entirety in English.

for Blanchot—and to Nietzsche. Blanchot's reading of Hegel bears the distinct mark of Bataille's; likewise, he shares his approach to Heidegger with Levinas to a certain extent. And when he quotes Nietzsche's hearty praise of suicide, we should also hear an echo of Kirilov's vacillating distress.

With Hegel, Blanchot recognizes negativity as the moving force of the dialectic. It is the power that informs history; it is death, creative and masterful, at work in the world. Indeed, Blanchot hails the impending completion of this labor which is the realization of human possibilities, the unfolding of truth. And he acknowledges that this progress—whereby meanings are determined, values assigned, mysteries solved; whereby man liberates himself from the unknown and imposes his autonomous will in the clear light of day—leaves art, the preserve of ambiguities and indecision, behind, just as it suppresses and surpasses the gods, the mysteries of the sacred. The work attains its ultimate and essential form, not in the work of art, but in that work which is the gradual achievement of human mastery and freedom: history—history as a whole, the total realization of that liberating process. And yet, Blanchot's attention is dedicated to that in the work which does not fit into this whole, this culmination. He has given himself up to something belonging only to art, which will not settle for the status assigned to art by history's sovereign movement (monument to man's creativity, repository of cultural values, or object offered up to pure esthetic enjoyment). In art Blanchot hears, murmuring with mute insistence, the very source of creativity. And this source is inexhaustible. Truth and its satisfactions cannot finish off the power of negativity.

This is the point at which we can grasp the importance of Bataille in Blanchot's thought. Indeed, much of *L'Espace littéraire* reads like a conversation between Blanchot and Bataille, a conversation that continues in *L'Entretien infini* (Paris: Gallimard, 1969), and *L'Amitié* (Paris: Gallimard, 1971). We hear it in works of Bataille as well (in *L'Expérience intérieure*, for example).[8] It is a conversation sustained by a common awareness of negativity as excess, foreign to purpose. Death is an infinitely futile *more*, which will not *serve* to achieve anything. Compared to this fruitless expenditure, the mastery which the use of death affords is perhaps a poor thing; in any case, it cannot use death up. Death subsists, and subsisting, proves itself to be a source of power

[8]Georges Bataille, *L'Expérience intérieure*, in *Oeuvres complètes* (Paris: Gallimard, 1973), vol. 5.

that power is powerless to exhaust — a nothing that exceeds everything. Never providing anything like satisfaction, it is unspeakably desirable. Both Blanchot and Bataille tell of desire, or the *experience* of the infinite remainder: power, reaching as high as it can, longs to reach its own possibility — death, its very source and essence — by undergoing the measurelessness of impotence. Both writers name the contradiction in such an alliance, or the intimacy of such strife, "communication." It risks, with the unjustifiable audacity Blanchot terms inspiration, all of language, everything that might ever be communicated, and the whole world that words put at our disposal.

Thus when Blanchot borrows Hegel's perspective and addresses us as if from the end of history when all that can be has been accomplished, he does so, not to announce the truth as it discloses itself in its realized wholeness to the mind whose comprehension is likewise complete, but rather in order to make us hear what Heidegger urges: let the sole be-ing — man — whose being stems from his capacity not to be, affirm that "not," the most proper of all his possibilities and the one proper to him alone, the possibility of impossibility (see *Being and Time*, sec. 50). This is the possibility which everything that is possible hides; it has had, in-deed, to be suppressed in order that anything be possible, in order that there be a world and the history of this world. But it must be resolutely acknowledged, if ever there is to be authenticity.

This demand is the one Blanchot associates with the work of art. The work requires death, the source, to *be* in the work; it demands that in it the ending, which initiates all beginnings, swell up as the essence of all swelling, all unfurling and flowering. It wants disappearance to come forth. It asks in other words that Being, which by receding opens the space in which beings appear, come into this clearing. The work asks that a retreat, an obscuring or effacement, show, or that the forgetfulness which inaugurates thought return to it.

Whenever Blanchot speaks about this care, this concern in the work for the origin of the work, we recognize his proximity to Heidegger. And all of *L'Espace littéraire* is imbued with care: *le souci de l'origine, le souci de l'oeuvre,* anxious solicitude for a time before the time when beings sup-plant being and submit to the command of the objectifying, acquisitive subject; concern for a time other than the time measured by the gradual reduction of the irreconcilably alien to the homogeneity of all that is com-prehensively mastered. To the extent that in the work of art the impossible is realized as such, art alone answers, with true fidelity, to the requirement of Heideggerian authenticity. Yet there is also in *L'Espace littéraire,* as in all of Blanchot—and this accounts for Blanchot's kinship with Levinas—concern for being's effacement itself: concern, precisely, *lest* it show, lest being be robbed of that indefiniteness, that seclusion, that *foreignness* from which it is inseparable. Together Blanchot and Levinas reverse the terms in which *Being and Time* poses the question of authenticity. Their concern is not to fail death through very resoluteness, forgetting that only forgetfulness keeps faith with it and that estrangement is its unique intimacy. The *unconcern*, however, which Blanchot locates at the very center of his concern, as well as his insistence upon the irreducibly *impersonal* character of the origin and his paradoxical way of making *breach* or *tear* synonymous with intimacy, turn this book more decisively in Bataille's direction than in Levinas's.

The estrangement from death, moreover, which Blanchot considers to be required of the writer by literature, even as literature requires of him that he greet and affirm death, determines that the writer never, properly speaking, be favored with any requirement at all. He has no vocation; he is one deprived of the very call that haunts him. That is why the quotations from Nietzsche in *L'Espace littéraire*, which almost all express the admirably bold refusal to cringe and hide from death, are presented with irony. The suicide manqué, indeed, even the baseness apparent in his inability to face death honestly—head-on—expresses more truly, perhaps, than anything else the essence of death, which is always to elude an authentic confrontation. It never presents itself for a duel, but represents itself; it comes disguising its coming. In fact, its essence is not to come at all—ever—but ever to come again. In later works by Blanchot, the Nietzsche of the Eternal Return is a constant reference. He is never cited in *L'Espace littéraire*, but he is never far.

For when disappearance appears, it is its *apparition*. Likewise, when the end begins, when it swells and blossoms as the truth of all beginnings (and that it should, we recall, is the demand Blanchot hears the work making), it is not the end itself that starts, and it is no real start that occurs. Rather, the impossibility of there ever being a first time starts over again, in the guise of an interminable ending. Then the work—at the very instant of its apotheosis, its devastating announcement that it *is*, and nothing more—subsides, engulfed in duplicity; it enters "the eternal torment of dying"; it draws the writer with it into this error which sustains no resolute being-for-death. It disguises what reveals it and only lets itself be discovered by what perverts it. Is that why it always seems to have the innocence of something never exposed, perfectly intact? Is it like a flower just on the sheer verge of blooming because clouds of inauthenticity enfold and conserve it? No one knows, as Blanchot regularly repeats.

His writing recedes toward such questions. They are the sole answers he presumes to propose. "The authentic answer is always the question's vitality," he writes. "It can close in around the question, but it does so in order to preserve the question by keeping it open." Perhaps this is a good way of suggesting once again the character of Blanchot's work which renders it somewhat alien to us in this country, but also fascinating, like a mirror. The Anglo-American critical tradition might be said to elucidate, and thus to honor, the actual object which writers offer us. We take the work to be what artists make in the course of a labor, a struggle perhaps, to which they alone are equal; or perhaps they bring it back to us from depths to which they alone descend. Attentive to masterful technique and perfected form, we seek to comprehend the profound *achievement* of the blackest text by Kafka, say. We try to do justice to its strong and genuine character, even if we acknowledge shifty ambiguity to be the necessary vehicle of this authenticity, or recognize playfulness as the special grace of this rigorous perfection, or understand that misery is what this treasure holds, weakness what this awesome manifestation of strength has to express. But the Kafka that concerns Blanchot is the nameless young man who cannot seem to write at all. He is reduced to lamentable games. The author of *The Metamorphosis* had to suppress and surpass him. The profundity of *The Metamorphosis* is, for Blanchot, the infinite depths of uncertainty and futility which its perfection masks—which the work shows *only* by masking—but which we seem actually to see laid bare sometimes when the masterpiece, like Eurydice when Orpheus looks back, disappears.

To *see* something *disappear*: again, this is an experience which cannot actually start. Nor, therefore, can it ever come to an end. Such, Blanchot insists, is the literary experience: an ordeal in which what we are able to do (for example, see), becomes our powerlessness; becomes, for instance, that terribly strange form of blindness which is the phantom, or the image, of the clear gaze—an incapacity to stop seeing what is not there to be seen.

I do not wish to overemphasize the problems of translation which I have encountered. By comparison to many French critical texts currently being translated, this one appears quite simple: word play, for example, is not striking in it, not immediately so in any event, and it does not depend upon any unusual terminology. However, I would like to discuss here three expressions in particular because they are something like the key words of the book; they also permit me to restate in more concrete terms some of the issues I have evoked above.

The first of these expressions appears in the title: *L'Espace littéraire*. The word *espace* recurs regularly in the titles of chapters: "Approche de l'espace littéraire," "L'Espace et l'exigence de l'oeuvre," "L'Oeuvre et l'espace de la mort." It means "space," the region toward which whoever reads or writes is drawn — literature's "domain." But, although words such as "region" or "domain" or "realm" are often used to designate this zone, it implies the withdrawal of what is ordinarily meant by "place"; it suggests the site of this withdrawal. Literature's space is like the place where someone dies: a nowhere, Blanchot says, which is *here*. No one enters it, though no one who is at all aware of it can leave: it is all departure, moving off, *éloignement*. It is frequently called *le dehors*, "the outside." Here we might think again of the dreamer we evoked earlier in this discussion who, dreaming that he only dreams, falls back into the dream to the very degree that he has the impression of freedom from it: it could just as well be said that he never enters the dream at all; he only ever dreams he does. Literature's "space" is likewise inaccessible *and* inescapable; it is its very own displacement or removal. It is the space separating this space from itself. In this strange ambiguity literature dwells, as in a preserve.

Yet "in" must always be taken back, for literature's space shelters nothing within it: it is also called *le vide*, "the void." Sometimes it is associated with the anonymity of big cities, sometimes with the gap left by the absence of the gods, but sometimes, too, with what Rilke calls "the Open," or the "world's inner space," the intimacy of an expansive welcome, the inward yes which death can say in the song of one who consents to fall silent and disappear. Or it is connected with the interval, which for Hölderlin is the sacred, between gods that abandon the world and men who, likewise, turn away from God — the sheer void in between, which the poet must keep pure. Almost always, it is the origin which is anterior to any beginning, the image or echo of beginning — that immense fund of impotence, the infinitely futile wherewithal to start over and over again. Literature's space, in other words — the void which literature introduces in place of the place it takes — is analogous to the "other time" in the time measured by achievements: sterile, inert time, "the time of distress." But the very freshness of every dawn is safeguarded in this distress and nowhere else, which is why literature demands that we return there (though this justification is never granted), risking the clear light of day in the name of sunshine, but more than just that: jeopardizing even this capacity of ours to take risks in the name of something, for some purpose.

With considerable regularity, literature's "space" is described as exile or banishment, and the writer as one wandering in the desert, like Kafka far from Canaan, too weak to collaborate in the active concerns of competent men; but then, too, the desert is a privileged zone of freedom and solitude, and if literature is exiled from the world of valuable achievements, it is also exempted from the world's demands. It has to bear no responsibility for anything; it is kept safe to itself: the desert is its refuge. Or it would be, if to be so gratuitous were not a grave danger for literature, and also if the desert were a *here* one could actually reach. Kafka is never quite convinced that he isn't still in Canaan after all.

Thus, *l'espace littéraire*, or *l'espace de l'oeuvre*, is the "distance" of the work, or of literature, with respect, not only to "every other object which exists," but with respect to itself. The work is remote from itself, or not quite itself. For example, when it isn't finished yet. But when it is done, when it comes into its own, this distance persists: it constitutes the opening of the work onto nothing but itself — this opening, this vacancy. And since the work appears, then, as pure deferral, a void or vacuum, it lends itself to being filled up with everything it isn't: with useful meanings, for example, which multiply and change as history progresses. Or this void can masquerade as the prestigious aura that surrounds the timeless masterpiece in its museum case. Yet these apparent travesties, these various ways in which the work is misrepresented and forgotten, sustain it; they protect its essence, which is to disappear. They provide it with its "space," which is *not* its location. But this is not to say that literature is to be found anywhere else.

I had thought of proposing as a title for this book "Literature's Remove." I hoped thereby to capture not only literature's distance from the world, and not only this distance as literature's preserve, but also that when "space" is literature's, it is space opened by that opening's absence: by the removal of that very interval, which is kept, as if for some other time, in reserve.

"Remove" could suggest a reflective distance, and it might be thought that literature involves a separation from the world permitting contemplation or critical interpretation of things and events. This sense of the term "remove" is in fact operative in *L'Espace littéraire*. Or rather, its mirror image is. For literature's "space," Blanchot emphasizes, is the resurgence of the distance at which we must place anything we wish to understand or aim to grasp. Literature is this remove coming back to us, returning like an echo; and now it is no longer a handy gap, a familiar and useful nothing, but an unidentifiable something, the strange immediacy, foreign to presence and to any present, of remoteness itself. It grasps *us*, and it removes us from our power to grasp or appropriate anything whatever—especially literature.

I have, in fact, used "remove" in the body of the text as one translation of *l'écart*, of *l'éloignement*, sometimes of *la distance*, occasionally of *la réserve*. But *l'espace*, which should surely be understood as related to these terms indicating separation (and linked thus to the French word *espacement*), is always translated somewhat lamely as "space," primarily in the interests of consistency. For the word *espace* is the main constant in this book, and if, in order not to sacrifice the significance of its repetition, I had translated it, each time it appears, as "remove," there would have been certain inaccuracies. "The Space of Literature," then, seeks to preserve a semblance of what seems to have been on Blanchot's part a move to unify the book (to give it the strangest unity): to associate in the title—*L'Espace littéraire*—"l'espace de l'oeuvre" and "l'espace de la mort," the work's space and death's.

The French text practically always distinguishes between the word *oeuvre* and the word *travail*: between the "work of art" and "work" in the sense of productive labor—man's action upon nature, his mastery and appropriation of the given. Thus, *le souci de l'oeuvre*, "concern for the work of art" (which is also the work's own troubled concern), is regularly contrasted with *le souci réalisateur*, "the concern for real achievements," which implies effective action. This real purposefulness is the process by which history unfolds, by which darkness is made to recede before the broad light of day. Man becomes free; he discovers his potentialities and fulfills them. All this takes place in what Blanchot regularly terms "the world," or on the level he calls "the worldly plane." The world is this historical process; it is its own gradual realization. But the artist is ineffectual. He has no place in the world. It is not that he belongs to what we ordinarily think of as the other world. If he is allied to the sacred, this is because he belongs neither to this world nor to any other, but to the "other of all worlds" in our own.

He is idle, inert, "désoeuvré." He is "out of work" to the very extent that his sole concern is for the *work*. For *l'oeuvre* is impotence endlessly affirmed. *Le travail*, on the other hand, is negativity in action, death as power and possibility.

L'oeuvre, then, immediately implies its revocation: perhaps one could say that in Blanchot *l'oeuvre* and *le désoeuvrement* are translations of each other. The difference, in other words, between *l'oeuvre* and *le travail* is that while *le travail* is diametrically opposed to inaction and passivity, *l'oeuvre* requires them. Indeed, Blanchot frequently describes *l'oeuvre*, not as the union of contraries, but as their restless alliance, their torn intimacy. He treats the word *oeuvre* the way he treats the word *inspiration*: the title of the section of this book devoted to inspiration is "Inspiration, Lack of Inspiration."

I have consistently used the English word "work" to refer to *l'oeuvre*, the work of art. For *travail* I have used various expressions such as "productive or purposeful activity," "labor," "effort," "real endeavor," "effective or useful action." I have most often translated *désoeuvrement* as "inertia," thereby emphasizing the paradox whereby the artist's relation to the work, the demand which he feels is made of him that there *be* a work, overwhelms him, not with creative powers, but on the contrary, with their exhaustion. The approach of the work does not elicit in him the strength to reach and achieve it, but immobilizes him. It calls upon his weakness, the incapacity in him to achieve anything at all; it *inspires* in him a kind of numbness or stupefaction. When Blanchot says of the writer that he is *désoeuvré*, I have written that the writer is idled or out of work, thereby emphasizing how the work to be realized requires nothing of him, gives him nothing to do—perversely demands that he *do*: nothing—but also stressing how the work excludes him, sets him *outside* it. He never knows the work except as the terrible immediacy of this dismissal. It must also be understood that the work thus presents itself to him as its absence. *Le désoeuvrement* is the absence of the work, "l'absence de l'oeuvre." I come closest to expressing this when I translate *désoeuvrement* as "lack of work."

Occasionally, Blanchot does use the word *oeuvre* to refer to something other than the work of art: notably, to history as a whole—completed history as mankind's *oeuvre*, the total realization of human freedom and the ultimate goal of humanity. The phrase *l'oeuvre humaine en général* recurs several times in section VII where, precisely, Blanchot is stressing a tendency on the part of the artist, who acknowledges only *l'oeuvre* as his task, to *confuse* this work with the work of history. Or, if he doesn't make this mistake—and to the very extent that he doesn't—his tendency to renounce his own task in favor of the other. I have translated *l'oeuvre humaine en général* as "the human undertaking as a whole," or "the overall work of humanity."

Finally, in three or four spots, the expressions "to be at work" (*à l'oeuvre*) and "to go back to work" (*se remettre à l'oeuvre*) appear in Blanchot's text. The writer, for example, inasmuch as he is "out of work," can only ever return to the work (*se remettre à l'oeuvre*): reapply himself to it tirelessly and uselessly, go back to what he cannot get to—*go back to work*. Or the interminably affirmative No, which keeps on revoking all achievements, is "at work" (*à l'oeuvre*) in the work—causing its presence endlessly to revert to absence, causing this regression infernally to emerge, causing the inexhaustibly persistent presence of absence. These examples account, I believe, for all departures from the general rule: "work" always means the "work of art," as opposed to *le travail*, just as lucidity in the deep of night means the phantom lucidity of the insomniac poet, as opposed both to the good sense of broad daylight and to the peaceful sleep, the honest oblivion, which reason requires at regular intervals.

My translation of the recurring word *exigence* is awkward. This word appears, for example, in one of the section titles quoted earlier: "L'Espace et l'exigence de l'oeuvre"; another section is entitled "Rilke et l'exigence de la mort." What is the *demand* of death? What does the work want? *L'exigence de l'oeuvre* means not simply what is required of the artist in order to make a work of art—the skill and patience that give form and coherence—though the work does demand these. Neither is *l'exigence de l'oeuvre* simply the demand that there *be* a work, although the implications of this demand are certainly part of Blanchot's concern. *L'exigence de l'oeuvre* does mean the peculiarly harsh demand that the work makes of the "creator," which is different from the demands of any other task: that all his powers be plunged in weakness, that he come into an immense wealth of silence and inertia. But still more, the work's demand is this: that Orpheus look back. That suddenly, desire should wreck everything—the desire to look at the dark *when this naked mask is showing*, and not when, veiled by clarity, clothed in the light, it can be seen.

No one begins to write, Blanchot says, who is not already somehow on the verge of this ruinous look back, and yet the sole approach to that turning point is writing. The form of the work's demand is circular. It is like the demand Blanchot imagines being made of Abraham: that, having no son, he kill his son. And thus it is like *l'exigence de la mort*. What is one to do to die? More than everything is required, less than nothing is called for.

Ann Smock

The
Space of
Literature

The
Essential
Solitude

❚

It seems that we learn something about art when we experience what the word *solitude* is meant to designate. This word has been much abused. Still, what does the expression *to be alone* signify? When is one alone? Asking this question should not simply lead us into melancholy reflections. Solitude as the world understands it is a hurt which requires no further comment here.

We do not intend to evoke the artist's solitude either — that which is said to be necessary to him for the practice of his art. When Rilke writes to the countess of Solms-Laubach (August 3, 1907), "For weeks, except for two short interruptions, I haven't pronounced a single word; my solitude has finally encircled me and I am inside my efforts just as the core is in the fruit," the solitude of which he speaks is not the essential solitude. It is concentration.

The Solitude of the Work

In the solitude of the work — the work of art, the literary work — we discover a more essential solitude. It excludes the complacent isolation of individualism; it has nothing to do with the quest for singularity. The fact that one sustains a stalwart attitude throughout the disciplined course of the day does not dissipate it. He who writes the work is set aside; he who has written it is dismissed. He who is dismissed, moreover, doesn't know it. This ignorance preserves him. It distracts him by authorizing him to persevere. The writer never knows whether the work is done. What he has finished in one book, he starts over or destroys in another. Valéry, celebrating this infinite quality which the work enjoys, still sees only its least problematic aspect. That the work is infinite means, for him, that the artist, though unable to finish it, can nevertheless make it the delimited site of an endless task whose incompleteness develops the mastery of the mind, expresses this mastery, expresses it by developing it in the form of power. At a certain moment, circumstances — that is, history, in the person of the publisher or in the guise of financial exigencies, social duties — pronounce the missing end, and the artist, freed by a dénouement of pure constraint, pursues the unfinished matter elsewhere.

The infinite nature of the work, seen thus, is just the mind's infiniteness. The mind wants to fulfill itself in a single work, instead of realizing itself in an infinity of works and in history's ongoing movement. But Valéry was by no means a hero. He found it good to talk about everything, to write on everything: thus the scattered totality of the world distracted him from the unique and rigorous totality of the work, from which he amiably let himself be diverted. The *etc.* hid behind the diversity of thoughts and subjects.

However, the work — the work of art, the literary work — is neither finished nor unfinished: it is. What it says is exclusively this: that it is — and nothing more. Beyond that it is nothing. Whoever wants to make it express more finds nothing, finds that it expresses nothing. He whose life depends upon the work, either because he is a writer or because he is a reader, belongs to the solitude of that which expresses nothing except the word *being*: the word which language shelters by hiding it, or causes to appear when language itself disappears into the silent void of the work.

The solitude of the work has as its primary framework the absence of any defining criteria. This absence makes it impossible ever to declare the work finished or unfinished. The work is without any proof, just as it is without any use. It can't be verified. Truth can appropriate it, renown draws attention to it, but the existence it thus acquires doesn't concern it. This demonstrability renders it neither certain nor real — does not make it manifest.

The work is solitary: this does not mean that it remains uncommunicable, that it has no reader. But whoever reads it enters into the affirmation of the work's solitude, just as he who writes it belongs to the risk of this solitude.

The Work, the Book

In order to examine more closely what such statements beckon us toward, perhaps we should try to see where they originate. The writer writes a book, but the book is not yet the work. There is a work only when, through it, and with the violence of a beginning which is proper to it, the word *being* is pronounced. This event occurs when the work becomes the intimacy between someone who writes it and someone who reads it. One might, then, wonder: if solitude is the writer's risk, does it not express the fact that he is turned, oriented toward the open violence of the work, of which he never grasps anything but the substitute — the approach and the illusion in the form of the book? The writer belongs to the work, but what belongs to him is only a book, a mute collection of sterile words, the most insignificant thing in the world. The writer who experiences this void believes only that the work is unfinished, and he thinks that a little more effort, along with some propitious moments, will permit him and him alone to finish it. So he goes back to work. But what he wants to finish by himself remains interminable; it involves him in an illusory task. And the work, finally, knows him not. It closes in around his absence as the impersonal, anonymous affirmation that it is — and nothing more. This is what is meant by the observation that the writer, since he only finishes his work at the moment he dies, never knows of his work. One ought perhaps to turn this remark around. For isn't the writer dead as soon as the work exists? He sometimes has such a presentiment himself: an impression of being ever so strangely out of work.[1]

Noli Me Legere

The same situation can also be described this way: the writer never reads his work. It is, for him, illegible, a secret. He cannot linger in its presence. It is a secret because he is separated from it. However, his inability to read the work is not a purely negative phenomenon. It is, rather, the writer's only real relation to what we call the work. The

[1]This situation is different from that of the man who labors and accomplishes his task only to have it escape him by being transformed in the world. What man makes undergoes transformation, but it undergoes this change in the world, and man recaptures it through the world. Or at least he can regain it if alienation is not immobilized — expropriated for the profit of certain others — but is pursued rather, right up to the world's own full realization.

On the contrary, what the writer aims at is the work, and what he writes is a book. The book, as such, can become an effective event in the world (an action, however, which is always reticent and insufficient), but it is not action that the writer aims at. It is the work. And what makes the book the substitute for the work suffices to make it a thing which, like the work, doesn't stem from the truth of the world, but is almost vain, inasmuch as it has neither the reality of the work nor the seriousness of genuine tasks undertaken in the world.

abrupt *Noli me legere* brings forth, where there is still only a book, the horizon of a different strength. This *Noli me legere* is a fleeting experience, although immediate. It is not the force of an interdict, but, through the play and the sense of words, the insistent, the rude and poignant affirmation that what is there, in the global presence of a definitive text, still witholds itself—the rude and biting void of refusal—or excludes, with the authority of indifference, him who, having written it, yet wants to grasp it afresh by reading it. The impossibility of reading is the discovery that now, in the space opened by creation, there is no more room for creation. And, for the writer, no other possibility than to keep on writing this work. No one who has written the work can linger close to it. For the work is the very decision which dismisses him, cuts him off, makes of him a survivor, without work. He becomes the inert idler upon whom art does not depend.

The writer cannot abide near the work. He can only write it; he can, once it is written, only discern its approach in the abrupt *Noli me legere* which moves him away, which sets him apart or which obliges him to go back to that "separation" which he first entered in order to become attuned to what he had to write. So that now he finds himself as if at the beginning of his task again and discovers again the proximity, the errant intimacy of the outside from which he could not make an abode.

Perhaps this ordeal points us toward what we are seeking. The writer's solitude, that condition which is the risk he runs, seems to come from his belonging, in the work, to what always precedes the work. Through him, the work comes into being; it constitutes the resolute solidity of a beginning. But he himself belongs to a time ruled by the indecisiveness inherent in beginning over again. The obsession which ties him to a privileged theme, which obliges him to say over again what he has already said—sometimes with the strength of an enriched talent, but sometimes with the prolixity of an extraordinarily impoverishing repetitiveness, with ever less force, more monotony—illustrates the necessity, which apparently determines his efforts, that he always come back to the same point, pass again over the same paths, persevere in starting over what for him never starts, and that he belong to the shadow of events, not their reality, to the image, not the object, to what allows words themselves to become images, appearances—not signs, values, the power of truth.

Tyrannical Prehension

Sometimes, when a man is holding a pencil, his hand won't release it no matter how badly he wants to let it go. Instead, the hand tightens rather than open. The other hand intervenes more successfully, but then the hand which one might call sick makes a slow, tentative movement and tries to catch the departing object. The strange thing is the slowness of this movement. The hand moves in a tempo which is scarcely human: not that of viable action, not that of hope either, but rather the shadow of time, the hand being itself the shadow of a hand slipping ghostlike toward an object that has become its own shadow. This hand experiences, at certain moments, a very great need to seize: it must grasp the pencil, it has to. It receives an order, an imperious command. This phenomenon is known as "tyrannical prehension."

The writer seems to be the master of his pen; he can become capable of great mastery over words and over what he wants to make them express. But his mastery only succeeds in putting him, keeping him in contact with the fundamental passivity where the word, no longer anything but its appearance — the shadow of a word — never can be mastered or even grasped. It remains the ungraspable which is also unreleasable: the indecisive moment of fascination.

The writer's mastery is not in the hand that writes, the "sick" hand that never lets the pencil go — that can't let it go because what it holds it doesn't really hold; what it holds belongs to the realm of shadows, and it is itself a shade. Mastery always characterizes the other hand, the one that doesn't write and is capable of intervening at the right moment to seize the pencil and put it aside. Thus mastery consists in the power to stop writing, to interrupt what is being written, thereby restoring to the present instant its rights, its decisive trenchancy.

We must start questioning again. We have said that the writer belongs to the work, but that what belongs to him, what he finishes by himself, is only a book: "by himself" corresponds to the restriction "only." The writer is never face to face with the work, and when there is a work, he doesn't know it; or, more precisely, even this ignorance is unknown to him, is only granted him in the impossibility of reading, the ambiguous experience that puts him back to work.

The writer goes back to work. Why doesn't he cease writing? Why, if he breaks with the work, as Rimbaud did, does this break strike us as a mysterious impossibility? Does he just desire a perfect product, and if he does not cease to work at it, is it simply because perfection is never perfect enough? Does he even write in the expectation of a work? Does he bear it always in mind as that which would put an end to his task, as the goal worthy of so much effort? Not at all. The work is never that in anticipation of which one can write (in prospect of which one would relate to the process of writing as to the exercise of some power).

The fact that the writer's task ends with his life hides another fact: that, through this task, his life slides into the distress of the infinite.

The Interminable, the Incessant

The solitude which the work visits on the writer reveals itself in this: that writing is now the interminable, the incessant. The writer no longer belongs to the magisterial realm where to express oneself means to express the exactitude and the certainty of things and values according to the sense of their limits. What he is to write delivers the one who has to write to an affirmation over which he has no authority, which is itself without substance, which affirms nothing, and yet is not repose, not the dignity of silence, for it is what still speaks when everything has been said. This affirmation doesn't precede speech, because it prevents speech from beginning, just as it takes away from language the right and the power to interrupt itself. To write is to break the bond that unites the word with myself. It is to destroy the relation which, determining that I speak toward "you," gives me room to speak within the understanding which my word receives from you (for my word summons you, and is the summons that begins in me because it finishes in you). To write is to break this bond. To write is, moreover, to withdraw language from the world, to detach it from what makes it a power according to which, when I speak, it is the world that declares itself, the clear light of day that develops through tasks undertaken, through action and time.

Writing is the interminable, the incessant. The writer, it is said, gives up saying "I." Kafka remarks, with surprise, with enchantment, that he has entered into literature as soon as he can substitute "He" for "I." This is true, but the transformation is much more profound. The writer belongs to a language which no one speaks, which is addressed to no one, which has no center, and which reveals nothing. He may believe that he affirms himself in this language, but what he affirms is altogether deprived of self. To the extent that, being a writer, he does justice to what requires writing, he can never again express himself, any more than he can appeal to you, or even introduce another's speech. Where he is, only being speaks — which means that language doesn't speak any more, but is. It devotes itself to the pure passivity of being.

If to write is to surrender to the interminable, the writer who consents to sustain writing's essence loses the power to say "I." And so he loses the power to make others say "I." Thus he can by no means give life to characters whose liberty would be guaranteed by his creative power. The notion of characters, as the traditional form of the novel, is only one of the compromises by which the writer, drawn out of himself by literature in search of its essence, tries to salvage his relations with the world and himself.

To write is to make oneself the echo of what cannot cease speaking — and since it cannot, in order to become its echo I have, in a way, to silence it. I bring to this incessant speech the decisiveness, the authority of my own silence. I make *perceptible*, by my silent mediation, the uninterrupted affirmation, the giant murmuring upon which language opens and thus becomes image, becomes imaginary, becomes a speaking depth, an indistinct plenitude which is empty. This silence has its source in the effacement toward which the writer is drawn. Or else, it is the resource of his mastery, the right of intervention which the hand that doesn't write retains — the part of the writer which can always say no and, when necessary, appeal to time, restore the future.

When we admire the tone of a work, when we respond to its tone as to its most authentic aspect, what are we referring to? Not to style, or to the interest and virtues of the language, but to this silence precisely, this vigorous force by which the writer, having been deprived of himself, having renounced himself, has in this effacement nevertheless maintained the authority of a certain power: the power decisively to be still, so that in this silence what speaks without beginning or end might take on form, coherence, and sense.

The tone is not the writer's voice, but the intimacy of the silence he imposes upon the word. This implies that the silence is still *his* — what remains of him in the discretion that sets him aside. The tone makes great writers, but perhaps the work is indifferent to what makes them great.

In the effacement toward which he is summoned, the "great writer" still holds back; what speaks is no longer he himself, but neither is it the sheer slipping away of no one's word. For he maintains the authoritative though silent affirmation of the effaced "I." He keeps the cutting edge, the violent swiftness of active time, of the instant.

Thus he preserves himself within the work; where there is no more restraint, he contains himself. But the work also retains, because of this, a content. It is not altogether its own interior.

The writer we call classic — at least in France — sacrifices within himself the idiom which is proper to him, but he does so in order to give voice to the universal. The calm of a regular form, the certainty of a language free from idiosyncrasy, where impersonal generality speaks, secures him a relation with truth — with truth which is beyond the person and purports to be beyond time. Then literature has the glorious solitude of reason, that rarefied life at the heart of the whole which would require resolution and courage if this reason were not in fact the stability of an ordered aristocratic society; that is, the noble satisfaction of a part of society which concentrates the whole within itself by isolating itself well above what sustains it.

When to write is to discover the interminable, the writer who enters this region does not leave himself behind in order to approach the universal. He does not move toward a surer world, a finer or better justified world where everything would be ordered according to the clarity of the impartial light of day. He does not discover the admirable language which speaks honorably for all. What speaks in him is the fact that, in one way or another, he is no longer himself; he isn't anyone any more. The third person substituting for the "I": such is the solitude that comes to the writer on account of the work. It does not denote objective disinterestedness, creative detachment. It does not glorify consciousness in someone other than myself or the evolution of a human vitality which, in the imaginary space of the work of art, would retain the freedom to say "I." The third person is myself become no one, my interlocutor turned alien; it is my no longer being able, where I am, to address myself and the inability of whoever addresses me to say "I"; it is his not being himself.

Recourse to the "Journal"

It is perhaps striking that from the moment the work becomes the search for art, from the moment it becomes literature, the writer increasingly feels the need to maintain a relation to himself. His feeling is one of extreme repugnance at losing his grasp upon himself in the interests of that neutral force, formless and bereft of any destiny, which is behind everything that gets written. This repugnance, or apprehension, is revealed by the concern, characteristic of so many authors, to compose what they call

their "journal." Such a preoccupation is far removed from the complacent attitudes usually described as Romantic. The journal is not essentially confessional; it is not one's own story. It is a memorial. What must
the writer remember? Himself: who he is when he isn't writing, when
he lives daily life, when he is alive and true, not dying and bereft of
truth. But the tool he uses in order to recollect himself is, strangely, the
very element of forgetfulness: writing. That is why, however, the truth
of the journal lies not in the interesting, literary remarks to be found
there, but in the insignificant details which attach it to daily reality.
The journal represents the series of reference points which a writer
establishes in order to keep track of himself when he begins to suspect
the dangerous metamorphosis to which he is exposed. It is a route that
remains viable; it is something like a watchman's walkway upon ram-
parts: parallel to, overlooking, and sometimes skirting around the
other path — the one where to stray is the endless task. Here true things
are still spoken of. Here, whoever speaks retains his name and speaks in
this name, and the dates he notes down belong in a shared time where
what happens really happens. The journal — this book which is apparently
altogether solitary — is often written out of fear and anguish at the solitude
which comes to the writer on account of the work.

The recourse to the journal indicates that he who writes doesn't
want to break with contentment. He doesn't want to interrupt the propriety of days which really are days and which really follow one upon the
other. The journal roots the movement of writing in time, in the humble succession of days whose dates preserve this routine. Perhaps what is
written there is already nothing but insincerity; perhaps it is said
without regard for truth. But it is said in the security of the event. It
belongs to occupations, incidents, the affairs of the world — to our active present. This continuity is nil and insignificant, but at least it is irreversible. It is a pursuit that goes beyond itself toward tomorrow, and
proceeds there definitively.

The journal indicates that already the writer is no longer capable of
belonging to time through the ordinary certainty of action, through the
shared concerns of common tasks, of an occupation, through the
simplicity of intimate speech, the force of unreflecting habit. He is no
longer truly historical; but he doesn't want to waste time either, and
since he doesn't know anymore how to do anything but write, at least he
writes in response to his everyday history and in accord with the preoccupations of daily life. It happens that writers who keep a journal are
the most literary of all, but perhaps this is precisely because they avoid,

thus, the extreme of literature, if literature is ultimately the fascinating realm of time's absence.

The Fascination of Time's Absence

To write is to surrender to the fascination of time's absence. Now we are doubtless approaching the essence of solitude. Time's absence is not a purely negative mode. It is the time when nothing begins, when initiative is not possible, when, before the affirmation, there is already a return of the affirmation. Rather than a purely negative mode, it is, on the contrary, a time without negation, without decision, when here is nowhere as well, and each thing withdraws into its image while the "I" that we are recognizes itself by sinking into the neutrality of a featureless third person. The time of time's absence has no present, no presence. This "no present" does not, however, refer back to a past. Olden days had the dignity, the active force of now. Memory still bears witness to this active force. It frees me from what otherwise would recall me; it frees me by giving me the means of calling freely upon the past, of ordering it according to my present intention. Memory is freedom of the past. But what has no present will not accept the present of a memory either. Memory says of the event: it once was and now it will never be again. The irremediable character of what has no present, of what is not even there as having once been there, says: it never happened, never for a first time, and yet it starts over, again, again, infinitely. It is without end, without beginning. It is without a future.

The time of time's absence is not dialectical. In this time what appears is the fact that nothing appears. What appears is the being deep within being's absence, which is when there is nothing and which, as soon as there is something, is no longer. For it is as if there were no beings except through the loss of being, when being lacks. The reversal which, in time's absence, points us constantly back to the presence of absence — but to this presence as absence, to absence as its own affirmation (an affirmation in which nothing is affirmed, in which nothing never ceases to affirm itself with the exhausting insistence of the indefinite) — this movement is not dialectical. Contradictions do not exclude each other in it; nor are they reconciled. Only time itself, during which negation becomes our power, permits the "unity of contraries." In time's absence what is new renews nothing; what is present is not contemporary; what is present presents nothing, but represents itself and belongs henceforth and always to return. It isn't, but comes back again. It comes already and forever past, so that my relation to it is not one of cognition, but of recognition, and this recognition ruins in me the power of knowing, the right to grasp. It makes what is ungraspable inescapable; it never lets me cease reaching what I cannot attain. And that which I cannot take, I must take up again, never to let go.

This time is not the ideal immobility which the name "eternal" glorifies. In the region we are trying to approach, here has collapsed into nowhere, but nowhere is nonetheless here, and this empty, dead time is a real time in which death is present — in which death happens but doesn't stop happening, as if, by happening, it rendered sterile the time in which it could happen. The dead present is the impossibility of making any presence real — an impossibility which is present, which is there as the present's double, the shadow of the present which the present bears and hides in itself. When I am alone, I am not alone, but, in this present, I am already returning to myself in the form of Someone. Someone is there, where I am alone. The fact of being alone is my belonging to this dead time which is not my time, or yours, or the time we share in common, but Someone's time. Someone is what is still present when there is no one. Where I am alone, I am not there; no one is there, but the impersonal is: the outside, as that which prevents, precedes, and dissolves the possibility of any personal relation. Someone is the faceless third person, the They of which everybody and anybody is part, but who is part of it? Never anyone in particular, never you and I. Nobody is part of the They. "They" belongs to a region which cannot be brought to light, not because it hides some secret alien to any revelation or even because it is radically obscure, but because it transforms everything which has access to it, even light, into anonymous, impersonal being, the Nontrue, the Nonreal yet always there. The They is, in this respect, what appears up very close when someone dies.[2]

When I am alone, the light of day is only the loss of a dwelling place. It is intimacy with the outside which has no location and affords no rest. Coming here makes the one who comes belong to dispersal, to the fissure where the exterior is the intrusion that stifles, but is also nakedness, the chill of the enclosure that leaves one utterly exposed. Here the only space is its vertiginous separation. Here fascination reigns.

[2]When I am alone, it is not I who am there, and it is not from you that I stay away, or from others, or from the world. So begins the reflection which investigates "the essential solitude and solitude in the world." See, on this subject, and under this title, certain pages in the Appendixes.

The Image

Why fascination? Seeing presupposes distance, decisiveness which separates, the power to stay out of contact and in contact avoid confusion. Seeing means that this separation has nevertheless become an encounter. But what happens when what you see, although at a distance, seems to touch you with a gripping contact, when the manner of seeing is a kind of touch, when seeing is *contact* at a distance? What happens when what is seen imposes itself upon the gaze, as if the gaze were seized, put in touch with the appearance? What happens is not an active contact, not the initiative and action which there still is in real touching. Rather, the gaze gets taken in, absorbed by an immobile movement and a depthless deep. What is given us by this contact at a distance is the image, and fascination is passion for the image.

What fascinates us robs us of our power to give sense. It abandons its "sensory" nature, abandons the world, draws back from the world, and draws us along. It no longer reveals itself to us, and yet it affirms itself in a presence foreign to the temporal present and to presence in space. Separation, which was the possibility of seeing, coagulates at the very center of the gaze into impossibility. The look thus finds, in what makes it possible, the power that neutralizes it, neither suspending nor arresting it, but on the contrary preventing it from ever finishing, cutting it off from any beginning, making of it a neutral, directionless gleam which will not go out, yet does not clarify—the gaze turned back upon itself and closed in a circle. Here we have an immediate expression of that reversal which is the essence of solitude. Fascination is solitude's gaze. It is the gaze of the incessant and interminable. In it blindness is vision still, vision which is no longer the possibility of seeing, but the impossibility of not seeing, the impossibility which becomes visible and perseveres—always and always—in a vision that never comes to an end: a dead gaze, a gaze become the ghost of an eternal vision.

Of whoever is fascinated it can be said that he doesn't perceive any real object, any real figure, for what he sees does not belong to the world of reality, but to the indeterminate milieu of fascination. This milieu is, so to speak, absolute. Distance is not excluded from it, but is immeasurable. Distance here is the limitless depth behind the image, a lifeless profundity, unmanipulable, absolutely present although not given, where objects sink away when they depart from their sense, when they collapse into their image. This milieu of fascination, where what one sees seizes sight and renders it interminable, where the gaze coagulates into light, where light is the absolute gleam of an eye one doesn't see but which one doesn't cease to see since it is the mirror image of one's own look—this milieu is utterly attractive. Fascinating. It is light which is also the abyss, a light one sinks into, both terrifying and tantalizing.

If our childhood fascinates us, this happens because childhood is the moment of fascination, is itself fascinated. And this golden age seems bathed in a light which is splendid because unrevealed. But it is only that this light is foreign to revelation, has nothing to reveal, is pure reflection, a ray which is still only the gleam of an image. Perhaps the force of the maternal figure receives its intensity from the very force of fascination, and one might say then, that if the mother exerts this fascinating attraction it is because, appearing when the child lives altogether in fascination's gaze, she concentrates in herself all the powers of enchantment. It is because the child is fascinated that the mother is fascinating, and that is also why all the impressions of early childhood have a kind of fixity which comes from fascination.

Whoever is fascinated doesn't see, properly speaking, what he sees. Rather, it touches him in an immediate proximity; it seizes and ceaselessly draws him close, even though it leaves him absolutely at a distance. Fascination is fundamentally linked to neutral, impersonal presence, to the indeterminate They, the immense, faceless Someone. Fascination is the relation the gaze entertains—a relation which is itself neutral and impersonal—with sightless, shapeless depth, the absence one sees because it is blinding.

Writing

To write is to enter into the affirmation of the solitude in which fascination threatens. It is to surrender to the risk of time's absence, where eternal starting over reigns. It is to pass from the first to the third person, so that what happens to me happens to no one, is anonymous insofar as it concerns me, repeats itself in an infinite dispersal. To write is to let fascination rule language. It is to stay in touch, through language, in language, with the absolute milieu where the thing becomes image again, where the image, instead of alluding to some particular feature, becomes an allusion to the featureless, and instead of a form drawn upon absence, becomes the formless presence of this absence, the opaque, empty opening onto that which is when there is no more world, when there is no world yet.

Why? Why should writing have to do with this essential solitude, the solitude whose essence is the dissimulation that appears in it?[3]

[3]We will not try here to answer this question directly. We will only ask: just as the statue glorifies the marble, and insofar as all art means to draw into the light of day the elemental deep which the world, in order to affirm itself, negates and resists, doesn't the language of the poem, of literature, compare to ordinary language as the image compares to the thing? One likes to think that poetry is a language which, more than others, favors images. This is probably an allusion to a much more essential transformation—the poem is not a poem because it contains a certain number of figures, metaphors, comparisons; on the contrary, the poem's particular character is that nothing in it functions as an image. So we must express what we are seeking differently: in literature, doesn't language itself become altogether image? We do not mean a language containing images or one that casts reality in figures, but one which is its own image, an image of language (and not a figurative language), or yet again, an imaginary language, one which no one speaks; a language, that is, which issues from its own absence, the way the image emerges upon the absence of the thing; a language addressing itself to the shadow of events as well, not to their reality, and this because of the fact that the words which express them are, not signs, but images, images of words, and words where things turn into images.

What are we seeking to represent by saying this? Are we not on a path leading back to suppositions happily abandoned, analogous to the one which used to define art as imitation, a copy of the real? If, in the poem, language becomes its own image, doesn't this mean that poetic language is always second, secondary? According to the common analysis, the image comes after the object. It is the object's continuation. We see, then we imagine. After the object comes the image. "After" seems to indicate subordination. We really speak, then we speak in our imagination, or we imagine ourselves speaking. Wouldn't poetic language be the copy, the dim shadow, the transposition—in a space where the requirements of effectiveness are attenuated—of the sole speaking language? But perhaps the common analysis is mistaken. Perhaps, before going further, one ought to ask: but what is the image? (See, in the Appendixes, the pages entitled "The Two Versions of the Imaginary.")

Approaching Literature's Space

||

The poem — literature — seems to be linked to a spoken word which cannot be interrupted because it does not speak; it is. The poem is not this word itself, for the poem is a beginning, whereas this word never begins, but always speaks anew and is always starting over. However, the poet is the one who has heard this word, who has made himself into an ear attuned to it, its mediator, and who has silenced it by pronouncing it. This word is close to the poem's origin, for everything original is put to the test by the sheer powerlessness inherent in starting over — this sterile prolixity, the surplus of that which can do nothing, which never is the work, but ruins it and in it restores the unending lack of work. Perhaps this word is the source of the poem, but it is a source that must somehow be dried up in order to become a spring. For the poet — the one who writes, the "creator" — could never derive the work from the essential lack of work. Never could he, by himself, cause the pure opening words to spring forth from what is at the origin. That is why the work is a work only when it becomes the intimacy shared by someone who writes it and someone who reads it, a space violently opened up by the contest between the power to speak and the power to hear. And the one who writes is, as well, one who has "heard" the interminable and incessant, who has heard it as speech, has entered into this understanding with it, has lived with its demand, has become lost in it and yet, in order to have sustained it, has necessarily made it stop — has, in this intermittence, rendered it perceptible, has proffered it by firmly reconciling it with this limit. He has mastered it by imposing measure.

Mallarmé's Experience

Here we must appeal to references that are well known today and that hint at the transformation to which Mallarmé was exposed as soon as he took writing to heart. These references are by no means anecdotal in character. When Mallarmé affirms, "I felt the very disquieting symptoms caused by the sole act of writing," it is the last words which matter. With them an essential situation is brought to light. Something extreme is grasped, something which has for its context and substance "the sole act of writing." Writing appears as an extreme situation which presupposes a radical reversal. Mallarmé alludes briefly to this reversal when he says: "Unfortunately, by digging this thoroughly into verse, I have encountered two abysses which make me despair. One is Nothingness" (the absence of God; the other is his own death). Here too it is the flattest expression that is rich with sense: the one which, in the most unpretentious fashion, seems simply to remind us of a craftsmanly procedure. "By digging into verse," the poet enters that time of distress which is caused by the gods' absence. Mallarmé's phrase is startling. Whoever goes deeply into poetry escapes from being as certitude, meets with the absence of the gods, lives in the intimacy of this absence, becomes responsible for it, assumes its risk, and endures its favor. Whoever digs at verse must renounce all idols; he has to break with everything. He cannot have truth for his horizon, or the future as his element, for he has no right to hope. He has, on the contrary, to despair. Whoever delves into verse dies; he encounters his death as an abyss.

The Crude Word and the Essential Word

When he seeks to define the aspect of language which "the sole act of writing" disclosed to him, Mallarmé acknowledges a "double condition of the word, crude or immediate on the one hand, essential on the other." This distinction itself is crude, yet difficult to grasp, for Mallarmé attributes the same substance to the two aspects of language which he distinguishes so absolutely. In order to characterize each, he lights on the same term, which is "silence." The crude word is pure silence: "It would, perhaps, be enough for anyone who wants to exchange human speech, silently to take or put in someone else's hand a coin." Silent, therefore, because meaningless, crude language is an absence of words, a pure exchange where nothing is exchanged, where there is nothing real except the movement of exchange, which is nothing. But it turns out the same for the word confided to the questing poet — that language whose whole force lies in its not being, whose very glory is to evoke, in its own absence, the absence of everything. This language of the unreal, this fictive language which delivers us to fiction, comes from silence and returns to silence.

Crude speech "has a bearing upon the reality of things." "Narration, instruction, even description" give us the presence of things, "represent" them. The essential word moves them away, makes them disappear. It is always allusive; it suggests, evokes. But what is it, then, to remove "a fact of nature," to grasp it through this absence, to "transpose it into its vibratory, almost-disappearance"? To speak, but also to think, essentially. Thought is the pure word. In thought we must recognize the supreme language, whose lack is all that the extreme variety of different tongues permits us to grasp. "Since to think is to write without appurtenances or whispers, but with the immortal word still tacit, the world's diversity of idioms keeps anyone from proffering expressions which otherwise would be, in one stroke, the truth itself materially." (This is Cratylus's ideal, but also the definition of automatic writing.) One is thus tempted to say that the language of thought is poetic language par excellence, and that sense — the pure notion, the idea — must become the poet's concern, since it alone frees us from the weight of things, the amorphous natural plenitude. "Poetry, close to the idea."

However, the crude word is by no means crude. What it represents is not present. Mallarmé does not want "to include, upon the subtle paper...the intrinsic and dense wood of trees." But nothing is more foreign to the tree than the word *tree*, as it is used nonetheless by everyday language. A word which does not name anything, which does not represent anything, which does not outlast itself in any way, a word which is not even a word and which disappears marvelously altogether and at once in its usage: what could be more worthy of the essential and closer to silence? True, it "serves." Apparently that makes all the difference. We are used to it, it is usual, useful. Through it we are in the world: it refers us back to the life of the world where goals speak and the concern to achieve them once and for all is the rule. Granted, this crude word is a pure nothing, nothingness itself. But it is nothingness in action: that which acts, labors, constructs. It is the pure silence of the negative which culminates in the noisy feverishness of tasks.

In this respect, the essential word is exactly the opposite. It is a rule unto itself; it is imposing, but it imposes nothing. It is also well removed from thought which always pushes back the elemental obscurity, for verse "attracts no less than it disengages," "polishes all the scattered ore, unknown and floating." In verse, words become "elements" again, and the word *nuit*, despite its brilliance, becomes night's intimacy.[1]

In crude or immediate speech, language as language is silent. But beings speak in it. And, as a consequence of the *use* which is its purpose — because, that is, it serves primarily to put us in connection with objects, because it is a tool in a world of tools where what speaks is utility and value — beings speak in it as values. They take on the stable appearance of objects existing one by one and assume the certainty of the immutable.

The crude word is neither crude nor immediate. But it gives the illusion of being so. It is extremely reflective; it is laden with history. But, most often — and as if we were unable in the ordinary course of events to know that we are the organ of time, the guardians of becoming — language seems to be the locus of an immediately granted revelation. It seems to be the sign that truth is immediate, always the same and always at our disposal. Immediate language is perhaps in fact a relation with the immediate world, with what is immediately close to us, our environs. But the immediacy which common language communicates to us is only veiled distance, the absolutely foreign passing for the habitual, the unfamiliar which we take for the customary, thanks to the veil which is language and because we have grown accustomed to words' illusion. Language has within itself the moment that hides it. It has within itself, through this power to hide itself, the

---

[1]Having regretted the fact that words are not "the truth materially" — that *jour*, by virtue of its sonority, is sombre and *nuit* brilliant — Mallarmé finds in this shortcoming of our various tongues the justification of poetry. Verse is their "superior complement." "Philosophically, it remunerates the lack in languages." What is this lack? Languages do not have the reality they express, for they are foreign to the reality of things, foreign to obscure natural profundity, and belong to that fictive reality which is the human world, detached from being and a tool for beings.

force by which mediation (that which destroys immediacy) seems to have the spontaneity, the freshness, and the innocence of the origin. Moreover, this power, which language exercises by communicating to us the illusion of immediacy when in fact it gives us only the habitual, makes us believe that the immediate is familiar; and thus language's power consists in making the immediate appear to us not as the most terrible thing, which ought to overwhelm us — the error of the essential solitude — but as the pleasant reassurance of natural harmonies or the familiarity of a native habitat.

In the language of the world, language as the being of language and as the language of being keeps still. Thanks to this silence, beings speak, and in it they also find oblivion and rest. When Mallarmé speaks of the essential language, part of the time he opposes it only to this ordinary language which gives us the reassuring illusion of an immediacy which is actually only the customary. At these junctures he takes up and attributes to literature the language of thought, that silent movement which affirms in man his decision not to be, to separate himself from being, and, by making this separation real, to build the world. This silence is the production and the expression of signification itself. But this language of thought is, all the same, "ordinary" language as well. It always refers us back to the world, sometimes showing it to us in the infinite qualities of a task and the risk of an undertaking, sometimes as a stable position where we are allowed to believe ourselves secure.

The poetic word, then, is no longer opposed only to ordinary language, but also to the language of thought. In poetry we are no longer referred back to the world, neither to the world as shelter nor to the world as goals. In this language the world recedes and goals cease; the world falls silent; beings with their preoccupations, their projects, their activity are no longer ultimately what speaks. Poetry expresses the fact that beings are quiet. But how does this happen? Beings fall silent, but then it is being that tends to speak and speech that wants to be. The poetic word is no longer someone's word. In it no one speaks, and what speaks is not anyone. It seems rather that the word alone declares itself. Then language takes on all of its importance. It becomes essential. Language speaks as the essential, and that is why the word entrusted to the poet can be called the essential word. This means primarily that words, having the initiative, are not obliged to serve to designate anything or give voice to anyone, but that they have their ends in themselves. From here on, it is not Mallarmé who speaks, but language which speaks itself: language as the work and the work as language.

From this perspective, we rediscover poetry as a powerful universe of words where relations, configurations, forces are affirmed through sound, figure, rhythmic mobility, in a unified and sovereignly autonomous space. Thus the poet produces a work of pure language, and language in this work is its return to its essence. He creates an object made of language just as the painter, rather than using colors to reproduce what is, seeks the point at which his colors produce being. Or again, the poet strives — as Rilke did during his Expressionist period, or as today perhaps Ponge does — to create the "poem-thing," which would be, so to speak, the language of mute being. He wants to make of the poem something which all by itself will be form, existence, and being: that is, the work.

We call this powerful linguistic construction — this structure calculated to exclude chance, which subsists by itself and rests upon itself — the work. And we call it being. But it is from this perspective neither one nor the other. It is a work, since it is constructed, composed, calculated; but in this sense it is a work like any work, like any object formed by professional intelligence and skillful know-how. It is not a work of art, a work which has art for its origin, through which art is lifted from time's absence where nothing is accomplished to the unique, dazzling affirmation of the beginning. Likewise, the poem, understood as an independent object sufficing to itself — an object made out of language and created for itself alone, a monad of words where nothing is reflected but the nature of words — is perhaps in this respect a reality, a particular being, having exceptional dignity and importance; but it is *a* being, and for this reason it is by no means close to being, to that which escapes all determination and every form of existence.

Mallarmé's Experience Proper

It seems that the specifically Mallarméan experience begins at the moment when he moves from consideration of the finished work which is always one particular poem or another, or a certain picture, to the concern through which the work becomes the search for its origin and wants to identify itself with its origin — "horrible vision of a pure work." Here lies Mallarmé's profundity; here lies the concern which, for Mallarmé, "the sole act of writing" encompasses. What is the work? What is language in the work? When Mallarmé asks himself, "Does something like Literature exist?," this question is literature itself. It is literature when literature has become concern for its own essence. Such a question cannot be relegated. What is the result of the fact that we have literature? What is implied about being if one states that "something like Literature exists"?

Mallarmé had the most profoundly tormented awareness of the particular nature of literary creation. The work of art reduces itself to being. That is its task: to be, to make present "those very words: *it is* . . . There lies all the mystery."[2] But at the same time it cannot be said that the work belongs to being, that it exists. On the contrary, what must be said is that it never exists in the manner of a thing or a being in general. What must be said, in answer to our question, is that literature does not exist or again that if it takes place, it does so as something "not taking place in the form of any object that exists." Granted, language is present — "made evident" — in it: language is affirmed in literature with more authority than in any other form of human activity. But it is wholly realized in literature, which is to say that it has only the reality of the whole; it is all — and nothing else, always on the verge of passing from all to nothing. This passage is essential; it belongs to the essence of language because, precisely, nothing operates in words. Words, we know, have the power to make things disappear, to make them appear as things that have vanished. This appearance is only that of disappearance; this presence too returns to absence through the movement of wear and erosion which is the soul and the life of words, which draws light from their dimming, clarity from the dark. But words, having the power to make things "arise" at the heart of their absence — words which are masters of this absence — also have the power to disappear in it themselves, to absent themselves marvelously in the midst of the totality which they realize, which they proclaim as they annihilate themselves therein, which they accomplish eternally by destroying themselves there endlessly. This act of self-destruction is in every respect similar to the ever so strange event of suicide which, precisely, gives to the supreme instant of *Igitur* all its truth.[3]

[2] A letter to Vielé-Griffin, 8 August 1891: ". . . There is nothing in this that I don't tell myself, less well, in the uneven whisperings of my solitary conversations, but where you are the diviner, it is, yes, relative to those very words: *it is;* they are the subject of notes I have been working on, and they reign in the furthest reaches of my mind. There lies all the mystery: to establish the secret identities through a two-by-two which wears and erodes objects, in the name of a central purity."

[3] We refer the reader to another section of this book, "The Work and Death's Space," the study specifically devoted to the *Igitur* experience. This experience can be discussed only when a more central point in literature's space has been reached. In his very important essay, *The Interior Distance*, Georges Poulet shows that *Igitur* is "a perfect example of philosophic suicide." He suggests thereby that for Mallarmé, the poem depends upon a profound

The Central Point

Such is the central point. Mallarmé always comes back to it as though he were returning to the intimacy of the risk to which the literary experience exposes us. This point is the one at which complete realization of language coincides with its disappearance. Everything is pronounced ("Nothing," as Mallarmé says, "will remain unproffered"); everything is word, yet the word is itself no longer anything but the appearance of what has disappeared—the imaginary, the incessant, and the interminable. This point is ambiguity itself.

On the one hand, in the work, it is what the work realizes, how it affirms itself, the place where the work must "allow no luminous evidence except of existing." In this sense, the central point is the presence of the work, and the work alone makes it present. But at the same time, this point is "the presence of Midnight," the point anterior to all starting points, from which nothing ever begins, the empty profundity of being's inertia, that region without issue and without reserve, in which the work, through the artist, becomes the concern, the endless search for its origin.

Yes, the center, the concentration of ambiguity. It is very true that only the work—if we come toward this point through the movement and strength of the work—only the accomplishment of the work makes it possible. Let us look again at the poem: what could be more real, more evident? And language itself is "luminous evidence" within it. This evidence, however, shows nothing, rests upon nothing; it is the ungraspable in action.

---

relation to death, and is possible only if death is *possible*: only if, through the sacrifice and strain to which the poet exposes himself, death becomes power and possibility in him, only if it is an act par excellence:

> Death is the only act possible. Cornered as we are between a true material world whose chance combinations take place in us regardless of us, and a false ideal world whose lie paralyzes and bewitches us, we have only one means of no longer being at the mercy either of nothingness or of chance. This unique means, this unique act, is death. Voluntary death. Through it we abolish ourselves, but through it we also found ourselves...It is this act of voluntary death that Mallarmé committed. He committed it in *Igitur*.

We must, however, carry Poulet's remarks further. *Igitur* is an abandoned narrative which bears witness to a certitude the poet was unable to maintain. For it is not sure that death is an act; it could be that suicide was not possible. Can I take my own life? Do I have the power to die? *Un Coup de dés jamais n'abolira le hasard* is something like the answer in which this question dwells. And the "answer" intimates that the movement which, in the work, is the experience of death, the approach to it and its use, is not the movement of possibility—not even of nothingness's possibility—but rather a movement approaching the point at which the work is put to the test by impossibility.

There are neither terms nor moments. Where we think we have words, "a virtual trail of fires" shoots through us—a swiftness, a scintillating exaltation. A reciprocity: for what is not is revealed in this flight; what there isn't is reflected in the pure grace of reflections that do not reflect anything. Then, "everything becomes suspense, fragmentary disposition with alternations and oppositions." Then, just as the tremor of the unreal turned into language gleams only to go out, simultaneously the unfamiliar presence is affirmed of real things turned into pure absence, pure fiction: a glorious realm where "willed and solitary celebrations" shine forth their splendor. One would like to say that the poem, like the pendulum that marks the time of time's abolition in *Igitur*, oscillates marvelously between its presence as language and the absence of the things of the world. But this presence is itself oscillating perpetuity: oscillation between the successive unreality of terms that terminate nothing, and the total realization of this movement—language, that is, become the whole of language, where the power of departing from and coming back to nothing, affirmed in each word and annulled in all, realizes itself as a whole, "total rhythm," "with which, silence."

In the poem, language is never real at any of the moments through which it passes, for in the poem language is affirmed in its totality. Yet in this totality, where it constitutes its own essence and where it is essential, it is also supremely unreal. It is the total realization of this unreality, an absolute fiction which says " being" when, having "worn away," "used up" all existing things, having suspended all possible beings, it comes up against an indelible, irreducible residue. What is left? "Those very words, *it is*." Those words sustain all others by letting themselves be hidden by all the others, and hidden thus, they are the presence of all words, language's entire possibility held in reserve. But when all words cease ("the instant they shimmer and die in a swift bloom upon some transparency like ether's"), "those very words, *it is*," present themselves, "lightning moment," "dazzling burst of light."

This lightning moment flashes from the work as the leaping brilliance of the work itself—its total presence all at once, its "simultaneous vision." This moment is the one at which the work, in order to give being and existence to the "feint"—that "literature exists"—declares the exclusion of everything, but in this way, excludes itself, so that the moment at which "every reality dissolves" by the force of the poem is also the moment the poem dissolves and, instantly done, is instantly undone. This is in itself extremely ambiguous. But the ambiguity touches something more essential. For this moment, which is like the work of the work, which outside of any signification, any historical or esthetic affirmation, declares that the work is, depends on the work's undergoing, at this very same moment, the ordeal which always ruins the work in advance and always restores in it the unending lack of work, the vain superabundance of inertia.

Inertia's Profundity

Here lies the most hidden moment of the experience. That the work must be the unique clarity of that which grows dim and through which everything is extinguished — that it can exist only where the ultimate affirmation is verified by the ultimate negation — this requirement we can still comprehend, despite its going counter to our need for peace, simplicity, and sleep. Indeed, we understand it intimately, as the intimacy of the decision which is ourselves and which gives us being only when, at our risk and peril, we reject — with fire and iron and with silent refusal — being's permanence and protection. Yes, we can understand that the work is thus pure beginning, the first and last moment when being presents itself by way of the jeopardized freedom which makes us exclude it imperiously, without, however, again including it in the appearance of beings. But this exigency, which makes the work declare being in the unique moment of rupture — "those very words: *it is*," the point which the work brilliantly illuminates even while receiving its consuming burst of light — we must also comprehend and feel that this point renders the work impossible, because it never permits arrival at the work. It is a region anterior to the beginning where nothing is made of being, and in which nothing is accomplished. It is the depth of being's inertia [désoeuvrement].

Thus it seems that the point to which the work leads us is not only the one where the work is achieved in the apotheosis of its disappearance — where it announces the beginning, declaring being in the freedom that excludes it — but also the point to which the work can never lead us, because this point is always already the one starting from which there never is any work.

Perhaps we make things too easy for ourselves when, tracing backwards along the movement of our active life, content to reverse this movement, we think we grasp thereby the movement of what we call art. It is the same facile procedure that persuades us we find the image by starting from the object, and that causes us to say, "First we have the object, afterwards comes the image," as if the image were simply the distancing, the refusal, the transposition of the object. Similarly we like to say that art does not reproduce the things of the world, does not imitate the "real," and that art is situated where, having taken leave of the ordinary world, the artist has bit by bit removed from it everything useful, imitable, everything pertaining to active life. Art seems, from this point of view, to be the silence of the world, the silence or the neutralization of what is usual and immediate in the world, just as the image seems to be the absence of the object.

Described thus, the movement in question permits itself the facilities of common analysis. This fluency lets us believe that we grasp art, because it furnishes us with a means of representing to ourselves the starting point of the artistic task. But this representation does not correspond to the psychology of creation. An artist could never ascend from the use he makes of an object in the world to a picture in which this object has become art. It could never suffice for him to bracket that use, to neutralize the object in order to enter into the freedom of the picture. On the contrary, it is because, through a radical reversal, he already belongs to the work's requirements that, looking at a certain object, he is by no means content to *see* it as it might be if it were out of use, but makes of the object the point through which the work's requirements pass and, consequently, the moment at which the possible is attenuated, the notions of value and utility effaced, and the world "dissolves." It is because he already belongs to another time, to time's other, and because he has abandoned time's labor to expose himself to the trial of the essential solitude where fascination threatens — it is because he has approached this "point" that, answering to the work's demands from within this original belonging, he seems to look at the objects of the ordinary world in a different way, neutralizing usefulness in them, rendering them pure, elevating them through continuous stylization to the simultaneity and symmetry in which they become pictures. In other words, one never ascends from "the world" to art, even by the movement of refusal and disqualification which we have described; rather, one goes always from art toward what appears to be the neutralized appearances of the world — appears so, really, only to the domesticated gaze which is generally ours, that gaze of the inadequate spectator riveted to the world of goals and at most capable of going from the world to the picture.

No one who does not belong to the work as origin, who does not belong to that other time where the work is concerned for its essence, will ever create a work. But whoever does belong to that other time also belongs to the empty profundity of inertia where nothing is ever made of being.

To express this in yet another way: when an all-too-familiar expression seems to acknowledge the poet's power to "give a purer sense to the words of the tribe," are we to understand that the poet is the one who, by talent or by creative savoir faire, is content to change "crude or immediate" language into essential language, elevating the silent nullity of ordinary language to the accomplished silence of the poem where, through the apotheosis of disappearance, all is present in the absence of all? By no means. That would be like imagining writing to consist merely in using ordinary words with more mastery, a richer memory, or an ear more attuned to their musical resources. Writing never consists in perfecting the language in use, rendering it purer. Writing begins only when it is the approach to that point where nothing reveals itself, where, at the heart of dissimulation, speaking is still but the shadow of speech, a language which is still only its image, an imaginary language and a language of the imaginary, the one nobody speaks, the murmur of the incessant and interminable which one has to *silence* if one wants, at last, to be heard.

When we look at the sculptures of Giacometti, there is a vantage point where they are no longer subject to the fluctuations of appearance or to the movement of perspective. One sees them absolutely: no longer reduced, but withdrawn from reduction, irreducible, and, in space, masters of space through their power to substitute for space the unmalleable, lifeless profundity of the imaginary. This point, whence we see them irreducible, puts us at the vanishing point ourselves; it is the point at which here coincides with nowhere. To write is to find this point. No one writes who has not enabled language to maintain or provoke contact with this point.

The
Work's Space
and Its
Demand

||||

The
Work
and the Errant
Word

What can be said about this point?

First, let us try to assemble some of the traits which the approach to literature's space has enabled us to recognize. Language, at this point, is not a power; it is not the power to tell. It is not at our disposal; there is in it nothing we can use. It is never the language I speak. I never express myself with it, I never address you, and I never invite your answer. All these features are negative in form. But this negation only masks the more essential fact that in language at this point everything reverts to affirmation: in this language what denies affirms. For this language speaks as absence. Wordless, it speaks already; when it ceases, it persists. It is not silent, because in this language silence speaks. The defining characteristic of ordinary language is that listening comprises part of its very nature. But at this point of literature's space, language is not to be heard. Hence the risk of the poetic function. The poet is he who hears a language which makes nothing heard.

It speaks, but without any beginning. It states, but does not refer back to something which is to be stated, something silent, like the meaning behind an expression, which would guarantee it. When neutrality speaks, only he who silences it prepares the conditions for hearing; and yet what is to be heard is this neutral word, which has always been said already, cannot stop its saying, and to which no hearing can be given.

This is an essentially errant word, for it is always cast out of itself. It designates the infinitely distended outside which takes the place of the spoken word's intimacy. It resembles the echo, when the echo does not simply say out loud what first is indistinctly murmured, but merges with the whispering immensity and is silence become reverberating space, all words' exterior. But here the outside is void, and the echo repeats in advance, "prophetic in the absence of time."

The Need to Write

The need to write is linked to the approach toward this point at which nothing can be done with words. Hence the illusion that if one maintained contact with this point even as one came back from it to the world of possibility, "everything" could be done, "everything" could be said. This need must be suppressed and contained. If not, it becomes so vast that there is no more room or space for its realization. One only begins to write when, momentarily, through a ruse, through a propitious burst of energy, or through life's distractions, one has succeeded in evading this impulse which remote control of the work must constantly awaken and subdue, protect and avert, master and experience in its unmasterable force. This operation is so difficult and dangerous that every writer and every artist is surprised each time he achieves it without disaster. And no one who has looked the risk in the face can doubt that many perished silently. It is not that creative resources are lacking — although they are in any event insufficient — but rather that the force of the writing impulse makes the world disappear. Then time loses its power of decision; nothing can really begin.

The work is the pure circle where, even as he writes the work, the author dangerously exposes himself to, but also protects himself against, the pressure which demands that he write. Hence — in part at least — the prodigious, the immense joy which, as Goethe says, is that of a deliverance: a tête-à-tête with the solitary omnipotence of fascination which one has faced resolutely, without betraying or fleeing it, but without renouncing one's own mastery either. This deliverance, it is true, will have consisted of enclosing oneself outside oneself.

It is regularly said of the artist that he finds in his work a convenient way of living while withdrawing from life's responsibilities. He is said to protect himself from the world where action is difficult by establishing himself in an unreal world over which he reigns supreme. This is, in fact, one of the risks of artistic activity: to exile oneself from the difficulties of time and of active pursuits in time without, however, renouncing the comfort of the world or the apparent easiness of pursuits outside of time. The artist often seems a weak being who cringes within the closed sphere of his work where, speaking as master and acting without any obstacles, he can take revenge for his failures in society.

Even Stendhal, even Balzac inspire this suspicion; Kafka, Hölderlin certainly do — and Homer is blind. But this perspective only expresses one side of the situation. The other side is that the artist who willingly exposes himself to the risks of the experience which is his does not feel free of the world, but, rather, deprived of it; he does not feel that he is master of himself, but rather that he is absent from himself and exposed to demands which, casting him out of life and of living, open him to that moment at which he cannot do anything and is no longer himself. It is then that Rimbaud flees into the desert from the responsibilities of the poetic decision. He buries his imagination and his glory. He says "adieu" to "the impossible" in the same way that Leonardo da Vinci does and almost in the same terms. He does not come back to the world; he takes refuge in it; and bit by bit his days, devoted henceforth to the aridity of gold, make a shelter for him of protective forgetfulness. If it is true, as doubtful sources have it, that in his last years he would not stand for any mention of his work or that he repeatedly said of himself, "absurd, ridiculous, disgusting," the violence of his disavowal, the refusal to remember himself shows the terror which he still felt and the force of the upheaval which he could not undergo to the limit. He is reproached with having sold out and deserted, but the reproach is easy for those who have not run the risk.

In the work, the artist protects himself not only against the world, but also against the requirement that draws him *out* of the world. The work momentarily domesticates this "outside" by restoring an intimacy to it. The work silences and gives the intimacy of silence to this outside bereft of intimacy and repose — this outside, this language of the original experience. But what the work encloses is also what opens it ceaselessly; and the work in progress runs one of two risks: it may either renounce its origin — exorcising it by endowing it with facile prestige — or the work may return ever closer to this origin by renouncing its own realization. Yet a third risk is that the author may want to maintain contact with the world, with himself, with the language he can use to say "I." He wants this, for if he loses himself, the work too is lost. But if, too cautiously, he remains himself, the work is *his* work, it expresses him, his gifts, and not the extreme demand of the work, art as origin.

Every writer, every artist is acquainted with the moment at which he is cast out and apparently excluded by the work in progress. The work holds him off, the circle in which he no longer has access to himself has closed, yet he is enclosed therein because the work, unfinished, will not let him go. Strength does not fail him; this is not a moment of sterility or fatigue, unless, as may well be the case, fatigue itself is simply the form this exclusion takes. This ordeal is awesome. What the author sees is a cold immobility from which he cannot turn away, but near which he cannot linger. It is like an enclave, a preserve within space, airless and without light, where a part of himself, and, more than that, his truth, his solitary truth, suffocates in an incomprehensible separation. And he can only wander astray around this separation; at the very most he can press himself hard against the surface beyond which he distinguishes nothing but an empty torment, unreal and eternal, until the moment when, through an inexplicable maneuver, through some distraction or through the sheer excessiveness of his patience, he finds himself suddenly inside the circle, joins himself there, and reconciles himself to its secret law.

A work is finished, not when it is completed, but when he who labors at it from within can just as well finish it from without. He is no longer retained inside by the work; rather, he is retained there by a part of himself from which he feels he is free and from which the work has contributed to freeing him. This ideal dénouement is, however, never altogether justified. Many a work moves us because we still see in it the imprint left by the author who has departed from it too hastily, impatient to finish with it, fearful that if he didn't have done with it, he would never be able to return to the light of day. In these works, which are too great, greater than those who bear them, the supreme moment — the nearly central point at which we know that if the author remains there, he will die in the undertaking — is always perceptible. It is from this mortal point that we see the great, heroic creators depart — but slowly, almost peacefully — and come back with an even step toward the surface which the firm, regular stroke of the radius permits to curve according to the perfections of the sphere. But how many others are there who can only tear themselves from the irresistible attraction of the center with an inharmonious violence, leaving behind them, like scars of badly knit wounds, the traces of their successive flights, their inconsolable returns, their aberrant comings and goings? The most sincere openly leave to abandon what they have themselves abandoned. Others hide the ruins, and this concealment becomes the only truth of their books.

The central point of the work is the work as origin, the point which cannot be reached, yet the only one which is worth reaching.

This point is the sovereign requirement. One can approach it only by means of the completed work, but one can complete the work only by means of the approach. Those who care only for brilliant success are nevertheless in search of this point where nothing can succeed. And whoever writes caring only for truth has already entered the magnetic field of this point from which truth is excluded. Certain artists, through no one knows what good fortune or bad luck, undergo its pull in an almost pure form: they have approached this instant by chance, as it were, and wherever they go, whatever they do, it retains them. It is an imperious and empty demand exerted all of the time, drawing them out of time. They do not desire to write: to them glory is vain, the immortality of works of art does not impress them, and the obligations of the calling are foreign to them. To live in the happy passion of beings — that is what they prefer. But their preferences are not taken into account, and they are themselves dismissed, propelled into the essential solitude from which they do not emerge except by writing a little.

Everyone knows the story of the painter whose patron had to imprison him to keep him from wasting his gifts, and who still managed to escape through a window. But the artist also has a "patron" within himself, who shuts him in where he cannot remain, and this time there is no escape. Moreover, this patron does not feed, but starves, him, presses him into service without honor, castigates him for no reason, makes of him a feeble and miserable being without any support except his own incomprehensible torment. And why? In view of a grandiose work? In view of a completely insignificant work? He himself has no idea, nor does anyone know.

It is true that many creators appear weaker than other men, less capable of living, and consequently more apt to marvel at life. Perhaps this is often the case. Still, one would have to add that their strength lies in their weakness, that a new strength is born in them at the very point where they succumb to the extremity of their weakness. And one must say still more: when, oblivious of their gifts, they set to work, many are normal beings, amiable people firmly planted in life, and it is to the work alone, to the demand which is in the work, that they owe this surplus of strength which can be measured only by the greatest weakness — this anomaly, the loss of the world and of themselves. So Goya, so Nerval.

The work requires of the writer that he lose everything he might construe as his own "nature," that he lose all character and that, ceasing to be linked to others and to himself by the decision which makes him an "I," he becomes the empty place where the impersonal affirmation emerges. This is a requirement which is no requirement at all, for it demands nothing; it has no content. It does not oblige anyone to do anything; it is only the air one has to breathe, the void on which one has to get a footing, daylight worn thin where the faces one loves best become invisible. Just as the most courageous men confront risk only through the veil of a subterfuge, many think that to respond to this call is to answer to the call of truth: they have something to say, a world within themselves to set free, a mandate to assume, their unjustifiable life to justify. And it is true that if the artist did not surrender to the original experience which sets him apart—which in this separation separates him from himself—if he did not abandon himself to the boundlessness of error and to the shifting sands of infinitely repeated beginnings, the word *beginning* would be lost. But this justification does not occur to the artist; it is not granted in the experience. It is, on the contrary, ruled out. And the artist can very well know it "in general," just as he believes in art "in general," but his work does not know it, and his search is ignorant of it. His search is pursued in the anxiety of this ignorance.

Kafka
and the
Work's
Demand

Someone begins to write, determined by despair. But despair cannot *determine* anything: "It has always, and right away, exceeded its
purpose" (Kafka, *Diaries*, 1910). And, likewise, writing cannot have as
its origin anything but "true" despair, the kind that leads to nothing,
turns us away from everything, and for a start withdraws the pen from
whoever writes. This means that the two movements — writing,
despair — have nothing in common except their own indeterminacy.
They have, that is, nothing in common but the sole, interrogative
mode in which they can be grasped. No one can say to himself, "I am in
despair," but only, "You are desperate?" And no one can affirm, "I am
writing," but only "You write? Yes? You are intending to write?"

Kafka's case is cloudy and complex.[1] Hölderlin's passion is pure
poetic passion; it draws him out of himself with a demand that bears no
other name. Kafka's passion is just as purely literary, but it is not always
only literary. Salvation is an enormous preoccupation with him, all the
stronger because it is hopeless, and all the more hopeless because it is
totally uncompromising. To be sure, this preoccupation is expressed
with surprising constancy through literature, and for quite a long time

---

[1] Almost all the texts quoted in the following pages are taken from the complete edition
of Kafka's Diaries. This edition reproduces the thirteen *in quarto* notebooks where, from
1910 to 1923, Kafka wrote everything that mattered to him: events in his personal life,
meditations upon these events, descriptions of persons and places, descriptions of his
dreams, narratives begun, interrupted, and begun again. His is thus not only a "Journal" as
we understand this genre today, but the very movement of the experience of writing, very
close to its beginning and in the essential sense which Kafka was led to give this term. It is
from this perspective that his diaries must be read and explored.

Max Brod states that he has made only a few insignificant deletions; there is no
reason to doubt this. On the other hand, it is certain that Kafka, at many decisive
moments, destroyed a large part of his notes. And after 1923, the *Diaries* are missing
altogether. We do not know whether the manuscripts destroyed at his request by Dora
Dymant included the continuation of his notebooks; it is very probable they did. It

it does not differentiate itself from literature. Then, for some time it continues to be expressed in literature, but it no longer blends with literature; it tends rather to use literature. And, since literature never consents to become a means, and since Kafka knows this, conflicts result which are obscure even for him—still more so for us—and an evolution which, difficult to elucidate, is nevertheless enlightening.

The Young Kafka

Kafka was not always the same. Until 1912, his desire to write is very great. It gives rise to works which do not persuade him of his gifts—works which are less persuasive to him than his direct awareness of devastatingly abundant, primitive forces within him with which he does practically nothing, for lack of time, but also because he cannot do anything with them, because he "fears these moments of exaltation as much as he desires them." In many respects, Kafka is at this point similar to every young man in whom a taste for writing develops, who recognizes writing as his vocation, but also recognizes that writing makes certain demands to which he has no assurance that he will be equal. The most striking sign that Kafka is, to a degree, a young writer

---

must be said, then, that after 1923, Kafka becomes unknown to us, for we do know that those who were closest to him judged him very differently from the way he pictured himself.

The *Diaries* (which the travel diaries complete) reveal to us practically nothing about his opinions on the great subjects that may have interested him. The *Diaries* speak to us of Kafka at that earlier stage when there are no opinions yet, and when there is scarcely even a Kafka. Such is its essential value. G. Janouch's book, *Conversations with Kafka*, allows us, on the contrary, to hear Kafka in the relaxation of more ordinary conversations where he speaks of the world's future, as well as of the Jewish problem, of Zionism, of religious forms, and sometimes of his books. Janouch met Kafka in 1920 in Prague. He noted down the conversations he reports almost immediately, and Brod has confirmed the authenticity of this echo. But in order not to misconstrue the import of these words, we should remember that they were spoken to a very young man, seventeen years old, whose youth, naïveté, and confident spontaneity touched Kafka, but probably also led him to soften his thoughts in order not to endanger such a youthful soul. Kafka, scrupulous in friendship, often feared troubling his friends by expressing a truth which was desolating only for him. This doesn't mean that he does not say what he thinks, but that he sometimes says what he does not think profoundly.

[For the passages cited from Kafka's *Diaries*, I have largely depended on the English translation by Martin Greenberg, *The Diaries of Franz Kafka* (New York: Schocken Books, 1949), but frequently I have departed somewhat from his text with an eye to Blanchot's French rendering of the original—Trans.]

like many others is the novel he begins to write in collaboration with Brod. Such a sharing of his solitude shows that Kafka is still skirting it. He perceives this very rapidly, as this note from the *Diaries* indicates:

> Max and I must really be different to the very core. Much as I admire his writings when they lie before me as a whole, resisting my and anyone else's encroachment, still, every sentence he writes for *Richard and Samuel* is bound up with a reluctant concession on my part which I feel painfully to my very depths. At least today. [November 1911]

If, up until 1912 he does not devote himself entirely to literature, he gives himself this excuse: "I cannot take the risk as long as I haven't succeeded in completing a more substantial work, capable of satisfying me fully." The night of September 22, 1912 brings him this success, this proof. That night he writes *The Verdict* at one stretch. It brings him unmistakably near the point where it seems that "everything can be expressed, that for everything, for the strangest of ideas a great fire is ready in which they perish and disappear." Soon afterwards, he reads this story to his friends, and the reading confirms his certainty: "I had tears in my eyes. The indubitable character of the story was confirmed." (This need to read what he has just written to friends, often to his sisters and even to his father, also belongs to the intermediary stage. He will never give it up altogether. It is not literary vanity—even though he himself denounces it—but a need to press himself physically against his work, to let it bear him up and draw him along, by causing it to unfold in the vocal space which his great gifts as a reader gave him the power to create.)

Kafka knows from then on that he can write. But this knowledge is no knowledge at all, this capability is not his. With few exceptions, he never finds in what he writes the proof that he is actually writing. His texts are at most preludes, investigative, preliminary attempts. Of *The Metamorphosis* he says, "I find it bad; perhaps there is no hope for me whatever," or later: "Great aversion for *The Metamorphosis*. Unreadable ending. Almost radically imperfect. It would have been much better if I had not been disturbed at the time by a business trip" (January 19, 1914).

The Conflict

This last entry alludes to a conflict that Kafka meets head-on and that exhausts him. He has a profession, a family. He belongs to the world and must belong to it. The world provides time, but takes it up. Throughout the *Diaries* — at least up until 1915 — there are despairing comments, where the thought of suicide recurs, because he lacks time: time, physical strength, solitude, silence. No doubt exterior circumstances are unfavorable: he has to write in the evenings and at night, his sleep is disturbed, anxiousness wears him out. But it would be vain to believe that the conflict could have been resolved by "better organization of [his] affairs." Later, when illness affords him leisure, the conflict persists; it deepens, changes form. There are no favorable circumstances. Even if one gives "all one's time" to the work's demands, "all" still is not enough, for it is not a matter of devoting time to the task, of passing one's time writing, but of passing into another time where there is no longer any task; it is a matter of approaching that point where time is lost, where one enters into the fascination and the solitude of time's absence. When one has all one's time, one no longer has time, and "favorable" exterior circumstances have become the — unfavorable — fact that there are no longer any circumstances.

Kafka cannot, or will not, consent to write "in little bits" — in the incompleteness of discontinuous moments. That is what the night of September 22 revealed to him. That night, having written without interruption, he grasped in its plenitude the limitless movement which enables him to write. "Writing is only possible thus, with that continuity, with that complete opening of the body and soul." And later (December 8, 1914): "Saw again that everything written in bits, and not at one stretch in the course of the greater part or the whole of a night, has less value, and that I am condemned by my mode of life to this lesser value." Here we have a first explanation for the numerous abandoned narratives of which the *Diaries*, in their current state, reveal the impressive shreds. Very often "the story" goes no further than a few lines; sometimes it rapidly attains coherence and density and yet stops at the end of a page; other times it continues for several pages, is affirmed, extended — and nonetheless halted. There are many reasons for this, but the first is that Kafka does not find in the time he has at his disposal the long stretch which would allow the story to develop, as it wants to, in all directions. The story is never anything but a fragment, then another fragment. "How, from pieces, can I weld a story capable of springing to life?" And so, never having been mastered, never having created the proper space where the need to write must at once be suppressed and expressed, the story cuts loose, loses its way; it returns to the night whence it came, there painfully to retain him who was unable to bring it forth into the light.

Kafka would require more time, but he would also need less world. The world is initially his family, whose constraints he finds hard to put up with even though he is never equal to freeing himself. Subsequently it is his fiancée, his essential desire to abide by the law which requires that a man fulfill his destiny in the world by establishing a family, having children, belonging to the community. Here the conflict takes on a new aspect. It contributes to a contradiction which Kafka's religious situation renders particularly harsh. When, on the occasion of his betrothal to F. B. — which later was broken, then renewed — he tirelessly examines, with increasing tension, "everything for or against my marrying," he always comes up against this requirement: solitude. "My unique aspiration and my sole vocation . . . is literature . . . Everything I have done is a result only of solitude . . . Married, I will never be alone again. Not that, not that." During his engagement celebration in Berlin, "I was bound like a criminal. If I'd been tied in a corner with real chains, policemen before me . . . it would have been no worse. And it was my engagement party, and everyone was doing his best to bring me to life and, not succeeding, to bear with me as I was." Soon afterwards, the engagement is broken off, but the aspiration persists — the desire for a "normal" life, to which the torment of having wounded someone dear lends a heartrending force. Kafka's story and the story of Kierkegaard's engagement have been compared, by Kafka himself among others. But the conflict is different. Kierkegaard can renounce Regine; he can renounce the ethical level. Access to the religious level is not thereby compromised; rather, it is made possible. But Kafka, if he abandons the earthly happiness of a normal life, also abandons the steadiness of a just life. He makes himself an outlaw, deprives himself of the ground and the foundation he needs in order to be and, in a way, deprives the law of this ground. His is Abraham's eternal dilemma. What is demanded of Abraham is not only that he sacrifice his son, but God himself. The son is God's future on earth, for it is time which is truly the Promised Land — the true, the only dwelling place of the chosen people and of God in his people. Yet Abraham, by sacrificing his only son, must sacrifice time, and time sacrificed will certainly not be given back in the eternal beyond. The beyond is nothing other than the future, the future of God in time. The beyond is Isaac.

For Kafka the ordeal is all the graver because of everything that makes it weigh lightly upon him. (What would the testing of Abraham be if, having no son, he were nevertheless required to sacrifice this son? He couldn't be taken seriously; he could only be laughed at. That laughter is the form of Kafka's pain.) The problem is thus so equivocally elusive that its indecisiveness overtakes whoever tries to face it. Other writers have known similar conflicts; Hölderlin struggles against his mother, who wants him to become a pastor. He cannot attach himself to any determined task, he cannot attach himself to the one he loves, and he loves precisely the one to which he cannot be attached. He feels these conflicts in all their force, and they practically destroy him, but they never put in doubt the absolute demand of poetry apart from which, at least after 1800, he no longer has any existence. For Kafka, everything is more unclear because he seeks to fuse the work's demand with the demand which could pertain to his salvation. If writing condemns him to solitude, if it makes of his existence a bachelor's existence without love and without attachments, and if nonetheless writing appears to him — at least often and for a long time — as the only activity which could justify him, this is because solitude threatens in any event, both within him and outside. For the community is no longer anything but appearances, and the law which still speaks in it is not even the law forgotten, but rather the concealment of its being forgotten. Then writing, in the heart of the distress and the weakness from which it is inseparable, again becomes a possibility of plenitude, a road without any goal at the end, but capable perhaps of corresponding to that goal without any road leading to it which is the one and only goal we must reach. When he is not writing, Kafka is not only alone — "alone like Franz Kafka," he will say to G. Janouch — but a prey to a sterile, cold solitude, a petrifying cold which he calls torpor and which seems to have been the great threat he feared. Even Brod, so anxious to represent Kafka as a man without anomalies, acknowledges that he was sometimes as if not there or dead. Again, this is very similar to Hölderlin: "I am dumb, I am made of stone." And Kafka: "My incapacity to think, to observe, to determine the truth of things, to remember, to speak, to take part in the life of others, becomes greater each day; I am turning into stone . . . . If I don't save myself in some work, I am lost" (July 28, 1914).

Salvation through Literature

"If I don't save myself in some work . . . . " But why should the effort of writing be able to save him? It seems that Kafka recognized in precisely this terrible state of self-dissolution, where he is lost for others and for himself, the center of gravity of writing's demand. His feeling profoundly destroyed is the first intimation of the profundity which replaces destruction with the possibility of the greatest creation. This is a marvelous reversal, a hope always equal to the greatest despair. And how understandable it is that he should draw from this experience confidence he will never willingly question. Thus the effort of writing, especially in his early years, becomes something like a means of psychological (not yet of spiritual) salvation: it is an effort to create something "which might be linked word for word with his life, which he draws into himself so that it might draw him from himself." He expresses this most naïvely and most forcefully in these terms: "Today I have a great yearning to write all my anxiety entirely out of me, write it into the depths of the paper just as it comes out of the depths of me, or write it down in such a way that I could draw what I had written into me completely" (December 8, 1911).[2] However somber it may become, this hope will never fail completely; always, at every period, we find in his *Diaries* notes of this sort: "The firmness which the most insignificant writing brings about in me is beyond doubt and wonderful. The comprehensive view I had of everything on my walk yesterday!" (November 27, 1913). At such moments writing is not a compelling call; it is not waiting upon grace, or an obscure prophetic achievement, but something simpler, more immediately pressing: the hope of not going under, or, more precisely, the hope of sinking faster than himself and thus of catching hold of himself at the last minute. This, then, is a duty more pressing than any other, and it leads him to note down on July 31, 1914 these remarkable words:

> I have no time. General mobilization. K. and P. have been called up. Now I receive the salary of solitude. But it is hardly a salary; solitude only brings punishments. It doesn't matter, I am not much affected by this misery, and more determined than ever . . . . I will write despite everything, at any price: it is my fight for survival.

A Change in Perspective

And yet it is the shock of the war — but still more the crisis set off by his betrothal, the movement of writing and his increasingly profound involvement with it, and all the difficulties he encounters in it — it is his unhappy situation in general that bit by bit will shed a different light

---

[2]Kafka adds, "This is not an artistic desire."

on the existence of the writer in him. This change is never explicit; it does not culminate in a decision; it is only an indistinct perspective. There are, however, certain indications. In 1914, for example, he is still striving passionately, desperately toward the sole end of finding a few free moments for writing — of obtaining two weeks leave to spend only writing, subordinating everything to this single, this supreme demand — writing. But in 1916, if he again asks for a leave, it is in order to enlist. "The immediate duty is unconditional; become a soldier." This project will have no results, but that is unimportant. The wish at its center shows how far Kafka already is from the "I will write despite everything" of July 31, 1914. Later, he will think seriously of joining the pioneers of Zionism and departing for Palestine. He says to Janouch: "I dreamed of leaving for Palestine as a worker or agricultural laborer. . . . — You would abandon everything here? — Everything, in order to find a life full of meaning in security and beauty." But since Kafka was already ill, this dream remained a dream, and we will never know whether, like another Rimbaud, he could have renounced his unique vocation for love of a desert where he would have found the security of a justified life — or, indeed, whether he would have found it. Of all the undertakings to which he applies himself in order to orient his life differently, he himself will say that they are nothing but broken attempts, so many radii making the center of that incomplete circle, his life, bristle with dots. In 1922, he counts up all his projects and sees only failures: the piano, the violin, languages, German studies, anti-Zionism, Zionism, Hebraic studies, gardening, wood carving, literature, attempts at marriage, living independently, and he adds: "When I happened to extend the radius a little further than usual — as in the case of my law studies or my engagement — it was all even worse just to the degree that it represented my effort to advance further" (January 13, 1922).

It would be unreasonable to extract from passing notes the absolute assertions they contain, and although he himself forgets it here, we cannot forget that he never stopped writing, that he will keep writing right up to the end. But still, between the young man who said to the person he considered his future father-in-law, "I am nothing but literature, and I neither can nor want to be anything else," and the mature man who, ten years later, puts literature on the same level with his little attempts at gardening, the interior distance is great, even if, seen from the outside, the writing force remains constant or even appears to us stronger and more rigorous toward the end, since to this later period we owe *The Castle*.

Where does this difference come from? To say would be to pose as an expert on the inner life of an infinitely reserved man, opaque even to his friends and, moreover, not very accessible to himself. No one can claim to reduce to a certain number of precise affirmations what for Kafka himself could not attain the transparency of comprehensible expression. Besides, a shared set of intentions would be necessary, and this common ground is not available. Perhaps we can at least avoid errors with regard to what shows outwardly if we say that although his confidence in the powers of art often remains great, his confidence in his own powers, because it is always more harshly tested, enlightens him about the test itself, about what it demands of him, and enlightens him especially about what he himself demands of art: no longer that it give reality and coherence to his person, that it save him, that is, from insanity, but that it save him from perdition. And when Kafka senses that, banished from this real world, he is perhaps already a citizen of another world where he has to struggle not only for himself but for that other world, then writing will begin to appear to him merely as a means of struggle — sometimes disappointing, sometimes marvelous — which he can lose without losing everything.

Let us compare the following two entries. The first is from January 1912:

> I must be given credit for a very efficient concentration on literary activity. When my organism realized that writing was the richest direction of my being, everything pointed itself that way, and all other capacities, those which had as objects the pleasures of sex, drink, food, philosophical meditation and especially music, were abandoned. I've thinned out in all those directions. This was necessary, because my strength, even when gathered all together and devoted to one aim, was so small that it could only half reach the goal of writing . . . . The compensation for all this is clear. I will now have only to reject work at the office — my development being complete and I myself having nothing more to sacrifice as far as I can see — to begin my real life . . . in the course of which my face will finally be able to grow old in a natural way according to the progress of my effort.

Doubtless we should not be deceived by the light tone of irony, and yet the lightness, the insouciance are noticeable, and they emphasize by contrast the tension of this other entry whose meaning is apparently the same (it is dated August 6, 1914):

> Seen from the point of view of literature, my destiny is very simple. The sense which leads me to portray my dreamlike inner life

has pushed all my other senses into the background, and they have atrophied terribly; they do not cease to atrophy. Nothing else can ever satisfy me. But now my strength for portraying cannot be counted on. Perhaps it has disappeared forever; perhaps it will come back again someday. The circumstances of my life are not naturally favorable to it. It is thus that I waver, continually fly toward the top of the mountain where I can scarcely maintain myself for an instant. Others waver too, but in lower regions, with greater strength. If they threaten to fall, a relative who walks next to them for this purpose holds them up. But I waver on the heights; it is, alas, not death, but the eternal torments of Dying.

Three movements cross here. First, an affirmation: "Nothing else (but literature) can satisfy me." Then, self-doubt, linked to the inexorably uncertain essence of his gifts, which "cannot be counted on." Finally, the feeling that this uncertainty — this fact that writing never is a power one has at one's command — belongs to what is extreme in the work, to the central, mortal demand, which "is, alas, not death," which is death but death held at a distance, "the eternal torments of Dying."

It can be said that these three movements, with their vicissitudes, constitute the ordeal which exhausts Kafka's fidelity to "his unique vocation" and which, coinciding with his religious preoccupations, leads him to read in the work's unique requirement something other, another demand which tends to subordinate the first or at least to transform it. The more Kafka writes, the less he is sure of writing. Sometimes he tries to reassure himself by thinking that "if one has once received knowledge of writing, it cannot fail or subside but that also, very rarely, something suddenly emerges which passes all measure." This is a faint consolation: the more he writes, the more he nears that extreme point toward which the work tends as toward its origin, but which cannot be looked upon by him who glimpses it except as the empty depths of the indefinite. "I can no longer continue to write. I am up against the definitive limit, at which I must perhaps remain for years before being able to begin again a new story which again will remain unfinished. This fate pursues me" (November 30, 1914).

It seems that in 1915–1916 (however vain it may be to try to date a movement which escapes time), the change in perspective is complete. Kafka renewed relations with his former fiancée. These relations —which will culminate in another engagement in 1917 and then immediately afterward end in the sickness which becomes apparent at that time—plunge Kafka into torments he cannot overcome. He finds more and more that he cannot live alone and that he cannot live with others. He is seized and obsessed by the guilt in his situation; his existence is dominated by what he calls the bureaucratic vices—stinginess, indecision, a calculating mentality. He has to escape bureaucracy whatever the cost, and he can no longer count on literature for his escape: the substance of literary efforts evaporates because they partake of imposture and irresponsibility, and because they require solitude but are also annihilated by solitude. Hence the decision: "Become a soldier." At the same time there appear in the *Diaries* allusions to the Old Testament, and the cries of a lost man are heard: "Take me in your arms, I am fallen very low, receive me in the depths; if you refuse now, then later." "Take me, take me, I am only a snarl of madness and pain." "Have pity on me, I am a sinner in all the reaches of my being . . . . Do not reject me among the damned."

Certain of these texts used to be translated into French with the word "God" added. It does not appear. The word "God" hardly ever figures in the *Diaries*, and never in a significant way. This does not mean that these invocations, in their uncertainty, do not have a religious direction; rather, it means that the force of their uncertainty must be conserved. Kafka must not be deprived of the reserve he always showed with regard to what was most important to him. These words of distress were written in July 1916 and correspond to a stay in Marienbad with F. B. This visit was at first not very happy, but in the end it brought them together intimately. A year later Kafka is again betrothed. A month later he coughs blood. In September he leaves Prague, but the sickness is still mild and does not become threatening until 1922 (it seems). In 1917 he writes the *Aphorisms*, the only text where spiritual affirmation (in a general form, which does not concern him in particular), sometimes escapes the test of a negative transcendence.

For the years that follow, almost nothing remains in the *Diaries*. In 1918, not a word. There are a few lines in 1919 when he becomes engaged for six months to a young girl about whom we know practically nothing. In 1920 he meets Milena Jasenka, a sensitive, intelligent young Czech woman, capable of great liberty of mind and passion, to whom for two years he is bound by violent feeling, full of hope and happiness at the beginning, later doomed to sorrow. The *Diaries* become more telling again in 1921 and especially in 1922 when the setbacks of this friendship, combined with the increasing gravity of his illness, bring him to a point of tension where his mind seems to vacillate between madness and a decisive commitment to salvation. Here we must quote two long passages. The first is dated January 28, 1922.

A little groggy, tired from the tobogganing. Weapons still exist for me, however seldom I may employ them, and I'm laboring toward them with so much difficulty because I do not know the joy of using them, for as a child I didn't learn. It is not only "Father's fault" that I didn't learn, but also because I wanted to disturb the "peace," upset the balance, and consequently never had the right to resurrect on the one hand someone I strove to bury on the other. It is true, I come back to "the fault," for why did I want to take leave of the world? Because "he" wouldn't let me live in it, in his world. Naturally, today I cannot judge clearly in this matter, for now I am already a citizen in this other world which compares with the ordinary world just as the desert compares to cultivated land (I have been forty years wandering from Canaan), and it is as a foreigner that I look back. Doubtless, in this other world as well I am only the littlest and most timid (I brought that with me, it is the paternal inheritance), and if I am capable of living out here, it is only because of the organization proper to this wilderness — an organization according to which, even for the least of persons, there are elevations at lightning speeds, and also, of course, crushing moments that last thousands of years as if under the weight of the seas. In spite of everything, shouldn't I be grateful? Wouldn't I have had to find the road leading this far? Might not "banishment" from one side, joined with rejection from this have crushed me at the border? And is it not thanks to the strength of my father that the expulsion was sufficiently forceful that nothing could resist it (it, not me)? Indeed, my situation is something like the wandering in the desert in reverse, with continual approaches toward the desert and childish hopes (particularly concerning women): "Perhaps I shall keep in Canaan after all?" And in the meantime I have been in the desert for a long time, and these are only visions born of despair, especially at the moments when, out here too, I am the most miserable of men and Canaan necessarily offers itself as the sole Promised Land, for there is no third land for men.

The second text is dated the next day:

Attacks on the road, in the evening, in the snow. There are conflicting thoughts always in my head, more or less thus: My situation in this world would seem to be a dreadful one, alone here in Spindlermühle, on a forsaken road, moreover, where one keeps slipping in the snow in the dark, a senseless road, moreover, without any earthly goal (it leads to the bridge? Why there? In any event I didn't even go that far); I too am forsaken in this place (I cannot consider the doctor to be any personal help, I didn't win his aid by my merits, at bottom the fee is my only relationship to him), incapable of striking up a friendship with anyone, unable to bear having any acquaintances, full, in fact, of an infinite astonishment before a cheerful company or before parents with their children (at the hotel, indeed, there is not much gaiety; I wouldn't go so far as to say that I am the cause, in my capacity as "man with too long a shadow," but as a matter of fact my shadow is too long, and with fresh astonishment I observe the capacity for resistance, the obstinacy of certain beings who want to live "in spite of everything" in this shadow, right in it — but there is much more than this to be said on the matter); forsaken moreover not only here but in general, even in Prague, my "home," and what is more, forsaken not by people (that would not be the worst — as long as I live I could chase after them), but rather by myself vis-à-vis people, by my strength with regard to them. I am fond of lovers, but I cannot love, I am too remote, I am excluded. Doubtless, since I am nonetheless a human being and my roots need nourishment, I have my proxies "down" (or up) there too, lamentable and inadequate actors, who can satisfy me (it is true, they do not satisfy me at all, and that is why I am so forsaken) only because my main nourishment comes from other roots in other climes. These roots too are lamentable, but still, more capable of life. This brings me to the conflict in my thoughts. If things were only as they seem to be on the road in the snow, it would be dreadful. I would be lost, and this is to be understood not as a threat; rather, as immediate execution. But I live elsewhere; it is only that the attraction of the world of men is immense. In an instant it can make you forget everything. But great also is the attraction of my world: those who love me love me because I am "forsaken" — not, I feel sure, on the principle of a Weissian vacuum but because they sense that in happy times I enjoy on another plane the freedom of movement which I lack completely here.

The Positive Experience

Commentary on these pages seems superfluous. Nevertheless we should notice how, at this date, deprivation of the world is reversed, becoming a positive experience,[3] that of another world where Kafka is already a citizen, where, granted, he is only the littlest and most anxious, but where he also knows staggering heights and enjoys a freedom whose value other men sense, whose prestige they acknowledge. However, in order not to alter the sense of such images, it is necessary to read them, not from the common Christian perspective (according to which there is this world, then the world beyond, the only one which has value, reality, and majesty), but always from the "Abraham" perspective. For, as far as Kafka is concerned, to be excluded from the world means to be excluded from Canaan, to wander in the desert, and it is this situation which makes his struggle pathetic, his hope hopeless. It is as if, cast out of the world, into the error of infinite migration, he had to struggle ceaselessly to make of this outside another world and of this error the principle, the origin of a new freedom. This struggle can have no ascertainable result. What he has to win is his own loss, the truth of exile and the way back into the very heart of dispersion. This struggle can be compared to profound Jewish speculations, when, especially after the Expulsion from Spain, religious minds tried to overcome exile by pushing it to its limit.[4] Kafka clearly associated "all this

[3]Certain letters to Milena also allude to the element of the unknown which persists in this terrible movement (see the studies that appeared in the *Nouvelle N.R.F.:* "Kafka et Brod" and "L'Echec de Milena," October and November, 1954).

[4]On this subject, we must refer to G.G. Scholem's book, *Major Trends in Jewish Mysticism:*

> The horrors of Exile were mirrored in the Kabbalistic doctrine of metempsychosis, which now won immense popularity by stressing the various stages of the soul's exile. The most fearful fate that could befall any soul — far more ghastly than the torments of hell — was to be "outcast" or "naked," a state precluding either rebirth or even admission to hell . . . . Absolute homelessness was the sinister symbol of absolute Godlessness, of utter moral and spiritual degradation. Union with God or absolute banishment were the two poles between which a system had to be devised in which the Jews could live under the domination of Law, which seeks to destroy the forces of Exile.

And again this: "There was an ardent desire to break down the Exile by enhancing its torments, by savoring its bitterness to the utmost (even to the night of the Exile of the Shekhina itself)" [Passages from *Major Trends*, 3d rev. ed. (1941; rpt. New York: Schocken Books, 1978), p. 250 — Trans.]. One could well imagine that the theme of *The Metamorphosis* (as well as the obsessive fictions of bestiality) is reminiscent of, or an

literature" (his own), with "a new Kabbala," "a new secret doctrine" which "could have developed" "if Zionism hadn't come along in the meantime" (January 19, 1922). One understands better why he is at the same time Zionist and anti-Zionist. Zionism is exile's cure – the affirmation that an earthly home is possible, that the Jewish people has for its dwelling not only a book, the Bible, but the earth, and belongs no longer to dispersion in time. Kafka wants this reconciliation profoundly. He wants it even if he is excluded from it, for the greatness of this rigorous conscience was always to hope for others more than for himself and not to measure mankind's unhappiness by his personal misfortune. "Magnificent, all that, except for me, and rightly so." He does not belong to this truth, and that is why he has to be anti-Zionist for himself, on pain of being condemned to immediate execution and to the despair of absolute impiety. He already belongs to the other shore, and his wandering does not consist in nearing Canaan, but in nearing the desert, the truth of the desert – in going always further in that direction even when, finding no favor in that other world either, and tempted again by the joys of the real world ("particularly with regard to women": this is a clear allusion to Milena), he tries to persuade himself that perhaps he still keeps in Canaan. If he weren't anti-Zionist for himself (that is only said, of course, figuratively), if there were only this world, then "the situation would be frightful." Then he would be lost right away. But he is "elsewhere," and if the force of the human world's attraction remains great enough to draw him back to the border and keep him there as though crushed, no less great is the pull of his own world, the one where he is free, where he has the liberty he speaks of with a tremor, a tone of prophetic authority which contrasts with his habitual modesty.

There is no doubt that this other world has something to do with literary activity. The proof is that Kafka, if he speaks of the "new Kabbala," speaks of it in connection, precisely, with "all this literature." But

---

allusion to, the tradition of Kabbalistic metempsychosis, even if it is not sure that "Samsa" recalls "Samsara" (Kafka and Samsa are related names, but Kafka rejects this comparison). Kafka sometimes asserts that he is not yet born: "Hesitation before birth: if there is a transmigration of souls, then I am not yet at the bottom rung; my life is hesitation before birth" (January 24, 1922). Let us recall that in *Preparations for a Country Wedding*, Raban, the hero of this early narrative, expresses playfully the wish to become an insect (*Käfer*) which could lie about in bed and escape the disagreeable duties of the community. The "shell" of solitude seems, thus, to be the image which was to be elaborated in the impressive theme of *The Metamorphosis*.

one also suspects that from here on the demand, the truth of that other world exceeds the work's demand — is not in his eyes exhausted by the work and is only imperfectly realized there. When writing becomes "a form of prayer," it is implied that there are probably other forms. And even if, as a consequence of this world's unhappiness, there were no other forms, to write is no longer from this perspective to approach the work, but rather to wait for that one moment of grace — Kafka acknowledged that he lay in wait for it — when one would have to write no longer. To Janouch, who asked him, "Do you mean that poetry tends toward religion?" he replies, "I will not say that, but toward prayer, certainly"; and opposing literature to poetry, he adds, "Literature strives to place things in an agreeable light; the poet is constrained to lift them into the realm of the true, the pure, and the constant." This is a significant response, for it corresponds to a note in the *Diaries* where Kafka wonders what joy literature can still hold for him: "I can still draw momentary satisfaction from works like *A Country Doctor*, provided I can still write such things (very unlikely). But happiness only if I can raise the world into the pure, the true, and the immutable" (September 25, 1917). Here the "idealist" or "spiritual" demand becomes categorical. Write, yes, continue to write, but only in order to "lift into infinite life what is perishable and isolated, into the realm of the law what belongs to chance," as he says again to Janouch. But no sooner is that said than this question arises: Is it possible, then? Is it sure that writing does not belong to evil? And isn't the consolation of writing an illusion, a dangerous illusion, one that must be resisted? "There is undeniably a certain happiness in being able calmly to write down: *suffocation is inconceivably horrible*. Of course it is inconceivable — that is why I have written nothing down" (December 20, 1921). And doesn't the humblest reality of the world have a solidity lacking in the strongest work?

> Writing's lack of independence: it depends on the maid who tends the fire, on the cat warming itself by the stove, even on that poor old human being warming himself. These are all autonomous activities, ruled by their own laws; only writing is helpless, cannot live in itself, is a joke and a despair (December 6, 1921).

A grimace, the grimace on the face that recoils from the light, "a defense of nothingness, a voucher for nothingness, a whiff of gaiety lent to nothingness" — such is art.

And yet, if the confidence of his early years gives place to an attitude of increasingly inflexible severity, still, even in his most difficult moments, when his very sanity seems threatened, when he undergoes almost palpable attacks from the unknown ("How it spies: for example, on the road going to the doctor's back there, constantly")—even then he continues to see in his work, not what threatens him, but what can help him and make salvation accessible to him.

The consolation of writing, remarkable, mysterious, perhaps dangerous, perhaps salutary: it is to leap out of the ranks of murderers; it is an observation which is an act (*Tat-Beobachtung*, the observation which has become act). There is an observation-act to the extent that a higher sort of observation is created—higher, not more acute, and the higher it is, the more inaccessible it is to the rank and file (of murderers), the less it is dependent, the more it follows the laws proper to its own movement, the more its road climbs, joyfully, incalculably. [January, 1922]

Here literature is proclaimed as the power which frees, the force that allays the oppressions of the world "where everything feels throttled"; it is the liberating passage from the first to the third person, from observation of oneself, which was Kafka's torment, to a higher observation, rising above mortal reality toward the other world, the world of freedom.

Why Art Is, Is Not, Justified

Why this confidence? One might well wonder. One could answer by reflecting that Kafka belongs to a tradition where the highest things are expressed in a book which is writing par excellence,[5] a tradition where the combination, the manipulation of letters has served as the basis of experiences of ecstasy, and where it is said that the world of letters, the letters of the alphabet, is the true world of beatitude.[6] To write is to conjure up spirits, perhaps freeing them against us, but this danger belongs to the essence of the power that liberates.[7]

[5]Kafka said to Janouch that "the task of the poet is a prophetic task: the right word is a guide, the wrong one a seducer; it is not by accident that the Bible is called Scripture."

[6]Hence Kafka's pitiless condemnation (which applies to himself) of Jewish writers who use German.

[7]"Yet what about this fact itself: being a poet? This act of writing is a gift, a silent and mysterious gift. But its price? In the night the answer always jumps out at me with

However, Kafka's was not a "superstitious" mind; there was in him a cold lucidity which made him say to Brod, as they left at the end of some Hassidic celebrations, "In fact it was more or less the same as a tribe of savages: gross superstitions."[8] We must not, then, limit ourselves to explanations which, while they may be correct, still do not help us understand why Kafka, so sensitive to the deviation implied in every one of the steps he takes, surrendered with such faith to that essential error which is writing. Nor would it suffice to recall in this connection that ever since his adolescence, he had been extraordinarily sensitive to the influence of artists such as Goethe and Flaubert, whom he was often ready to place above everyone because they placed their art above everything. Probably Kafka never entirely separated himself internally from this conception. But if the passion of art was from the beginning so strong and appeared to him for such a long time to be salutary, this is because, from the start, and by "Father's fault," he found himself cast out of the world, condemned to a solitude for which he had literature, not to blame, but rather to thank—for brightening this solitude, making it fertile, opening it onto another world.

It can be said that his debate with his father pushed the negative aspect of the literary experience into the background for him. Even when he sees that his work requires his ruin, even when, still more grave, he sees the opposition between his work and his marriage, he by no means concludes that there is in this work a fatal power, a voice which decrees "banishment" and condemns to the desert. He does not come to this conclusion, because the world has been lost for him ever since the beginning; real existence has been withdrawn from him, or it was never granted him, and when again he speaks of his exile and of the impossibility of escaping it, he will say, "I have the impression of never

---

dazzling clarity: writing is wages received of the diabolical powers one has served. This surrender to obscure forces, this unleashing of forces ordinarily held in check, these impure embraces and everything else that happens in the depths, does one still know anything about all this when one writes stories in the full light, in the broad daylight? . . . Does the surface retain some trace of it? Perhaps there is some other way to write? For my part, I know only this way, in the nights when anguish torments me at the edge of sleep" (cited by Brod).

[8]But later, Kafka appears to become ever more attentive toward this form of devotion. Dora Dymant belonged to a "respected Jewish Hassidic family." And Martin Buber may have influenced him.

having come here at all, but of having been pushed already as a little child and then chained to the spot" (January 24, 1922). Art did not cause him this misfortune: art did not even contribute to it, but on the contrary has shed light upon it — has been the "consciousness of unhappiness," its new dimension.

Art is primarily the consciousness of unhappiness, not its compensation. Kafka's rigor, his fidelity to the work's demand, his fidelity to the demands of grief, spared him that paradise of fictions where so many weak artists whom life has disappointed find satisfaction. Art has for its object neither reveries nor "constructions." But it does not describe truth either. Truth needs neither to be known nor to be described — it cannot even know itself — just as earthly salvation asks not to be discussed or represented, but to be achieved. In this sense there is no place for art: rigorous monism excludes all idols. But, in this same sense, if art is not justified in general, it is at least justified for Kafka alone. For art is linked, precisely as Kafka is, to what is "outside" the world, and it expresses the profundity of this outside bereft of intimacy and of repose — this outside which appears when even with ourselves, even with our death, we no longer have relations of possibility. Art is the consciousness of "this misfortune." It describes the situation of one who has lost himself, who can no longer say "me," who in the same movement has lost the world, the truth of the world, and belongs to exile, to the *time of distress* when, as Hölderlin says, the gods are no longer and are not yet. This does not mean that art affirms another world, at least not if it is true that art has its origin, not in another world, but in the other of all worlds (it is on this point, we now see — but in the notes which represent his religious experience rather than in his work — that Kafka takes or is ready to take the leap which art does not authorize).[9]

Kafka vacillates pathetically. Sometimes he seems to do everything to create for himself a dwelling place among men whose "attractiveness is monstrously strong." He tries to get engaged, he gardens, he practices manual tasks, he thinks about Palestine, he procures lodgings in Prague in order to win not only solitude but the independence of a mature,

---

[9]Kafka does not fail to denounce the temptation — the tempting simplicity — in the excessively determined distinction between these two worlds: "Usually, the division (of these two worlds) seems to me too determined, dangerous in its determination, sad and too domineering" (January 30, 1922).

vigorous man. On this level, the debate with the father remains essential, and all the new notes of the *Diaries* confirm this. They show that Kafka hides nothing from himself of what psychoanalysis could reveal to him. His dependence on his family not only rendered him weak, a stranger to manly tasks (as he himself affirms), but, since this dependence horrifies him, it makes all forms of dependence just as unbearable to him — and, to start with, marriage, which reminds him repulsively of his parents', [10] of the family life from which he would like to free himself but to which he would also like to commit himself, for that is obedience to the law, that is the truth, the truth of the father, which attracts him as much as he resists it, so that "really I stand up before my family, and in its circle I ceaselessly brandish knives to hurt it but at the same time to protect it." "This on the one hand."

But on the other hand he always sees more, and sickness naturally helps him see: that he belongs to the other shore; that, banished, he must not bargain with this banishment; neither must he, as though crushed against its border, remain passively turned toward a reality from which he feels excluded and in which he has never even lived since he is not yet born. This new perspective might be merely that of absolute despair, the nihilistic perspective which is too hastily attributed to him. There is no denying that distress is his element. It is his abode and his "time." But this distress is never without hope. This hope is often only the torment of distress — which does not give hope, but prevents one from getting enough even of despair and determines that "condemned to die, one is also condemned to defend oneself right up to the last" — and perhaps at that point assigned to reverse condemnation into deliverance. In this new perspective, the perspective of distress, it is essential not to turn toward Canaan. The wanderer has the

---

[10]We must quote at least this passage from a draft of a letter to his fiancée in which he specifies with the greatest lucidity his relations with his family:

> But I stem from my parents, I am linked to them just as to my sisters by blood. In everyday life, and because I devote myself to my own goals, I don't feel it, but fundamentally this bond has more value for me than I know. Sometimes, too, I pursue it with my hatred: the sight of the conjugal bed, of the rumpled sheets, the night clothes carefully spread out, makes me want to vomit; it pulls all my insides out. It's as if I were not definitively born, as if I were always coming into the world out of that obscure life in that obscure room; it's as if I had always to search there again for confirmation of myself, and as if I were, at least to a certain extent, indissolubly linked to these repulsive things. This still impedes my feet which want to run; my feet are still stuck in the formless original soup. [October 18, 1916]

desert for a destination, and it is his approach to the desert which is now the true Promised Land. "Is it out there you are leading me?" Yes, out there. But where is that, out there? It is never in sight; the desert is even less certain than the world; it is never anything but the approach to the desert. And in this land of error one is never "here," but always "far from here." And yet, in this region where the conditions of a real dwelling lack, where one has to live in an incomprehensible separation, (an exclusion from which one is, somehow, excluded, just as one is excluded from oneself) — in this region which is the region of error because in it one does nothing but stray without end, there subsists a tension: the very possibility of erring, of going all the way to the end of error, of nearing its limit, of transforming wayfaring without any goal into the certitude of the goal without any way there.

The Move outside Truth: The Landsurveyor

We know that the story of the landsurveyor represents the most impressive image of this move. From the very beginning, this hero of inflexible obstinacy is described to us as having renounced his world, his home, the life which includes wife and children, forever. Right from the start, then, he is outside salvation, he belongs to exile, that region where not only is he away from home, but away from himself. He is in the outside itself — a realm absolutely bereft of intimacy where beings seem absent and where everything one thinks one grasps slips away. The tragic difficulty of the undertaking is that in this world of exclusion and radical separation, everything is false and inauthentic as soon as one examines it, everything lacks as soon as one seeks support from it, but nevertheless the depth of this absence is always given anew as an indubitable, absolute presence. And the world *absolute*, which means "separated," is in its proper place here. For it is as if separation, experienced in all its rigor, could reverse itself and become the absolutely separated, the absolutely absolute.

This must be put more precisely: Kafka — that exacting mind by no means satisfied with the dilemma of all or nothing which he nevertheless conceives more intransigently than anyone else — hints that in this move outside the true there are certain rules. They are perhaps contradictory and indefensible, but still they authorize a sort of possibility. The first is given in error itself: one must stray and not be indolent as Joseph K. is in *The Trial*, imagining as he does that things are always going to continue and that he is still in the world when, from the first sentence, he is cast out of it. Joseph's fault, similar probably to the one with which Kafka reproached himself at the time he was writing this book, is that he wants to win his trial in the world itself, to which he thinks he still belongs, but where his cold, empty heart, his bachelor bureaucrat's existence, his lack of concern for his family—all character traits which Kafka found in himself—already prevent him from getting a footing. Granted, his indifference yields bit by bit, but that is a result of the trial, just as the beauty which shines in the faces of the accused and makes them attractive to women is the reflection of their own dissolution, of death advancing in them like a truer light.

The trial, the banishment, is no doubt a great misfortune; it is perhaps an incomprehensible injustice or an inexorable punishment. But it is also—to be sure, only to a certain extent (and this is the hero's excuse, the trap he falls into)—a given which it does no good to protest by invoking in hollow speeches some higher justice. On the contrary, one must try to gain from it, according to the rule which Kafka made his own: "You must limit yourself to what you still possess." The trial has at least the advantage of making known to K. what is really the case. It dissipates illusion—the deceptive consolations which, because he had a good job and a few indifferent pleasures, allowed him to believe in his existence, in his existence as a man of the world. But the trial is not, for all that, the truth. It is, on the contrary, a process of error, like everything which is linked to the outside, that "exterior" darkness where one is cast by the force of banishment. The trial is a process where if one hope remains, it is for him who advances, not against the current, in futile opposition, but in the very direction of error.

The Essential Fault

The landsurveyor is almost entirely free of Joseph K.'s faults. He does not seek to return home. Gone is life in Canaan; effaced is the truth of this world; he scarcely even remembers it in brief, pathetic moments. He is not indolent either, but always on the move, never stopping, almost never getting discouraged, going from failure to failure in a tireless movement which evokes the cold disquietude of the time which affords no rest. Yes, he goes ahead, with an inflexible obstinacy, always in the direction of extreme error, disdaining the village which still has some reality, but wanting the Castle, which perhaps has none, detaching himself from Frieda, who retains some glints of life, to turn toward Olga, sister of Amalia, the doubly excluded, the rejected — Amalia who, still worse, in a fearful decision, voluntarily chose to be so. Everything ought to proceed, then, for the best. But nothing of the sort. For the landsurveyor falls incessantly into the fault which Kafka designates as the gravest: impatience.[11] The impatience at the heart of error is the essential fault, because it misconstrues the very trueness of error which, like a law, requires that one never believe the goal is close or that one is coming nearer to it. One must never have done with the indefinite; one must never grasp — as if it were the immediate, the already present — the profundity of inexhaustible absence.

To be sure, it is inevitable that one should do so, and therein lies the desolating character of such a quest. Whoever is not impatient is indolent. Whoever surrenders to the disquietude of error loses the indifference that would exhaust time. Scarcely having arrived, understanding nothing about this ordeal of exclusion in which he finds himself, K. sets out right away to get quickly to the end. He won't expend any energy on the intermediaries; in their regard he is indolent. This is probably to his credit: doubtless it demonstrates the force of his tense striving towards the absolute. But his aberration is not any the less glaring. It consists in taking for the end what is only an intermediary, a representation befitting his "lights."

Surely we are as deceived as the landsurveyor when we think we recognize in the bureaucratic phantasm the fitting symbol of a superior world. This figure merely befits our impatience. It is the palpable form of the error through which, before the impatient gaze, the inexorable force of the evil infinite is ceaselessly substituted for the absolute. K. always wants to reach the goal before having reached it. This demand for a premature dénouement is the principle of figuration: it engenders the *image*, or, if you will, the idol, and the curse which attaches to it is that which attaches to idolatry. Man wants unity right away; he wants it in separation itself. He represents it to himself, and this representation, the image of unity, immediately reconstitutes the element of dispersion where he loses himself more and more. For the image as such can never be attained, and moreover it hides from him the unity of which it

---

[11]"There are two main human sins from which all the others derive: impatience and indolence. Because of impatience, they were banished from Paradise. Because of indolence, they do not return. Perhaps there is only one main sin, impatience. Because of impatience, they were driven out, because of impatience, they do not return" (*Aphorisms*) [English translation from "Reflections on Sin, Suffering, Hope, and the True Way," in *Wedding Preparations*, trans. Eithne Wilkins and Ernst Kaiser, Jr. (London: Secker & Warburg, 1954) — Trans.].

is the image. It separates him from unity by making itself inaccessible and by making unity inaccessible.

Klamm is by no means invisible. The landsurveyor wants to see him, and he sees him. The Castle, supreme goal, is by no means out of sight. As an image, it is constantly at his disposal. Naturally when you look at them closely, these figures are disappointing. The Castle is only a cluster of village huts; Klamm, a big heavy man seated in front of a desk. There is nothing here that isn't very ordinary and ugly. But this is the landsurveyor's good luck — the truth, the deceptive honesty of these images: they are not seductive in themselves, they possess nothing to justify the fascinated interest people take in them. Thus they remind us that they are not the true goal. In this insignificance, however, the other truth lets itself be forgotten. And the other truth is that these images are, all the same, images of the goal; they partake of its glow, of its ineffable value, and not to attach oneself to them is already to turn away from the essential.

We could summarize this situation as follows: it is impatience which makes the goal inaccessible by substituting for it the proximity of an intermediary figure. It is impatience that destroys the way toward the goal by preventing us from recognizing in the intermediary the figure of the immediate.

We must limit ourselves here to these few indications. The bureaucratic phantasm, all the bustling idleness which characterizes it, and those double beings who are its functionaries, guards, aides, messengers, who always go two by two as if to show clearly that they are only each other's reflections and the reflection of an invisible whole; moreover, that whole chain of metamorphoses, that methodical enlarging of the distance which is never defined as infinite but necessarily expands indefinitely through the transformation of the goal into obstacles, but also of obstacles into intermediaries leading to the goal — all this powerful imagery does not represent the truth of a superior world, or even its transcendence. It represents, rather, the favorable and unfavorable nature of figuration — the bind in which the man of exile is caught, obliged as he is to make out of error a means of reaching truth and out of what deceives him indefinitely the ultimate possibility of grasping the infinite.

The Work's Space

To what extent was Kafka aware of the analogy between this move outside truth and the movement by which the work tends toward its origin — toward that center which in the only place the work can be achieved, in the search for which it is realized and which, once reached, makes the work impossible? To what extent did he connect the ordeal of his heroes with the way in which he himself, through art, was trying to make his way toward the work and, through the work, toward something true? Did he often think of Goethe's words, "It is by postulating the impossible that the writer procures for himself all of the possible"? This much at least is strikingly evident: the fault which he punished in K. is also the one with which the artist reproaches himself. Impatience is this fault. It wants to hurry the story toward its dénouement before the story has developed in all its directions, exhausted the measure of time which is in it, lifted the indefinite to a true totality where every inauthentic movement, every partially false image can be transformed into an unshakable certitude. This is an impossible task, a task which, if it were accomplished fully, would destroy that very truth toward which it tends, just as the work is wrecked if it touches the point which is its origin. Many considerations restrain Kafka from finishing almost any of his "stories" and cause him, when he has scarcely begun one, to leave it in search of peace in another. He states that he often feels the torment of the artist exiled from his work at the moment it affirms itself and closes up. He also says that he sometimes abandons a story in anguish lest, if he didn't abandon it, he could never come back toward the world, but it is not certain that this concern was in his case the strongest. That he often abandons a story because every dénouement bears in itself the happiness of a definitive truth which he hasn't the right to accept, to which his existence does not yet correspond — this reason also appears to have played a considerable role. But all these hesitations can be summarized as follows: Kafka, perhaps without knowing it, felt deeply that to write is to surrender to the incessant; and, out of anxiety — fear of impatience — and scrupulous attention to the work's demand, he most often denied himself the leap which alone permits finishing, the insouciant and happy confidence by which (momentarily) a limit is placed upon the interminable.

What has so inappropriately been called his realism reveals this same instinctive effort to exorcise the impatience within him. Kafka often showed that his genius was a prompt, a ready one; he was capable of reaching the essential in a few swift strokes. But more and more he imposed upon himself a minuteness, a slow approach, a detailed precision (even in the description of his own dreams), without which a man exiled from reality is rapidly condemned to the errors of confusion and the approximations of the imaginary. The more one is lost outside, in the strangeness and insecurity of this loss, the more one must appeal to the spirit of rigor, scruple, exactitude; the more one must concentrate on absence through a multitude of images, through their determined and modest appearance — modest because disengaged from fascination — and through their energetically sustained coherence. Anyone who belongs to reality can forego all these details which, as we know, in no way correspond to the form of a real vision. But he who belongs to the depths of the limitless and the remote, to the distress of the immeasurable, yes, that person is condemned to an excess of measure and to strive for continuity without a single misstep, without any missing links, without the slightest inconsistency. And condemned is the right word. For if patience, exactitude, and cold mastery are qualities indispensable for not getting lost when nothing subsists that one could hold onto, patience, exactitude, and cold mastery are also faults which, dividing difficulties and stretching them out indefinitely, may well retard the shipwreck, but surely retard deliverance, by ceaselessly transforming the infinite into the indefinite. In the same way it is measure which, in the work, prevents the limitless from ever being achieved.

Art and Idolatry

"Thou shalt not make unto thee any graven image or any likeness of any thing that is in heaven above or that is in the earth beneath or that is in the water under the earth." Felix Weltsch, Kafka's friend, who has spoken very pertinently of Kafka's struggle against impatience, thinks that he took the Biblical commandment to heart. If this is so, then imagine a man upon whom this essential interdiction weighs, who must, on pain of death, exile himself from images and who, suddenly, discovers himself exiled in the imaginary without any dwelling place or subsistence except images and the space of images. There he is, then, obliged to live off his death and constrained in his despair, and in order to escape despair—immediate execution—to make of his condemnation the only road to salvation. Was Kafka consciously this man? No one can say. Sometimes one has the feeling that the more he seeks to remember the essential prohibition (for it is in any case forgotten, since the community in which it was alive is more or less destroyed)—the more he seeks to remember the religious sense which lives hidden in this prohibition, and seeks this with an ever greater rigor, emptying himself and the space all around him so that idols might find no welcome there, the more he seems prepared, contradictorily, to forget that this interdiction ought also to be applied to his art. The result is a very unstable equilibrium. This equilibrium, in the illegitimate solitude which is his, allows him to be faithful to an ever more rigorous spiritual monism while abandoning himself to a certain artistic idolatry. Then it commits him to purifying this idolatry by all the rigors of an asceticism which condemns literary realities (he leaves his works unfinished, is unwilling to publish, refuses to believe himself a writer, etc.), and which furthermore—this is still more grave—tends to subordinate art to his spiritual condition. Art is not religion, "it doesn't even lead to religion." But in the time of distress which is ours, the time when the gods are missing, the time of absence and exile, art is justified, for it is the intimacy of this distress: the effort to make manifest, through the image, the error of the imaginary, and eventually the ungraspable, forgotten truth which hides behind this error.

That there is, in Kafka, a tendency at first to let literature's demand relieve religion's and then, especially toward the end, an inclination to allow his religious experience to take over from his literary one—that there is in him a tendency to mix the two in a rather confusing way by passing from the desert of faith to faith in a world which is no longer the desert but another world, where liberty will be returned to him—all this is suggested by the notes in the *Diaries*. "Do I live now in the other world? Do I dare say it?" (January 30, 1922). On one of the pages we have quoted, Kafka recalls that according to him men have no other choice than this one: either to seek the Promised Land in Canaan or to seek it in the other world, which is the desert, "for," he adds, "there is no third land for men." Certainly there is not, but perhaps one should say more. Perhaps it must be said that the artist—the man Kafka also wanted to be, the "poet," concerned for his art and in search of its origin—is he for whom there exists not even one world. For there exists for him only the outside, the glistening flow of the eternal outside.

The
Work and
Death's
Space
IV

Death
as
Possibility

The Word Experience

The work draws whoever devotes himself to it toward the point where it withstands its impossibility. The work comes through this test and is, in this respect, experience. But what does that word mean? In a passage from *Malte*, Rilke says that "poetry is not sentiment, it is experience. In order to write a single line, one must have seen many cities, men and things." Rilke does not mean, however, that poetry is the expression of a rich personality, capable of living and of having lived. Memories are necessary, but only that they may be forgotten: in order that in this forgetfulness — in the silence of a profound metamorphosis — there might at last be born a word, the first word of a poem. "Experience" here means contact with being, renewal of oneself in this contact — an experiment, but one that remains undetermined.

Valéry writes in a letter: "All his life the true painter seeks painting: the true poet, Poetry, etc. For these are not determined activities. In them one must create the need, the goal, the means, and even the obstacles." Valéry is alluding here to another form of experience. Poetry is not granted the poet as a truth and a certainty against which he could measure himself. He does not know whether he is a poet, but neither does he know what poetry is, or even whether it is. It depends on him, on his search. And this dependence does not make him master of what he seeks; rather, it makes him uncertain of himself and as if nonexistent. Every work, and each moment of the work, puts everything into question all over again; and thus he who must live only for the work has no way to live. Whatever he does, the work withdraws him from what he does and from what he can do.

Apparently these remarks take into consideration only the technical activity in the work. They imply that art is difficult, that the artist, in the practice of his art, lives on uncertainty. In his almost naïve concern to protect poetry from insoluble problems, Valéry tried to present it as an activity all the more demanding in that it has few secrets and is little able to seclude itself in the vagueness of its profundity. Poetry, in his eyes, is a convention which envies mathematics and appears to require nothing but uninterrupted effort or attention. It seems, then, that art, this strange activity which has to create everything — need, goal, means — above all creates for itself what hampers it, what renders it not only supremely difficult, but also useless to all living beings and especially to one living being in particular, the artist. This activity is not even a game, although it has the innocence and vanity of games. Yet there comes a moment when it appears as the most necessary of all activities. Poetry is only an exercise, but this exercise is the mind, the mind's purity, the pure point at which consciousness — that empty power to exchange itself for everything — becomes a real power, enclosing its infinite number of constructs and the whole range of its maneuvers within strict limits. Art now has a goal, and this goal is the mind's mastery. And Valéry considers that his poems have no interest for him other than that of teaching him how they were fashioned, how a work of the mind is produced. Art has a goal; it is this very goal. It is not simply a way of exercising the mind; it *is* mind — which is nothing if it is not a work. And what is the work? The exceptional moment when possibility becomes power, when the mind — law or empty form rich only in undetermined potentiality — becomes the certainty of a realized form, becomes this body which is form and this beautiful form which is a lovely body. The work is mind, and the mind is the passage, within the work, from the supreme indeterminacy to the determination of that extreme. This unique passage is real only in the work — in the work which is never real, never finished, since it is only the realization of the mind's infiniteness. The mind, then, sees once again in the work only an opportunity to recognize and exercise itself ad infinitum. Thus we return to our point of departure.

This movement, and the terrible constraint, so to speak, which makes it circular, show that one can never simply make an allowance for artistic experience. Reduced to a purely formal investigation, it makes form the ambiguous point through which everything passes.[1] Everything becomes enigma, an enigma with which there is no possible compromise, for it

---

[1] Valéry's singularity is that he gives to the work the name "mind," but mind *equivocally* conceived by him as *form*: form which sometimes has the sense of an empty

requires that one do and be nothing which it has not drawn into itself. "All his life the true painter seeks painting; the true poet, Poetry."*"All his life"*: those are three demanding words. They do not mean that the painter turns his life into painting or that he tries to discover painting in his life. Yet neither do they mean that life remains intact when through and through it becomes the search for an activity which is sure neither of its goals nor of its means but only of this uncertainty and of the absolute passion which it commands.

We have two answers so far. Poetry is experience, linked to a vital approach, to a movement which is accomplished in the serious, purposeful course of life. In order to write a single line, one must have exhausted life. And now, the other answer: to write a single line, one must have exhausted art, one must have exhausted one's life in the search for art. These two answers share the idea that art is experience because it is experimental: because it is a search – an investigation which is not undetermined but is, rather, determined by its indeterminacy, and involves the whole of life, even if it seems to know nothing of life.

Yet another answer would be André Gide's: "I wanted to indicate in *Tentative amoureuse* the influence of the book upon the writer, during the writing itself. For, emerging from us, it changes us, it modifies the course of our life".[2] This answer, however, is more limited. Writing changes us. We do not write according to what we are; we are according to what we write. But where does what is written come from? Still from us? From a possibility in ourselves which is discovered and affirmed only through literary endeavors? All endeavors transform us; every action we accomplish acts upon us. Does the act which consists in making a book modify us more profoundly? And if so, is it really the act itself, the effort, the patience, the attention in this act which is responsible for the change? Is it not rather a question of a more original demand, a necessary prior

---

power, a capacity of substitution which precedes and makes possible an infinite number of realizable objects – while at other times it has the plastic, concrete reality of a realized form. In the first instance, it is *mind* which is the master of forms; in the second, it is *body* which is mind's form and power. Poetry, creation, is thus the ambiguity of one and the other. As mind, poetry is only pure intellectual exercise and tends to accomplish nothing; it is the empty, though admirable, movement of the indefinite. But as already embodied and formed, as the form and reality of a beautiful body, poetry is as if indifferent to "meaning," to mind. In language as body, in the physicalness of language, poetry tends only toward the perfection of a finished thing.

[2]Thirty years later, Gide returns to this point of view and refines it: "It seems to me that each of my books was not so much the product of a new inner disposition, as, on the

change which is perhaps achieved through the work, toward which the work leads us but which, through an essential contradiction, is not just prior to the work's completion but goes back even further to the point where nothing can be done at all? "I no longer have any personality other than the one which suits this work." But what suits the work is perhaps that "I" have no personality. Clemens Brentano, in his novel *Godwi*, speaks eloquently of "the nullification of oneself" which is effected in the work. And perhaps it is a question of a still more radical change which does not consist in a new disposition of the soul and mind, which is not limited to removing me from myself, "nullifying" me, and which is not linked to the particular content of a given book either, but rather to the fundamental demand of the work.

To Die Content

Kafka, in a note from his *Diaries*, makes a remark which bears reflection:

On the way home, I said to Max that on my deathbed, provided the suffering is not too great, I will be very content. I forgot to add, and later I omitted this on purpose, that the best of what I have written is based upon this capacity to die content. All the good passages, the strongly convincing ones, are about someone who is dying and who finds it very hard and sees in it an injustice. This, at least in my opinion, is all very moving for the reader. But for me, since I think I can be content on my deathbed, such descriptions are secretly a game. I even enjoy dying in the character who is dying. Thus I calculatingly exploit the reader's attention which I have concentrated upon death; I keep a much clearer head than he, who will lament, I suppose, on his deathbed. My lamentation is thus as perfect as possible. It does not interrupt itself abruptly the way real lamentation does, rather it follows its beautiful, pure course.

This is dated December, 1914. One cannot be sure that it expresses a point of view which Kafka would still have entertained later. It is, in

---

contrary, its cause and the first provocation of that disposition of soul and mind in which I had to maintain myself in order to bring the book's elaboration to a successful finish. I would like to express this in a simpler fashion: the book, as soon as it is conceived, disposes of me entirely; and all within me, including the most profound in me, orchestrates itself for the book. I have no personality other than that which suits this work" (*Journals*, July 1922).

fact, what he keeps quiet about, as if he were aware of its offensive aspect. But, precisely because of its irritating insincerity, it is revealing. The whole passage might be summarized as follows: you cannot write unless you remain your own master before death; you must have established with death a relation of sovereign equals. If you lose face before death, if death is the limit of your self-possession, then it slips the words out from under the pen, it cuts in and interrupts. The writer no longer writes, he cries out — an awkward, confused cry which no one understands and which touches no one. Kafka feels deeply here that art is a relation with death. Why death? Because death is the extreme. He who includes death among all that is in his control controls himself extremely. He is linked to the whole of his capability; he is power through and through. Art is mastery of the supreme moment, supreme mastery.

The sentence, "The best of what I have written is based on this capacity to die content," has an attractive aspect stemming from its simplicity; nevertheless, it remains difficult to accept. What is this capacity? What is it that gives Kafka this assurance? Has he already come close enough to death to know how he will bear himself when he faces it? He seems to suggest that in the "good passages" of his writings — where someone is dying, dying an unjust death — he is himself at stake. Is it a matter, then, of an approach toward death accomplished under the cover of writing? The text does not say exactly that. It probably indicates an intimacy between the unhappy death which occurs in the work and the writer who enjoys this death. It excludes the cold, distant relation which allows an objective description. A narrator, if he knows the art of moving people, can recount in a devastating manner devastating events which are foreign to him. The problem in that case is one of rhetoric and the right one may or may not have to use it. But the mastery of which Kafka speaks is different, and the calculating tactic which authorizes it is more profound. Yes, one has to die in the dying character, truth demands this. But one must be capable of satisfaction in death, capable of finding in the supreme dissatisfaction supreme satisfaction, and of maintaining, at the instant of dying, the clearsightedness which comes from such a balance. Contentment is then very close to Hegelian wisdom, if the latter consists in making satisfaction and self-consciousness coincide, in finding in extreme negativity — in death become possibility, project, and time — the measure of the absolutely positive.

Yet here Kafka does not situate himself directly in so ambitious a perspective. Neither, when he links his capacity to write well with the power to die well, does he allude to a conception which would concern death in general. Rather, he alludes to his own experience. For one reason or another he lies down untroubled upon his death bed, and that is why he can direct upon his heroes an untroubled gaze and share their death with clear-sighted intimacy. Which of his writings is he thinking of? Probably *In der Strafkolonie, In the Penal Colony*. A few days earlier he had presented to his friends a reading of this story, which gave him courage. He then writes *The Trial*, and several unfinished narratives which do not concern death directly. We should mention *The Metamorphosis* and *The Verdict* as well. To recall these works is to recognize that Kafka is not thinking of a realistic description of death scenes. In all these narratives, those who die do so in a few quick and silent words. This confirms the idea that not just when they die but apparently while they are alive Kafka's heroes carry out their actions in death's space, and that it is to the indefinite time of "dying" that they belong. They are experiencing, feeling this strangeness out, and Kafka, in them, is also standing a test. But it seems to him that he won't be able to bring it to a "happy conclusion," draw from it a story and a work unless, in a certain way, he is in tune beforehand with the extreme moment of this trial—unless he is death's equal.

What disturbs us in his reflection is that it seems to authorize art to cheat. Why describe as unjust an event that he himself feels capable of welcoming with equanimity? Why does he make death frightful for us when he is content with it? This gives the text a cruel shallowness. Perhaps art demands that one play with death; perhaps it introduces a game, a bit of play in the situation that no longer allows for tactics or mastery. But what does this play mean? "Art flies around the truth, with the decided intention not to burn itself." Here it flies around death. It does not burn itself, but makes us feel the burn and becomes what burns and moves us—coldly and falsely. This perspective would suffice to condemn art. But to be fair to Kafka's remark, one must also take it differently. To die content is not in his eyes an attitude that is good in itself, for what it expresses primarily is discontent with life, exclusion from the happiness of living—that happiness which one must desire and love above everything. "The capacity to die content" implies that relations with the normal world are now and henceforth severed. Kafka is in a sense already dead. This is given him, as exile was given him; and this gift is linked to that of writing. Naturally, the fact of being exiled from normal possibilities does not in itself afford mastery over the extreme possibility. The fact of being deprived of life does not guarantee the happy possession of death; it does not make death acceptable except in a negative fashion (one is content to finish with the discontent of life). Hence the insufficiency and the superficial character of the remark. But the same year precisely, and twice over Kafka writes in his *Diary*, "I do not separate myself from men in order to live in peace, but in order to be able to die in peace." This separation, this need for solitude is imposed upon him by his work. "If I do not save myself in some work, I am lost. Do I know this distinctly enough? I do not hide from men because I want to live peacefully, but because I want to perish peacefully." The work in question is writing. Kafka cuts himself off from the world in order to write, and he writes in order to die in peace. Here death, tranquil death, is represented as the wages of art; it is the aim and the justification of writing. Write to perish peacefully. Yes, but how to write? What allows one to write? We know the answer: you cannot write unless you are able to die content. The contradiction situates us back in the profundity of the experience.

The Circle

Whenever thought is caught in a circle, this is because it has touched upon something original, its point of departure beyond which it cannot move except to return. Perhaps we would come closer to that original movement if we modified the focus of Kafka's formulae by removing the words "peacefully" and "content." The writer, then, is one who writes in order to be able to die, and he is one whose power to write comes from an anticipated relation with death. The contradiction subsists, but is seen in a different light. Just as the poet only exists once the poem faces him, only after the poem, as it were — although it is necessary that first there be a poet in order for there to be a poem — so one senses that if Kafka goes toward the power of dying through the work which he writes, the work itself is by implication an experience of death which he apparently has to have been through already in order to reach the work and, through the work, death. But one can also sense that the movement which, in the work, is the approach to death, death's space and its use, is not exactly the same movement which would lead the writer to the *possibility* of dying. One can even suppose that the particularly strange relations between artist and work, which make the work depend on him who is only possible within the work — one can even suppose that such an anomaly stems from the experience which overpowers the forms of time, but stems more profoundly still from the ambiguity of that experience, from its double aspect which Kafka expresses with too much simplicity in the sentences we ascribe to him: *Write to be able to die—Die to be able to write.* These words close us into their circular demand; they oblige us to start from what we want to find, to seek nothing but the point of departure, and thus to make this point something we approach only by quitting it. But they also authorize this hope: the hope, where the interminable emerges, of grasping the term, of bringing it forth.

Naturally, Kafka's words may seem to express a somber view peculiar to him. They are in conflict with generally accepted ideas about art and the work of art which André Gide, in the wake of so many others, called upon: "The reasons which lead me to write are many, and the most important are, it seems to me, the most secret. Especially, perhaps, this one: to shelter something from death" (*Journals*, July 27, 1922). To write in order not to die, to entrust oneself to the survival of the work: this motive is apparently what keeps the artist at his task. Genius confronts death; the work is death rendered vain, or transfigured, or, in the evasive words of Proust, made "less bitter," "less inglorious," and "perhaps less probable." Perhaps. We will not rebut these traditional dreams attributed to creators by remarking that they are recent—that, belonging to our modern, occidental world, they are connected to the development of humanistic art, where man seeks to glorify himself in his works and to act in them, perpetuating himself in this action. All this is certainly important and meaningful. But art, at this juncture, is no longer anything but a memorable way of becoming one with history. Great historical figures, heroes, great men of war no less than artists shelter themselves from death in this way: they enter the memory of peoples; they are examples, active presences. This form of individualism soon ceases to be satisfying. It soon becomes clear that if what is important is primarily the process which is history—action in the world, the common striving toward truth—it is vain to want to remain oneself above and beyond one's disappearance, vain to desire immutable stability in a work which would dominate time. This is vain and, moreover, the opposite of what one wants, which is not to subsist in the leisurely eternity of idols, but to change, to disappear in order to cooperate in the universal transformation: to act anonymously and not to be a pure, idle name. From this perspective, creators' dreams of living on through their works appear not only small-minded but mistaken, and any true action, accomplished anonymously in the world and for the sake of the world's ultimate perfection, seems to affirm a triumph over death that is more rigorous, more certain. At least such action is free of the wretched regret that one cannot be oneself for longer.

These dreams, which are so strong and which are linked to a transformation of art at a time when art is not yet present to itself—at a time when man, who believes he is the master of art, wants to make himself present, wants to be the one who creates and by creating escapes destruction even if only just barely—these dreams, then, are striking in this: they show "creators" engaged in a profound relation with death. And this relation, despite appearances, is the one Kafka pursued also. Both he and they want death to be possible: he in order to grasp it, they in order to hold it at a distance. The differences are negligible. They are set in one perspective, which is the determination to establish with death a relation of freedom.

Can I Die?

At first glance, the preoccupation of the writer who writes in order to be able to die is an affront to common sense. It would seem we can be sure of at least one event: it will come without any approach on our part, without our bestirring ourselves at all; yes, it will come. That is true, but at the same time it is not true, and indeed quite possibly it lacks truth altogether. At least it does not have the kind of truth which we feel in the world, which is the measure of our action and of our presence in the world. What makes me disappear from the world cannot find its guarantee there; and thus, in a way, having no guarantee, it is not certain. This explains why no one is linked to death by *real* certitude. No one is sure of dying. No one doubts death, but no one can think of certain death except doubtfully. For to think of death is to introduce into thought the supremely doubtful, the brittleness of the unsure. It is as if in order to think authentically upon the certainty of death, we had to let thought sink into doubt and inauthenticity, or yet again as if when we strive to think on death, more than our brain—the very substance and truth of thought itself—were bound to crumble. This in itself indicates that if men in general do not think about death, if they avoid confronting it, it is doubtless in order to flee death and hide from it, but that this escape is possible only because death itself is perpetual flight before death, and because it is the deep of dissimulation. Thus to hide from it is in a certain way to hide in it.

So the ability to die ceases to be a meaningless issue, and we can understand how a man's goal might be the search for death's possibility. This search, however, only becomes significant when it is necessary. In the great religious systems, death is an important event, but it does not have the paradoxical character of a brute fact bearing no truth. It is a relation to another world where, precisely, truth is believed to have its origin. It is the true way, and if it lacks the guarantee of the comprehensible certitudes which are ours here in this world, it does have the guarantee of the incomprehensible but unshakable certitudes of the eternal. Thus in the great religious systems of the West, it is not at all difficult to hold that death is true. Death always takes place in a world, it is an event of the greatest world, an event which can be located and which gives us a location.

Can I die? Have I the power to die? This question has no force except when all the escape routes have been rejected. It is when he concentrates exclusively upon himself in the certainty of his mortal condition that man's concern is to make death possible. It does not suffice for him that he is mortal; he understands that he has to become mortal, that he must be mortal twice over: sovereignly, extremely mortal. That is his human vocation. Death, in the human perspective, is not a given, it must be achieved. It is a task, one which we take up actively, one which becomes the source of our activity and mastery. Man dies, that is nothing. But man *is*, starting from his death. He ties himself tight to his death with a tie of which he is the judge. He makes his death; he makes himself mortal and in this way gives himself the power of a maker and gives to what he makes its meaning and its truth. The decision to be without being is possibility itself: the possibility of death. Three systems of thought—Hegel's, Nietzsche's, Heidegger's—which attempt to account for this decision and which therefore seem, however much they may oppose each other, to shed the greatest light on the destiny of modern man, are all attempts at making death possible.

Kirilov

It would seem that the most immediately pressing consequence of such an attitude is to make us wonder whether, among all the forms of death, there is not one which is more human, more mortal, and whether voluntary death is not perhaps an exemplary death. To take one's own life: is this not the shortest road from man to himself, from animal to man and, as Kirilov will add, from man to God? "I recommend my death to you, voluntary death, which comes to me because I want it to." "To eliminate oneself is the most praiseworthy of acts; it practically grants us the right to live." Natural death is death "in the most contemptible conditions, a death which is not free, which does not come when it should, a coward's death. Love of life should make us wish for an altogether different death, a free and conscious death, one which is no accident and holds no surprises." Nietzsche's words resound like an echo of liberty. One doesn't kill oneself, but one can. This is a marvelous resource. Without this supply of oxygen close at hand we would smother, we could no longer live. Having death within reach, docile and reliable, makes life possible, for it is exactly what provides air, space, free and joyful movement: it is possibility.

Voluntary death appears to pose a moral problem: it accuses and it condemns; it makes a final judgment. Or else it seems a challenge in defiance of an exterior omnipotence. "I will kill myself to affirm my insubordination, my new and terrifying liberty." What is new in Kirilov's undertaking is that he not only considers himself to be rising up against God by taking his own life, but expects by so doing to prove the nonexistence of this God — to prove it for himself just as he demonstrates it to others. As long as he has not killed himself, he himself does not know how this matter stands. Perhaps he is a believer, "having more faith even than a priest," suggests Dostoyevsky, apparently abandoning him to forlorn wanderings among contradictory feelings. Yet this remark is not inconsistent. On the contrary. For it is his preoccupation with God — the urgency of his need to become certain about God's nonexistence — that suggests suicide to Kirilov. Why suicide? If he dies freely, if he experiences and proves to himself his liberty in death and the liberty of his death, he will have attained the absolute. He will be that absolute. He will be absolutely man, and there will be no absolute outside of him. In fact more is involved here than a proof. In this obscure combat not only Kirilov's knowledge concerning the existence of God, but that existence itself is at stake. God is gambling his own existence in this freely chosen death which a resolute man takes upon himself. If someone becomes his own master even in death, master of himself through death, he will be master also of that omnipotence which makes itself felt by us through death, and he will reduce it to a dead omnipotence. Kirilov's suicide thus becomes the death of God. Hence his strange conviction that this suicide will inaugurate a new era, that it will mark the turning point in the history of humanity, and that, precisely, after him men will no longer need to kill themselves. His death, by making death possible, will have liberated life and rendered it wholly human.

Kirilov's words have an unsteady but attractive rhythm. He constantly loses his bearings among clear arguments which he does not pursue to the end because of the intervention, the call of an obscure argument which he cannot grasp but never ceases to hear. To all appearances his plan is that of a calm and collected rationalist. If men do not kill themselves, he thinks, it is because they are afraid of death; fear of death is the origin of God; if I can die in opposition to this fear, I will have liberated death from fear and overthrown God. This is a plan which, requiring the serenity of a man who keeps to reason's undeviating paths, conflicts with the lamp burning before the icon, with the religious torment to which Kirilov confesses, and above all with the terror that makes him falter at the end. Yet the starts and stops of this disoriented thinking, this madness which we feel envelops it and even its dizzy fear—beneath the mask it wears, which is shame at being afraid—are solely responsible for the fascinating interest of Kirilov's undertaking. Speaking of death, he speaks of God, as if he needed this supreme name to understand and evaluate such an event, to confront it in its supremacy. God is, for him, the face of his death. But is it God that is at issue? Is not the omnipotence in whose shadow Kirilov wanders (sometimes seized by a happiness which shatters time, sometimes delivered to horror against which he defends himself with puerile ideologies)—is not this power fundamentally anonymous? Does it not make of him a nameless, powerless being, essentially cowardly and surrendered to dispersion? This power is death itself, and what is at issue behind Kirilov's undertaking is death's possibility. Can I kill myself? Have I the power to die? How far can I go freely into death, in full control of my freedom? Even when, with an ideal and heroic resolve, I decide to meet death, isn't it still death that comes to meet me, and when I think I grasp it, does it not grasp me? Does it not loosen all hold upon me, deliver me to the ungraspable? Do I die, humanly, a death which will be that of a man and which I will imbue with all of human intention and freedom? Do I myself die, or do I not rather die always other from myself, so that I would have to say that properly speaking *I* do not die? Can I die? Have I the power to die?

The critical problem that torments Kirilov in the form of a God he would like to believe in is the problem of his suicide's possibility. When someone says to him, "But many people kill themselves," he does not even understand. As far as he is concerned, no one has yet killed himself: no one has ever died by his own hand in a real coming to grips, a full and heartfelt grasping of the situation which would make this act an authentic action. Or again, no one has seen in death the possibility of taking it himself instead of receiving it, dying "for the idea" as Kirilov puts it, dying that is, in a purely ideal manner. Certainly, if he succeeds in making death a possibility which is his and fully human, he will have attained absolute freedom. He will have attained it as a man, and he will have given it to men. Or, in other words, he will have been conscious of disappearing and not consciousness disappearing; he will have entirely annexed to his consciousness its own disappearance; he will be, thus, a realized totality, the realization of the whole, the absolute. Certainly this privilege is far superior to that of being immortal. Immortality, if it is mine to enjoy by definition, is not mine. It is rather my limit and my constraint. Thus in this context my whole vocation as a man consists in making of this immortality which is imposed upon me something I can gain or lose: hell or heaven. But immortality in itself, over which I have no power, is nothing to me. On the other hand, immortality might become one of science's conquests. Then it would have the value — beneficial or not — of a cure for sickness. It would not be altogether without consequences, but it would have none for Kirilov, who would still ask himself — and with a passion made greater by the greater strangeness of the problem: Do I retain the power to die? Immortality, guaranteed by science, would have no weight in his destiny unless it signified the impossibility of death. But then it would be, precisely, the symbolic representation of the question he embodies. For a human race weirdly destined to be immortal, suicide would constitute perhaps the only chance to remain human, the only way out toward a human future.

What might be called Kirilov's task — death, when death becomes the search for its possibility — is not exactly the task of voluntary death, the exercise of the will in a struggle with death. Is suicide always the act of a man whose thought is already obscured, whose will is sick? Is it always an involuntary act? That is what is said by certain psychiatrists who, in any event, do not know it to be the case; some well-meaning theologians think so, in order to cover up the scandal, and Dostoyevsky, who gives his character the appearance of madness, also draws back from the abyss that has been opened up before him by Kirilov. But this is not the important problem: does Kirilov truly die? Does he prove through his death the possibility which he received in advance from his death, that power of not being which permitted him to be himself — to be, that is, though freely linked to himself, always other than himself — the power to act, speak, take risks, and be without being? Can he maintain even in death this sense of death, sustain even in death this active and industrious death which is the power to finish, the power that has its source in the end? Can he act in such a way that death will still be for him the force of the negative, the cutting edge of decision, the moment of supreme possibility where even his own impossibility will come to him in the form of a power? Or, on the contrary, is the experience one of radical reversal, where he dies but cannot die, where death delivers him to the impossibility of dying?

In this search of his, it is not his own decisiveness that Kirilov is testing, but death as resolution. He wants to know whether the purity, whether the integrity of his act can triumph over the limitlessness of the indecisive, over the immense irresolution: over death. He wants to know whether, by the force of his action, he can render death active and by the affirmation of his freedom assert himself in death, appropriate it, make it true. In the world he is mortal, but in death — in this finish without definition — does he not risk becoming infinitely mortal? The question is his task. To answer it is his torment, which drags him toward death, toward the death he wants to master through the exemplary value of his own, by making "death understood" its only content.

Arria

To master death does not simply mean to remain one's own master in the face of death. That is the indifferent sovereignty which Stoic serenity expresses. It is true that when, upon seeing her husband, Caecina Poetus, hesitate, Arria plunges a dagger into her own breast, draws it back out, and offers it to him saying, "It is not painful," her steadiness — her stiffness — is impressive. Restraint is a feature of great and tranquil death scenes which gives pleasure. To die well means to die with propriety, in conformity with oneself and with respect for the living. To die well is to die in one's own life, turned toward one's life and away from death; and this good death shows more consideration for the world than regard for the depth of the abyss. The living appreciate this reserve, they prefer those who do not abandon themselves. The pleasure we take in a decent end, our desire to make death humane and proper, to free it from its inhuman quality — which, before killing men degrades them through fear and transforms them into something repulsively foreign — can lead us to praise suicide for doing away with death. This is Nietzsche's position. In his effort to eliminate the somber importance which Christianity attaches to the last hour, he regards this final moment as totally insignificant and not even worth a thought: a moment which is nothing to us and takes nothing from us. "There is nothing more banal than death." "I am happy to see that men refuse absolutely to want to think about death!" Kirilov would also like to say this to us. He himself thinks constantly about death, but in order to deliver us from the thought of it. This is the outermost limit of the process of humanization; it is Epicurus's external exhortation: if you are, death is not; if it is, you are not. Stoics want indifference before death because they want it to be free of all passion. Thus they attribute indifference to death; it is an indifferent moment. Ultimately, it is nothing, it is not even the last moment, which still belongs to life. At this point they have completely vanquished the old enemy and they can say, "O death, where is thy victory?" They can say this, providing they add, "Where is thy sting?" For, having freed themselves from death, they have in the same stroke deprived themselves of true life — the life which "does not shun death or keep clear of destruction, but endures its death and in death maintains its being." Hegel called it the life of Mind.

It does not suffice, then, to approach the adversary with the strength of a combative mind that wants to conquer, but from afar and in such a way, apparently, as to prevent death's approach. A death that is free, useful, and conscious, that is agreeable to the living, in which the dying person remains true to himself, is a death which has not met with death. It is a death in which there is much talk of life, but in it is not heard the unheard language from which speech emerges like a new gift. Those who do not abandon themselves elude thus the absolute abandon. We are spared the worst, but the essential escapes us.

That is why, with his sense of what is profound and also from the perspective of his theoretical intentions which were to show that militant atheism was a mad dream, Dostoyevsky did not give Kirilov an impassive destiny, the cold resolve which is the heritage of the ancients. This hero of certain death is neither indifferent nor master of himself, nor is he certain, and he does not go to his nullification as toward a pale nothing, purified and proportioned to fit him. The fact that his end is an extraordinary fiasco; that, in killing himself, he also kills his companion and double, with whom he had maintained a sullen silence; that he has for his last interlocutor and finally for his sole adversary only the most sinister figure, in whose countenance he can look upon the failure of his undertaking in all its truth — these circumstances are not simply part of his share of existence in the world, but emerge from the sordid intimacy of the abyss. We believe, as we die, that we are engaged in a noble combat with God, and finally it is Verkhovensky we meet, a much truer image of that base power with which one has to compete in bestiality. We enter thus the greatest contradictions. The deliberateness in suicide, its free and imposing side, whereby we strive to remain ourselves, serves essentially to protect us from what is at stake in this event. It would seem that through our effort to remain ourselves, we elude the essential; it would seem that we interpose ourselves illegitimately between something unbearable and ourselves, still seeking, in this familiar death that comes from us, not to meet anyone but ourselves, our own resolution and our own certitude. Purposeless passion, unreasonable and vain: this is, on the contrary, what we read upon Kleist's face, and it is this which seems to us imposing — this passion which seems to reflect the immense passivity of death, which escapes the logic of decisions, which can perfectly well speak but remains secret, mysterious, and indecipherable because it bears no relation to light. Thus in voluntary death it is still *extreme passivity* that we perceive — the fact that action here is only the mask of a fascinated dispossession. For this point of view, Arria's impassivity is no longer the sign of the preservation of her mastery, but the sign of an absence, of a hidden disappearance, the shadow of someone impersonal and neutral. Kirilov's feverishness, his instability, his steps which lead nowhere, do not signify life's agitation or a still vital force; they indicate, rather, that he belongs to a space where no one can rest, and which is in that respect a nocturnal space: no one is welcomed there; there nothing can abide. Nerval, it is said, wandered adrift in the streets before hanging himself. But aimless wandering is already death; it is the mortal error he must finally interrupt by immobilizing himself. Hence the hauntingly repetitive character of suicidal gestures. He who, through clumsiness, has missed his own death, is like a ghost returning only to continue to fire upon his own disappearance. He can only kill himself over and over. This repetition is as frivolous as the eternal and as grave as the imaginary.

Thus it is not certain that suicide is an answer to the call of possibility in death. Suicide doubtless asks life a question — is life possible? But it is more essentially a questioning of itself: *Is suicide possible?* The psychological contradiction encumbering such a project is simply the consequence of this deeper contradiction. He who kills himself says, "I withdraw from the world, I will act no longer." And yet this same person wants to make death an act; he wants to act supremely and absolutely. This illogical optimism which shines through voluntary death — this confidence that one will always be able to triumph in the end by disposing sovereignly of nothingness, by being the creator of one's own nothingness and by remaining able, in the very midst of the fall, to lift oneself to one's full height — this certitude affirms in the act of suicide the very thing suicide claims to deny. That is why he who espouses negation cannot allow it to be incarnated in a final decision which would be exempt from that negation. The anguish which opens with such assurance upon nothingness is not essential; it has drawn back before the essential; it does not yet seek anything other than to make of nothingness the road to salvation. Whoever dwells with negation cannot use it. Whoever belongs to it can no longer, in this belonging, take leave of himself, for he belongs to the neutrality of absence in which already he is not himself anymore. This situation is, perhaps, despair — not what Kierkegaard calls "sickness unto death," but the sickness in which dying does not culminate in death, in which one no longer keeps up hope for death, in which death is no longer to come, but is that which comes no longer.

The weakness of suicide lies in the fact that whoever commits it is still too strong. He is demonstrating a strength suitable only for a citizen of the world. Whoever kills himself could, then, go on living: whoever kills himself is linked to hope, the hope of finishing it all, and hope reveals his desire to begin, to find the beginning again in the end, to inaugurate in that ending a meaning which, however, he means to challenge by dying. Whoever despairs cannot hope to die either voluntarily or naturally: he has no time, he has no present upon which to brace himself in order to die. He who kills himself is the great affirmer of the *present*. I want to kill myself in an "absolute" instant, the only one which will not pass and will not be surpassed. Death, if it arrived at the time we choose, would be an apotheosis of the *instant;* the instant in it would be that very flash of brilliance which mystics speak of. And surely because of this, suicide retains the power of an exceptional affirmation. It remains an event which one cannot be content to call voluntary, an event which one can look neither back upon nor forward to.

The Strange Project, or Double Death

One cannot "plan" to kill oneself. This apparent project sets out after something never attained, toward a goal impossible to aim for. I cannot conceive of the end as an end in itself. But this implies that death eludes the workday, the time which is nevertheless death made active and capable. This is equivalent to thinking that death is somehow doubled: there is one death which circulates in the language of possibility, of liberty, which has for its furthest horizon the freedom to die and the capacity to take mortal risks; and there is its double, which is ungraspable. It is what I cannot grasp, what is not linked to *me* by any relation of any sort. It is that which never comes and toward which I do not direct myself.

Thus one begins to understand what is strange and superficial, fascinating and deceptive about suicide. To kill oneself is to mistake one death for the other; it is a sort of bizarre play on words. I go to meet the death which is in the world, at my disposal, and I think that thereby I can reach the other death, over which I have no power—which has none over me either, for it has nothing to do with me, and if I know nothing of it, it knows no more of me; it is the empty intimacy of this ignorance. That is why suicide remains essentially a bet, something hazardous: not because I leave myself a chance to survive, as sometimes happens, but because suicide is a leap. It is the passage from the certainty of an act that has been planned, consciously decided upon, and vigorously executed, to something which disorients every project, remains foreign to all decisions—the indecisive and uncertain, the crumbling of the inert and the obscurity of the nontrue. By commiting suicide I want to kill myself at a determined moment. I link death to now: yes, now, now. But nothing better indicates the illusion, the madness of this "I want," for death is never present. There is in suicide a remarkable intention to abolish the future as the mystery of death: one wants in a sense to kill oneself so that the future might hold no secrets, but might become clear and readable, no longer the obscure reserve of indecipherable death. Suicide in this respect does not welcome death; rather, it wishes to eliminate death as future, to relieve death of that portion of the yet-to-come which is, so to speak, its essence, and to make it superficial, without substance and without danger. But this tactic is vain. The most minute precautions, all the most carefully considered and precise arrangements have no power over this essential indeterminacy—the fact that death is never a relation to a determined moment any more than it bears any determined relation to myself.

One cannot "plan" to kill oneself. One prepares to do so, one acts in view of the ultimate gesture which still belongs to the normal category of things to do, but this gesture does not have death in view, it does not look at death, it does not keep death before it. Hence the attention to minutiae often symptomatic in those who are about to die—the love for details, the patient, maniacal concern for the most mediocre realities. Other people are surprised at this, and they say, "When you really want to die, you don't think about so many little things." But the explanation is that you don't *want* to die, you cannot make of death an object of the will. You cannot want to die, and the will, arrested thus at the uncertain threshold of what it cannot attain, redirects itself, with its calculating wisdom, toward everything it still can grasp in the area around its limit. You think of so many things because you cannot think of something *else,* and this is not for fear of looking into the face of too grave a reality; it is because there is nothing to see. Whoever wants to die can only want the borders of death, the utilitarian death which is in the world and which one reaches through the precision of a workman's tools. Whoever wants to die does not die, he loses the will to die. He enters the nocturnal realm of fascination wherein he dies in a passion bereft of will.

Art, Suicide

What a strange, contradictory undertaking is this effort to act where immeasurable passivity reigns, this striving to maintain the rules, to impose measure, and to fix a goal in a movement that escapes all aims and all resolution. This contest seems to make death superficial by making it into an act like any other — something to do; but it also gives the impression of transfiguring action, as if to reduce death to the level of a project were a unique opportunity to elevate the project toward that which exceeds it. This is madness, but it is madness we could not be spared without being excluded from the human condition (a humanity that could no longer kill itself would lose its balance, would cease to be normal). Suicide is an absolute right, the only one which is not the corollary of a duty, and yet it is a right which no real power reinforces. It would seem to arch like a delicate and endless bridge which at the decisive moment is cut and becomes as unreal as a dream, over which nevertheless it is necessary really to pass. Suicide is a right, then, detached from power and duty, a madness required by reasonable integrity and which, moreover, seems to succeed quite often. It is striking that all these traits can be applied equally well to another experience, one that is apparently less dangerous but perhaps no less mad: the artist's. Not that the artist makes death his work of art, but it can be said that he is linked to the work in the same strange way in which the man who takes death for a goal is linked to death.

This is evident at first glance. Both the artist and the suicide plan something that eludes all plans, and if they do have a path, they have no goal; they do not know what they are doing. Both exert a resolute will, but both are linked to what they want to achieve by a demand that knows nothing of their will. Both strive toward a point which they have to approach by means of skill, savoir faire, effort, the certitudes which the world takes for granted, and yet this point has nothing to do with such means; it is a stranger to the world, it remains foreign to all achievement and constantly ruins all deliberate action. How is it possible to proceed with a firm step toward that which will not allow itself to be charted? It seems that both the artist and the suicide succeed in doing something only by deceiving themselves about what they do. The latter takes one death for another, the former takes a book for the work. They devote themselves to this misunderstanding as if blind, but their dim consciousness of it makes of their task a proud bet. For it is as if they were embarking upon a kind of action which could only reach its term at infinity.

This comparison of art to suicide is shocking in a way. But there is nothing surprising about it if, leaving aside appearances, one understands that each of these two movements is testing a singular form of *possibility*. Both involve a power that wants to be power even in the region of the ungraspable, where the domain of goals ends. In both cases an invisible but decisive leap intervenes: not in the sense that through death we pass into the unknown and that after death we are delivered to the unfathomable beyond. No, the act of dying itself constitutes this leap, the empty depth of the beyond. It is the fact of dying that includes a radical reversal, through which the death that was the extreme form of my power not only becomes what loosens my hold upon myself by casting me out of my power to begin and even to finish, but also becomes that which is without any relation to me, without power over me — that which is stripped of all possibility — the unreality of the indefinite. I cannot represent this reversal to myself, I cannot even conceive of it as definitive. It is not the irreversible step beyond which there would be no return, for it is that which is not accomplished, the interminable and the incessant.

Suicide is oriented toward this reversal as toward its end. The work seeks this reversal as its origin. That is a first difference. Suicide, to a certain extent, denies the reversal, doesn't take account of it, and is only "possible" in this refusal. Voluntary death is the refusal to see the other death, the death one cannot grasp, which one never reaches. It is a kind of sovereign negligence, an alliance made with visible death in order to exclude the invisible one, a pact with the good, faithful death which I use constantly in the world, an effort to expand its sphere, to make it still viable and true beyond itself, where it is no longer anything but the other death. The expression "I kill myself" suggests the doubling which is not taken into account. For "I" is a self in the plenitude of its action and resolution, capable of acting sovereignly upon itself, always strong enough to reach itself with its blow. And yet the one who is thus struck is no longer I, but another, so that when I kill myself, perhaps it is "I" who does the killing, but it is not done to me. Nor is it my death — the one I dealt — that I have now to die, but rather the death which I refused, which I neglected, and which is this very negligence — perpetual flight and inertia.

The work wants, so to speak, to install itself, to dwell in this *negligence*. A call from there reaches it. That is where, in spite of itself, it is drawn, by something that puts it absolutely to the test. It is attracted by an ordeal in which everything is risked, by an essential risk where being is at stake, where nothingness slips away, where, that is, the right, the power to die is gambled.

The
Igitur
Experience

From this point of view one can sense how it was that in Mallarmé concern for the work became confused for a time with the affirmation of suicide. But one also sees how this same concern led Rilke to seek a relationship with death that would be more "exact" than that of voluntary death. These two experiences merit reflection.

Mallarmé acknowledged, in a letter to Cazalis (November 14, 1896), that *Igitur* is an undertaking in which poetry itself is at stake. "It is a tale with which I want to conquer the old monster Impotence, which is, moreover, its subject, in order to cloister myself in a great labor already planned and replanned. If it gets finished (the tale), I shall be cured." The great labor was *Hérodiade,*[3] and also poetic work in the largest sense. *Igitur* is an attempt to make the work possible by grasping it at the point where what is present is the absence of all power, impotence. Mallarmé feels deeply here that the state of aridity which he knows so well is linked to the work's demand, and is neither simply deprivation of the work nor a psychological state peculiar to him.

"Unfortunately, by digging this thoroughly into verse, I have encountered two abysses which make me despair. One is Nothingness . . . . The other void which I have found is the one in my breast." "And now, having reached the horrible vision of a pure work, I have almost lost my reason and the meaning of the most familiar words." "Everything which, as a result, my being has suffered during this long agony is indescribable, but fortunately I am perfectly dead . . . . Which is to convey to you that I am now impersonal, and no longer Stéphane whom you know." When one recalls these remarks, one cannot doubt that *Igitur* was born of the obscure, essentially hazardous experience into which the

[3]Mallarmé may, however, have had another text in mind.

craft of poetry, over the course of years, drew Mallarmé. This risk affects his normal relationship to the world, his habitual use of language; it destroys all ideal certainties, deprives the poet of the physical assurance of living. It exposes him finally to death — the death of truth, the death of his person; it yields him up to the impersonality of death.

The Exploration and Purification of Absence

Igitur's interest does not come directly from the thought which serves as its theme, which is such that thinking would smother it, and which is similar in this respect to Hölderlin's. Hölderlin's is, however, richer, more active. He was familiar from youth with Hegel, whereas Mallarmé received only an impression of Hegelian philosophy. And yet this impression corresponds to the deep current which drew him, precisely, to the "frightful years." Everything is summed up for Mallarmé by the relationship among the words *thought, absence, language,* and *death.* The materialist profession of faith ("Yes, I know, we are but vain forms of matter"), is not Mallarmé's point of departure. Such a revelation would have obliged him to reduce thought, God, and all the other figures of the ideal to nothing. Quite obviously it is from this *nothing* that he starts. He felt its secret vitality, its force and mystery in his contemplation and accomplishment of the poetic task. His Hegelian vocabulary would merit no attention, were it not animated by an authentic experience, and this experience is that of the power of the negative.

One can say that Mallarme saw this nothing in action; he experienced the activity of absence. In absence he grasped a presence, a strength still persisting, as if in nothingness there were a strange power of affirmation. All his remarks on language tend to acknowledge the word's ability to make things absent, to evoke them in this absence, and then to remain faithful to this value of absence, realizing it completely in a supreme and silent disappearance. In fact, the problem for Mallarmé is not to escape from the real in which he feels trapped, according to a still generally accepted interpretation of the sonnet on the swan. The true search and the drama take place in the other sphere, the one in which pure absence affirms itself and where, in so doing, it eludes itself, causing itself still to be present. It subsists as the dissimulated presence of being, and in this dissimulation it persists as chance which cannot be abolished. And yet this is where everything is at stake, for the work is possible only if absence is pure and perfect, only if, in the presence of Midnight, the dice can be thrown. There alone the work's origin speaks; there it begins, it finds there the force of the beginning.

More precisely: the greatest difficulty does not come from the pressure of beings, from what we call their reality, their persistent affirmation, whose action can never be altogether suspended. It is in unreality itself that the poet encounters the resistance of a muffled presence. It is unreality from which he cannot free himself; it is in unreality that, disengaged from beings, he meets with the mystery of "those very words: *it is*." And this is not because in the unreal something subsists — not because the rejection of real things was insufficient and the work of negation brought to a halt too soon — but because when there is nothing, it is this nothing itself which can no longer be negated. It affirms, keeps on affirming, and it states nothingness as being, the inertia of being.

This is the situation which would form the subject of *Igitur*, were it not necessary to add that the narrative avoids this situation, seeking to surmount it by putting a term to it. These are pages in which some readers have thought they recognized the somber hues of despair. But actually they carry a youthful expression of great hope. For if *Igitur* were to be right — if death is true, if it is a genuine act, not a random occurrence but the supreme possibility, the extreme moment in which negation is founded and completed — then the negation that operates in words, and "this drop of nothingness" which is the presence of consciousness in us, the death from which we derive the power not to be which is our essence, also partake of truth. They bear witness to something definitive; they function to "set a limit upon the infinite." And so the work which is linked to the purity of negation can in its turn arise in the certainty of that distant Orient which is its origin.

The Three Movements toward Death.

Igitur is thus not only an exploration but a purification of absence — it is an attempt to make absence possible and to glean possibility from it. The whole interest of this narrative lies in the way three movements are accomplished together. To a certain extent they are distinct from each other, and yet they are so closely linked that their interdependence remains hidden. All three movements are necessary to reach death; but which controls the others, which is the most important? The act by which the hero leaves the chamber, descends the staircase, drinks the poison, and enters the tomb apparently constitutes the initial decision, the "deed" which alone gives reality to absence and authenticates nothingness. But in fact this is not the case. This accomplishment is only an insignificant moment. What is done must first be dreamed, thought, grasped in advance by the mind, not in a moment of psychological contemplation, but through an actual movement — a lucid effort on the part of the mind to advance outside of itself, to see itself disappear and to appear to itself in the mirage of this disappearance, to gather itself all up into this essential death which is the life of the consciousness and, out of all the various acts of death through which we are, to form the unique act of the death to come which thought reaches at the same time that it reaches, and thereby liquidates, itself.

Here voluntary death is no longer anything but a dying in spirit, which seems to restore to the act of dying its pure, inward dignity — but not according to the ideal of Jean-Paul Richter, whose heroes, "lofty men," die in a pure desire to die, "their eyes gazing steadfastly beyond the clouds" in response to the call of a dream which disembodies and dissolves them. The idea of suicide found in *Igitur* is more akin to what Novalis means when he makes suicide "the principle of his entire philosophy." "The truly philosophical act is suicide; the real beginning of all philosophy lies in it; all the philosopher's desires tend toward it. Only this act fulfills all the conditions and bears all the marks of a trans-worldly action." Yet these last words indicate a horizon unknown to *Igitur*. Novalis, like most of the German Romantics, seeks in death a further region beyond death, something more than death, a return to the transfigured whole — in that night, for example, which is not night but the peaceful oneness of day and night. Moreover, in Novalis the movement toward death is a concentration of the will, an affirmation of its magical force, an energetic expenditure or yet again an unruly affection for the remote. But *Igitur* does not seek to surpass itself or to discover, through this voluntary move, a new point of view on the other side of life. It dies by the spirit — through the spirit's very development, through its presence to itself, to its own profound, beating heart, which is precisely absence, the intimacy of absence, night.

Midnight

Night: here is where the true profundity of *Igitur* is to be felt, and it is here that we can find the third movement, which, perhaps, commands the two others. If the narrative begins with the episode called

"Midnight" — with the evocation of that pure presence where nothing but the subsistence of nothing subsists — this is certainly not in order to offer us a choice literary passage, nor is it, as some have claimed, in order to set the scene for the action: the empty chamber and its lavish furnishings enveloped, however, in shadows, the image of which is, in Mallarmé, something like the original medium of poetry. This "décor" is in reality the center of the narration whose true hero is Midnight and whose action is the ebb and flow of Midnight.

The story begins with the end, and that is what forms its troubling truth. With the very first words, the chamber is empty, as if everything were already accomplished, the poison drunk, the vial emptied, and the "lamentable personage" laid out upon his own ashes. Midnight is here; the hour when the cast dice have absolved all movement is here; night has been restored to itself, absence is complete, and silence pure. Thus everything has come to an end. Everything the end must make manifest, all that Igitur seeks to create by means of his death — the solitude of darkness, the deep of disappearance — is given in advance, and seems the condition for this death: its anticipated appearance, its eternal image. A strange reversal. It is not the youth who, by disappearing into death, institutes disappearance and therein establishes the night. It is the absolute presence of this disappearance, its dark glistening, which alone permits him to die. It alone introduces him to his mortal decision and act. It is as though death had first to be anonymous in order to occur with certainty in someone's name, or as if, before being my death, a personal act in which my person deliberately comes to an end, death had to be the neutrality and impersonality in which nothing is accomplished, the empty omnipotence which consumes itself eternally.

We are now a long way away from that voluntary death which the final episode let us see. Drawing back from the precise action which consists in emptying the vial, we have returned to a thought, the ideal act, already impersonal, where thinking and dying explored each other in their reciprocal truth and their hidden identity. But now we find ourselves before the immense passivity which, in advance, dissolves all action, even the action by which Igitur wants to die, the momentary master of chance. It seems that three figures of death confront each other here in a motionless simultaneity. All three are necessary for death's accomplishment, and the most secret is apparently the substance of absence, the deep of the void created when one dies, the eternal outside — a space formed by my death and yet whose approach is alone what makes me die. From such a perspective the event could never happen (death could never become an event): that is what is inscribed in this prerequisite night. The situation could also be expressed as follows: in order for the hero to be able to leave the chamber and for the final chapter, "Leaving the Chamber," to be written, it is necessary that the chamber already be empty and that the word to be written have returned forever into silence. And this is not a difficulty in logic. This contradiction expresses everything that makes both death and the work difficult. One and the other are somehow unapproachable, as Mallarmé said in notes that seem, precisely, to concern *Igitur*: "The Drama is only insoluble because unapproachable." And he comments further in the same passage: "The Drama is caused by the Mystery of what follows—Identity (Idea) Self—of the Theater and the Hero through the Hymn. *Operation.* —the Hero disengages—the (maternal) hymn which creates him, and he restores himself to the Theater which it was—of the Mystery where this hymn was hidden." If the "Theater" here means Midnight's space, a moment which is a place, then theater and hero are indeed identical, through the hymn which is death become word. How can Igitur "disengage" this death my making it become song and hymn, and thereby restore himself to the theater, to the pure subsistence of Midnight where death was hidden? That is the "operation." It is an end which can only be a return to the beginning, as the last words of the narrative say: "Nothingness having departed, there remains the Castle of purity," that empty chamber in which everything persists.

The "Act of Night"

The way Mallarmé nevertheless tries to approach the drama, in order to find a solution to it, is very revealing. Among night, the hero's thoughts, and his real acts, or, in other words, among absence, the thought of this absence, and the act by which it is realized, an exchange is established, a reciprocity of movements. First we see that this Midnight, eternal beginning and eternal end, is not so immobile as one might think. "Certainly a presence of Midnight subsists." But this subsisting presence is not a presence. This substantial present is the negation of the present. It is a vanished present. And Midnight, where first "the absolute present of things" (their unreal essence) gathered itself together, becomes "the pure dream of a Midnight vanished into itself": it is no longer a present, but the past, symbolized, as is the end of history in Hegel, by a book lying open upon the table, "page and usual décor of Night." Night is the book: the silence and inaction of a book when, after everything has been proffered, everything returns into the silence that alone speaks — that speaks from the depth of the past and is at the same time the whole future of the word. For present Midnight, that hour at which the present lacks absolutely, is also the hour in which the past touches and, *without the intervention of any timely act whatever*, immediately attains the future at its most extreme. And such, we have seen, is the very instant of death, which is never present, which is the celebration of the absolute future, the instant at which one might say that, in a time without present, what has been will be. This is announced to us in two famous sentences of *Igitur*: "I *was* the hour which *is to* make me pure"; and, more exactly, in Midnight's farewell to night — a farewell which can never end because it never takes place now, because it is present only in night's eternal absence: "Adieu, night, that I *was*, your own tomb, but which, surviving shade, *will* change into Eternity."[4]

However, this structure of Night has already given us back a movement: its immobility is constituted by this call of the past to the future, the muffled scansion by which what has been affirms its identity with what will be beyond the wrecked and sunken present, the abyss of the present. With this "double beat," the night stirs, it acts, it becomes an act, and this act opens the gleaming doors of the tomb, creating the solution which makes the "exit from the chamber" possible.[5] Here Mallarmé discovers the motionless sliding which causes things to move forward at the heart of their eternal annulment. There is an imperceptible exchange among the inner oscillation of the night, the pulse of the clock, the back and forth of the doors of the open tomb, the back and forth of consciousness which returns to and goes out from itself, which divides and escapes from itself, wandering distantly from itself with a rustling of nocturnal wings, a phantom already confused with the ghosts of those who have already died. This "rhythm," in all these forms, is the movement of a disappearance, the movement of return to the heart of disappearance — a "faltering beat," however, which bit by bit affirms itself, takes on body, and finally becomes the living heart of Igitur, that heart whose too lucid certainty then "troubles" him and summons him to the real act of death. Thus we have come from the most interior to the most exterior. Indefinite absence, immutable and sterile, has imperceptibly transformed itself. It has taken on the look

[4]In his essay on Mallarmé (*The Interior Distance*), Georges Poulet is right to say that this hour can "never be expressed by a present, always by a past or a future."

[5]"The hour formulates itself in this echo, at the threshold of the open doors by its *act* of night."

and the form of this youth, and having become real in him, it finds in this reality the means of realizing the decision that annihilates him. Thus night, which is Igitur's intimacy, the pulsating death which is the heart of each of us, must become life itself, the sure heart of life, so that death may ensue, so that death may for an instant let itself be grasped, identified — in order that death might become the death of an identity which has decided it and willed it.

The earlier versions of Mallarmé's narrative show that in the death and the suicide of Igitur he initially saw the death and the purification of night. In these pages (in particular in scholium d), it is no longer either Igitur or his consciousness that acts and keeps watch, but night itself, and all the events are lived by the night. The heart which, in the definitive text, Igitur recognizes as his own — "I hear the pulsating of my own heart. I do not like this noise: this perfection of my certitude troubles me; everything is too clear" — this heart, then, is, in the earlier versions, the night's heart: "Everything was perfect; night was pure Night, and it heard its own heart beat. Still, this heart troubled it, gave it the disquietude of too much certainty, of a proof too self-confident. Night wanted in its turn to plunge back into the darkness of its unique tomb and to abjure the idea of its form." The night is Igitur, and Igitur is that portion of night which the night must "reduce to the state of darkness" in order to become again the liberty of night.

The Igitur Catastrophe

It is significant that, in the most recent version, Mallarmé modified the whole perspective of the work by making it Igitur's monologue. Although in this prolóngation of Hamlet's soliloquy there is no very ringing affirmation of the first person, that wan "I" which from moment to moment presents itself behind the text and supports its diction is clearly perceptible. In this way, everything changes. On account of this voice which speaks, it is no longer night that speaks, but a voice that is still very personal, no matter how transparent it makes itself; and where we thought we were in the presence of the secret of Midnight, the pure destiny of absence, we now have only the speaking presence, the rarefied but certain evidence of a consciousness which, in the night which has become its mirror, still contemplates only itself. That is remarkable. It is as though Mallarmé had drawn back before what he will call, in *Un Coup de dés*, "the identical neutrality of the abyss." He seemed to do justice to the night, but it is to consciousness that he delegates all rights. Yes it is as though he had feared to see everything dissipate, "waver, subside, madness," if he did not introduce, surreptitiously, a living mind which, from behind, could still sustain the absolute nullity that he claimed to evoke. Whoever wishes to speak of a "catastrophe" in *Igitur* might well find it here. Igitur does not leave the chamber: the empty chamber is simply he—he who merely goes on speaking of the empty chamber and who, to make it absent, has only his word, founded by no more original absence. And if, in order to accede sovereignly to death, it is truly necessary that he expose himself to the presence of sovereign death—that pure medium of a Midnight which "crosses him out" and obliterates him—this confrontation, this decisive test is missed, for it takes place under the protection of consciousness, with its guarantee, and without consciousness's running any risk.

Finally there remains only the act in the obscurity of its resolve: the vial that is emptied, the drop of nothingness that is drunk. Granted, this act is imbued with consciousness, but its having been decided upon does not suffice to make it decisive; it bears in itself the cloudiness of the decision. Igitur ends his monologue rather feebly with these words, "The hour has struck for me to depart," in which we see that everything remains to be done. He has not taken so much as one step toward the "therefore" which his name represents—that conclusion of himself which he wants to draw from himself, believing that solely by virtue of understanding it, knowing it in its quality as chance, he can rise to the level of necessity and annul his end as chance by adjusting himself precisely to that nullity. But how could Igitur know chance? Chance is the night he has avoided, in which he has contemplated only proof of himself and his constant certitude. Chance is death, and the dice according to which one dies are cast by chance; they signify only the utterly hazardous movement which reintroduces us within chance. Is it at Midnight that "the dice must be cast"? But Midnight is precisely the hour that does not strike until after the dice are thrown, the hour which has never yet come, which never comes, the pure, ungraspable future, the hour eternally past. Nietzsche had already come up against the same contradiction when he said, "Die at the right time." That right moment which alone will balance our life by placing opposite it on the scales a sovereignly balanced death can be grasped only as the unknowable secret: only as that which could never be elucidated unless, already dead, we could look at ourselves from a point from which it would be granted us to embrace as a whole both our life and our death—the point which is perhaps the truth of the night from which Igitur would like, precisely, to take his leave, in order to render his leave-taking possible and correct, but which he reduces to the poverty of a reflection. "Die at the right time." But death's rightful quality is impropriety, inaccuracy—the fact that it comes either too soon or too late, prematurely and as if after the fact, never coming until after its arrival. It is the abyss of present time, the reign of a time without a present, without that exactly positioned point which is the unstable balance of the instant whereby everything finds its level upon a single plane.

Un Coup de dés

Is *Un Coup de dés* the recognition of such a failure? Is it the renunciation of the wish — to master the measurelessness of chance through a sovereignly measured death? Perhaps. But this cannot be said with certainty. Rather, it is *Igitur*, a work not simply unfinished but left dangling, that announces this failure—announces it by being thus forsaken. And thereby it recovers its meaning. It escapes the naïveté of a successful undertaking to become the force and the obsession of the interminable. For thirty years *Igitur* accompanied Mallarmé, just as all his life the hope of the "great Work" kept its vigil by his side. He evoked this Work mysteriously before his friends, and he eventually made its realization credible even in his own eyes and even, for a time, in the eyes of the man who had the least confidence in the impossible, Valéry—Valéry who, startled by his own credence, never recovered from this hurt, so to speak, but hid it beneath the demands of a contrary commitment.

Un Coup de dés is not *Igitur*, although it resurrects almost all of *Igitur's* elements. It is not *Igitur* reversed, the challenge abandoned, the dream defeated, hope changed to resignation. Such comparisons would be worthless. *Un Coup de dés* does not answer *Igitur* as one sentence answers another, as a solution answers a problem. That reverberating proclamation itself—A THROW OF THE DICE NEVER WILL ABOLISH CHANCE—the force of its affirmation, the peremptory brilliance of its certitude, which makes it an authoritative presence holding the whole work together physically—this lightning which seems to fall upon the mad faith of *Igitur* in order to destroy and consume it, does not contradict *Igitur*, but on the contrary gives it its last chance, which is not to annul chance, even by an act of mortal negation, but to abandon itself entirely to chance, to consecrate chance by entering without reserve into its intimacy, with the abandon of impotence, *"without the ship that is vain no matter where."* In an artist so fascinated by the desire for mastery, nothing is more impressive than that final phase in which the work shines suddenly above him, no longer necessary but as a "perhaps" of pure chance, in the uncertainty of "the exception," not necessary but the absolutely unnecessary, a constellation of doubt which only shines in the forgotten sky of perdition. The night of *Igitur* has become the sea, *"the gaping deep," "the identical neutrality of the abyss," "a whirlpool of hilarity and horror."* But Igitur was still searching only for himself in the night, and he wanted to die in the heart of his thought. To make impotence a power — these were the stakes; this has been conveyed to us. In *Un Coup de dés,* the youth, who has matured, however, who is now "the Master," the man of sovereign mastery, does perhaps hold the successful throw of the dice in his hand, *"the unique Number which does not want to be another"*; but he does not take his unique chance to master chance any more than a man who always holds in his hand the supreme power, the power to die, can exercise that power. He dies outside this power, *"cadaver pulled away by the arm from the secret he holds."* This massive image rejects the challenge of voluntary death, where the hand holds the secret by which we are cast out of the secret. And this chance which is not taken, which remains idle, is not even a sign of wisdom, the fruit of a carefully considered and resolute abstention. It is itself something random, linked to the happenstance of old age and its incapacities, as if impotence had to appear to us in its most devastated form, where it is nothing but misery and abandon, the ludicrous future of an extremely old man whose death is only useless inertia. *"A shipwreck that."* But what happens in this shipwreck? Can the supreme conjunction, the game which in the fact of dying is played not against or with chance, but in its intimacy, in that region where nothing can be grasped — can this relation to impossibility still prolong itself? Can it give rise to an *"as if"* with which the dizziness of the work would be suggested — a delirium contained by *"a small rigorous reason,"* a sort of *"worried" "laughter," "mute"* and *"expiatory"*? To this no answer is offered, no other certainty than the concentration of chance, its stellar glorification, its elevation to the point where its rupture *"rains down absence," "some last point which sanctifies it."*

"If it gets finished (the tale), I shall be cured." This hope is touching in its simplicity. But the tale was not finished. Impotence — that abandon in which the work holds us and where it requires that we descend in the concern for its approach — knows no cure. That death is incurable. The absence that Mallarmé hoped to render pure is not pure. The night is not perfect, it does not welcome, it does not open. It is not the opposite of day—silence, repose, the cessation of tasks. In the night, silence is speech, and there is no repose, for there is no position. There the incessant and the uninterrupted reign—not the certainty of death achieved, but "the eternal torments of Dying."

Rilke
and
Death's
Demand

When Rilke, in order to live up to his poet's destiny, does his best to accommodate that greater dimension of himself which must not exclude what he becomes by dying, he cannot be said to recoil from the difficult sides of the experience. He faces what he calls the horror. It is most terrible. It is too great a force for us: it is our own force which outdoes us [nous dépasse] and which we do not recognize. But, for that reason, we must draw it toward us, bring it close, and in it bring ourselves close to what is close to it.

Sometimes he speaks of overcoming death. The word *overcome* is one of the words poetry needs. To overcome means to outdo [dépasser], but to outdo what outdoes us by undergoing it, without turning away from it or aiming at anything beyond. Perhaps it is in this sense that Nietzsche intends Zarathustra's formula: "Man is something that must be overcome." It is not that man must attain something beyond man; he has nothing to attain, and if he is what exceeds him, this excess is not anything he can possess, or be. *To overcome,* then, is also very different from *to master.* One of the errors of voluntary death lies in the desire to be master of one's end and to impose one's form and limit even upon this last movement. Such is the challenge of *Igitur:* to assign a limit to chance, to die centered within oneself in the transparency of an event which one has made equal to oneself, which one has annihilated and by which, thus, one can be annihilated without violence. Suicide remains linked to this wish to die by doing without death [en se passant de la mort].

When Rilke contemplates the suicide of the young Count Wolf Kalckreuth — and his contemplation takes the form of a poem — what he cannot accept is the impatience and the inattention which this form of death shows. Inattention is an offense against a certain profound maturity which is the opposite of the modern world's brutal agitation—that officiousness which hurries to action and bustles about in the empty urgency of things to do. Impatience is also an offense against suffering: by refusing to suffer the frightful, by eluding the unbearable, one eludes the moment when everything reverses and the greatest danger becomes the essential security. The impatience in voluntary death is this refusal to wait to reach the pure center where we would find our bearings again in that which exceeds us.

> Why did you not wait until the burden
> became unbearable: then it reverses itself
> and is only so heavy because it is so pure.[6]

Thus we see that too prompt a death is like a child's caprice, a failure in attentiveness, a gesture of inattention which leaves us strangers to our end—leaves us to die, despite the resolute character of the event, in a state of distraction and impropriety. He who too willingly dies—that too passionately mortal being, man, who with all his might wants to cease living—is as if whisked from death by the violence of the élan that tears him from life. One must not desire to die too much; one must not obfuscate death by casting the shadow of an excessive desire upon it. Perhaps there are two distracted deaths: the one in which we have not matured, which does not belong to us, and the one which has not matured in us and which we have acquired by violence. In both cases—on the one hand because death is not our own, and on the other because it is more our desire than our death—we might well fear perishing for lack of death by succumbing in the ultimate state of inattention.

1. The Search for a Proper Death

It seems, then, that outside all religious or moral systems, one is led to wonder whether there are not a good and a bad death: a possibility of dying authentically, on good terms with death, and also a danger of dying badly, as if inadvertently, an inessential and false death—a danger so great that all of life could depend upon this legitimate relation to death, this clear-sighted gaze directed toward the profundity of an exact

---

[6][In translating Blanchot's quotations from Rilke's poems, I have consulted J.B. Leishman's English verse translations of the original texts, *Selected Works* (New York: New Directions, 1967), vol. 1; but my English seeks to be as close as possible to Blanchot's French version of Rilke—Trans.]

death. When one reflects upon this concern that death be valid, and this need to link the word *death* with the word *authenticity* — a need which Rilke lived intensely in several forms — one sees that for him it had a double origin.

A. To Die Faithful to Oneself

O Lord, grant to each his own death,
the dying which truly evolves from this life
in which he found love, meaning and distress.

This wish is rooted in a form of individualism which belongs to the end of the nineteenth century and which was endowed with its noble pride by a narrowly interpreted Nietzsche. Nietzsche too wishes to die his own death. Hence the excellence which he sees in voluntary death. "He dies *his* death, victorious, who accomplishes it himself." "But detestable . . . is your grimacing death, which advances in its belly like a thief." "If not, your death will suit you ill." To die an individual death, still oneself at the very last, to be an individual right up to the end, unique and undivided: this is the hard, central kernel which does not want to let itself be broken. One wants to die, but in one's own time and one's own way. One doesn't want to die just anybody's undistinguished death. Contempt for anonymous death, for the "They die," is the disguised anguish to which the anonymous character of death gives rise. Or again, one is glad to die: it is noble to die, but not to decease.

The Anguish of Anonymous Death

Contempt plays no part in Rilke's discreet and silent intimacy. But the anguish of anonymous death confirmed him in the concern which the views of Simmel, Jacobsen, and Kierkegaard had first awakened in him. *Malte* gave this anguish a form which we would not be able to separate from that book if our era had not, at closer range, contemplated impersonal death and the particular look it gives men. In fact, Malte's anguish has more than a little to do with the anonymous existence of big cities — to that distress which makes vagrants of some, men fallen out of themselves and out of the world, already dead of an unwitting death never to be achieved. Such is the true perspective of this book: the apprenticeship of exile, proximity to error which takes the concrete form of the vagabond existence into which the young foreigner slips, banished from his station in life, cast into the insecurity of a space where he cannot live or die "himself."

This fear which arises in Malte, which leads him to discover "the existence of the terrible" in every particle of air—this anguish born of oppressive strangeness, when all protective security is gone and suddenly the idea of a human nature, of a human world in which we could take shelter collapses: Rilke confronted it lucidly and endured it bravely. He stayed in Paris, in that town too big and "full to the brim with sadness," stayed there "precisely because it is difficult." He saw there the decisive test, the one which transforms and teaches to see, a starting point for "a beginner learning the conditions of his own life." "If one manages to work here, one advances far in profundity." Nevertheless, when he tries to give form to this test in the third part of the *Book of Hours*, why does he seem to turn away from death as he saw it, the frightful approach of an empty mask, and replace it with the hope for another death, which would be neither foreign nor heavy? Doesn't this faith which he expresses—this thought that one can die greeted by a death of one's own, familiar and amicable—mark the point at which he eluded the experience by enveloping himself in a hope meant to console his heart? One can't fail to recognize this backing off. But there is something else as well. Malte does not encounter anguish only in its pure form of the terrible; he also discovers the terrible in the form of the absence of anguish, daily insignificance. Neitzsche had seen this too, but he accepted it as a challenge: "There is nothing more banal than death." Death as banality, death degrading itself and becoming a vulgar nullity: that is what made Rilke back away. He shrank from the moment when death reveals itself as it also is, when dying and killing have no more importance than "taking a drink of water or cutting the head of a cabbage." Mass-produced death, ready-made in bulk for all and in which each disappears hastily; death as an anonymous product, an object without value, like the things of the modern world which Rilke always rejected: if only from these comparisons one sees how he slips from death's essential neutrality to the idea that this neutrality is but an historical and temporary form of death, the sterile death of big cities.[7] Sometimes, when fear seizes him, he cannot avoid hearing the anonymous hum of "dying" which is by no means the fault of the times or

---

[7] "It is evident that with accelerated production, each individual death is not so well executed, but that doesn't matter much anyway. It's the quantity that counts. Who still attaches any importance to a well-wrought death? No one. Even rich people, who can pay for luxury, have ceased to care about it; the desire to have one's own death

people's negligence. In all times we all die like the flies that autumn forces indoors, into rooms where they circle blindly in an immobile dizziness, suddenly dotting the walls with their mindless death. But, the fear past, Rilke reassures himself by evoking the happier world of another time, and that nil death which made him shudder seems to him to reveal only the indigence of an era devoted to haste and idle amusement.

When I think back to my home (where there is nobody left now), it always seems to me that formerly it must have been otherwise. Formerly one knew — or maybe one guessed — that one had one's death within one, as the fruit its core. Children had a little one, adults a big one. Women carried it in their womb, men in their breast. They truly had their death, and that awareness gave dignity, a quiet pride.

And so the image of a loftier death arises in Rilke, that of the Chamberlain, where death's sovereignty, at the same time that it exceeds our habitual human perspectives with its monumental omnipotence, retains at least the features of an aristocratic superiority, which one fears, but which one can admire.

The Task of Dying and the Artistic Task

In this terror before mass-produced death there is the sadness of the artist who honors well-wrought things, who wants to make a work and make of death his work. Death is thus from the start linked to the movement, so difficult to bring to light, of the artistic experience. This does not mean that, like the much-admired personalities of the Renaissance, we are to be artists of ourselves, to make of our life and of our death an art, and of art a sumptuous affirmation of our person. Rilke enjoys neither the tranquil innocence of this pride nor its naïveté. He is sure neither of himself nor of the work, since he lives in a critical period which obliges art to feel unjustified. Art is perhaps a road toward ourselves — Rilke is the first to think so — and perhaps also toward a death which would be ours. But where is art? The road that leads to it is

---

is becoming more and more rare. Shortly it will be as rare as a life of one's own" (*The Notebooks of M.-L. Brigge*). [In translating Blanchot's quotations from this book, I have been guided by M.D. Herter Norton's English translation of the original, *The Notebooks of Malte Laurids Brigge* (New York: Norton Press, 1949) — Trans.]

unknown. Granted, the work demands effort, application, knowledge; but all these forms of aptitude are plunged in an immense ignorance. The work always means: not knowing that art exists already, not knowing that there is already a world.

The search for a death that would be mine sheds light, thanks to the obscurity of its paths, upon precisely what is difficult in artistic "realization." When one considers the images that serve to sustain Rilke's thought (death "ripens" in our very heart; it is the "fruit," the sweet, obscure fruit, or else a fruit still "green," without sweetness, which we, "leaves and bark," must bear and nourish),[8] one sees clearly that he seeks to make of our end something other than an accident which would arrive from outside to terminate us hastily. Death must exist for me not only at the very last moment, but as soon as I begin to live and in life's intimacy and profundity. Death would thus be part of existence, it would draw life from mine, deep within. It would be made of me and, perhaps, for me, as a child is the child of its mother. These are images which Rilke also uses frequently: we engender our death, or else we bring our death into the world dead, a stillborn child. And he prays:

And grant us now (after all women's pains)
the serious motherhood of men.

These are grave and troubling figures which, however, keep their secret. Rilke appeals to the image of vegetable or organic maturation only in order to turn us toward what we prefer to stay clear of — in order to show us that death has a kind of existence, and to train our attention upon this existence, awaken our concern. Death exists, but what form of existence does it have? What relation does this image establish between him who lives and the fact of dying? One might believe in a natural link; one might think, for example, that I produce my death as the body produces cancer. But that is not the case: despite the biological reality of the event, one must always reflect, beyond the organic phenomenon, upon death's being. One never dies simply of an

[8]In there is Death. Not the one whose voice
Wonderfully greeted them in their childhood,
but the little death as it is understood in there,
while their own end hangs in them like a
sour, green fruit, which doesn't ripen . . . .
For we are only the leaf and the bark.
The great death which each bears in himself
is the fruit around which all revolves.

illness, but of one's death, and that is why Rilke shied so stubbornly from learning of *what* he was dying: he did not want to put between himself and his end the mediation of any general knowledge.

My intimacy with my death seems, then, unapproachable. It is not within me like the vigilance of the species or like a vital necessity which over and above my person would affirm the larger view of nature. All such naturalistic conceptions are foreign to Rilke. I remain responsible for this intimacy which I cannot approach. I can, according to an obscure choice incumbent upon me, die of the great death which I bear within me, but also of that little death, sour and green, which I have been unable to make into a lovely fruit, or yet again of a borrowed, random death:

> . . . it's not our death, but one that takes us in the end
> only because we have not ripened our own.

This foreign death makes us die in the distress of estrangement.

My death must become always more inward. It must be like my invisible form, my gesture, the silence of my most hidden secret. There is something I must do to accomplish it; indeed, everything remains for me to do: it must be my work. But this work is beyond me, it is that part of me upon which I shed no light, which I do not attain and of which I am not master. Sometimes Rilke, in his respect for thoughtful effort and tasks carefully done, says of such a death:

> . . . it was a death which good work
> had profoundly formed, this proper death
> which has so great a need of us because we live it,
> and to which we are never nearer than here.

Death would seem, then, to be the dearth which we must generously fill, essential poverty which resembles that of God, "the absolute want that wants our aid," and which is terrifying only because of the distress that separates it from us. To sustain, to fashion our nothingness — such is the task. We must be the figurers and the poets of our death.

Patience

Such is the task: it invites us once more to associate poetic labors and the effort we must put into dying, but it clarifies neither one nor the other. The impression of a singular activity, scarcely graspable, essentially different from what is ordinarily called acting and doing, alone persists. The image of the fruit's slow maturation, the invisible growth of that other fruit, the child, suggest the idea of unhurried efforts, where relations with time are profoundly changed, as are relations with our will which projects and produces. Although the perspective is different, we find again here the same condemnation of impatience which we have recognized in Kafka: the feeling that the shortest road is an offense against the indefinite if it leads us toward what we want to reach without making us reach what exceeds all will.[9] Time as it is expressed in our habitual activities is time that decides, that negates; it is the hasty movement between points that must not retain it. Patience tells another time, another sort of task whose end one doesn't see, which assigns us no goal we can steadfastly pursue. Here patience is essential because impatience is inevitable in this space (the space of death's approach and of the work's), where there are neither milestones nor forms, where one has to suffer the unruly call of the remote. Impatience is inevitable and necessary. Were we not impatient, we would have no right to patience; we would not know that great appeasement which in the greatest tension no longer tends toward anything. Patience is the endurance of impatience, its acceptance and welcome, the accord which wants still to persist in the most extreme confusion.[10]

This patience, though it separates us from all forms of daily activity, is not inactive. But its procedure is mysterious. The task of forming our death leaves us to guess: it seems that we are to do something which, however, we cannot do, which does not depend upon us, but we upon it, upon which we do not even depend, for it escapes us and we escape it. To say that Rilke affirms the immanence of death in life is no doubt to speak correctly, but it is also to construe only one side of his

[9]Van Gogh constantly appeals to patience: "What is it to draw? How does one come to do it? It is the action of making one's way through an invisible iron wall which seems to be between what one *feels* and what one is *capable* of. How is one to get through this wall, for it is no use beating on it, one must undermine it and file one's way through slowly and patiently in my judgment."

"I am not an artist—how imprecise—even to think this of oneself—how could one not have patience, not learn from nature to have patience, have patience by seeing the wheat silently rise, things grow—how could one judge oneself to be a thing so absolutely dead as to think that one can no longer even grow. . . . I say this to show how stupid I find it to speak of artists' being gifted or not."

[10]If one compared this patience to the dangerous mobility of Romantic thought, patience would appear as its intimacy, but also as the inner pause, the expiation at the very heart of the fault (although in Rilke, patience often signifies a humbler attitude, a return to the silent tranquility of things as opposed to the feverishness of tasks, or yet again, as obedience to the fall which, drawing a thing toward the center of gravity of pure forces, makes it come to rest and rest itself in its immobile plenitude).

thought. This immanence is not given; it is to be achieved. It is our task, and such a task consists not only in humanizing or in mastering the foreignness of our death by a patient act, but in respecting its "transcendence." We must understand in it the absolutely foreign, obey what exceeds us, and be faithful to what excludes us. What must one do to die without betraying this high power, death? There is, then, a double task: I must die a death which does not betray *me*, and I myself must die without betraying the truth and the essence of death.

B. To Die Faithful to Death

It is at this juncture that we come back to the other requirement at the origin of Rilke's image of personal death. The anguish of anonymous death, the anguish of the "They die" and the hope for an "I die" in which individualism retrenches, tempts him at first to want to give *his* name and *his* countenance to the instant of dying: he does not want to die like a fly in the hum of mindlessness and nullity; he wants to possess his death and be named, be hailed by this unique death. From this perspective he suffers the obsession of the "I" that wants to die without ceasing to be "I"—a remainder of the need for immortality. This "I" wants to die concentrated in the very fact of dying, so that my death might be the moment of my greatest authenticity, the moment toward which "I" propel myself as if toward the possibility which is absolutely proper to me, which is proper only to me and which secures me in the steadfast solitude of this pure "I."

However, Rilke does not think only of the anguish of ceasing to be himself. He also thinks of death, of the supreme experience it represents, an experience which, because it is supreme, is terrifying, whose terror keeps us at a distance and which is impoverished by this distance. Men have recoiled from the obscure part of themselves, they have rejected and excluded it, and thus it has become foreign to them. It is an enemy to them, an evil power which they evade through constant distractions or which they denature by the dread which separates them from it. This is a great sorrow. It makes our life a desert of dread, doubly impoverished: impoverished by the poverty of this dread which is a bad dread, impoverished because deprived of the death which this poor dread thrusts obstinately outside us. And so, to make death my death is no longer at this point to remain myself even in death; it is to stretch this self as far even as death, to expose myself to death, no longer excluding but including it — to regard it as mine, to read it as my secret truth, the terribleness in which I recognize what I am when I am greater than myself, absolutely myself or the absolutely great.

And so the concern that will bit by bit displace the center of Rilke's thoughts is affirmed: will we continue to regard death as the foreign and incomprehensible, or will we learn to draw it into life, to make of it the other name, the other side of life? This concern becomes more pressing and more painful with the war. The horror of war sheds its somber light upon all that is inhuman for man in this abyss: yes, death is the adversary, the invisible opponent that wounds the best in us and by which all our joys perish. This view weighs heavily with Rilke, whom the ordeal of 1914 ravages in every way. Hence the energy he clearly devotes to keeping his gaze level before the ghastly sight of all the graves. In the *Bardo Thödol*, the Tibetan Book of the Dead, the deceased, during a period of indecision when he continues to die, sees himself confronted with the clear primordial light, then with the peaceful deities, then with the terrifying figures of the angry deities. If he lacks the strength to recognize himself in these images, if he does not see in them the projection of his own horrified soul, avid and violent — if he seeks to flee them — he will give them reality and density and thus fall back into the errors of existence. It is to a similar purification during life itself that Rilke calls us, with the difference that death is not the denunciation of the illusory appearances in which we live, but forms a whole with life, forms the generous space of the two domains' unity. Confidence in life and, for life's sake, in death: if we refuse death it is as if we refused the somber and difficult sides of life. It is as if we sought to welcome in life only its minimal parts. So, then, would our pleasures be minimal. "Whoever does not consent to the frightful in life and does not greet it with cries of joy never enters into possession of the inexpressible powers of our life. He remains marginal. When the time for judgment comes, he will have been neither alive nor dead."[11]

[11]In this effort to "strengthen a familiar trust in death by basing it upon the profoundest joys and splendors of life," Rilke seeks, above all, to master our fear. What we dread as an enigma is only unknown because of the error, our fear, which prevents it from making itself known. Our horror creates the horrible. It is the force with which we exclude death that confronts us, when death arrives, with the horror of being excluded from our own milieu. Rilke does not put death on a pinnacle; he seeks first and foremost a reconciliation: he wants us to trust in this obscurity that it might clarify itself. But, as

The Malte Experience

The *Malte* experience was decisive for Rilke. This book is mysterious because it turns around a hidden center which the author was unable to approach. This center is the death of Malte, or the instant of his collapse. The whole first part of the book announces it: all Malte's experiences tend to undermine life with the proof of its impossibility; a bottomless space opens where he slips, falls—but this fall is hidden from us. Moreover, as it is written, the book seems to develop only in order to forget this truth, and ramifies into diversions where the unexpressed signals to us from further and further away. In his letters Rilke always spoke of the young Malte as a being struggling in an ordeal which he was bound to lose.

Has this test not surpassed his strength, has he not failed to withstand it even though he was convinced in his mind of its necessity, so convinced that he pursued it with such instinctive perseverence that in the end it attached itself to him never again to leave him? This book of *Malte Laurids Brigge,* if ever it is written, will be nothing but the book of this discovery, presented in someone for whom it was too strong. Perhaps, after all, he did stand the test victoriously, for he wrote the death of the Chamberlain. But, like Raskolnikov, exhausted by his action, he remained on the road, incapable of continuing to act at the moment the action was to

---

happens in all mediations, what was the reality and the force that surpass us runs the risk, by modifying itself according to our measure, of losing the significance of its immoderation. Strangeness surmounted dissolves into a pallid intimacy which only teaches us our own knowledge. Rilke said of death: "Be satisfied to believe that it is a friend, your profoundest friend, perhaps the only friend never to be alienated by our actions and waverings, never." Perhaps the experience ceases, thus, utterly to derail us, but thus it leaves us on the old track of our habitual reality. In order to be "the awakener," it must be "the stranger." One cannot at once draw death close and hope that it will teach us the truth of the remote. Rilke also says, "Death is not beyond our strength; it is the measuring mark at the top of the vase; we are full each time we want to reach it, and for us to be filled means to be heavy: that is all." Here, death is the sign of a full existence: the fear of dying would be fear of that weight by which we are plenitude and authenticity; it would be tepid preference for insufficiency. The desire to die would express, on the contrary then, a certain need for plenitude; it would be the aspiring movement toward the brim, the impulse of liquid that wants to fill the vase. But is reaching the brim enough? "To overflow"; that is the secret liquid passion, the one that knows no measure. And overflowing does not signify plenitude, but emptiness, the excess by comparison to which fullness is still lacking.

begin, so that his liberty, conquered anew, turned against him and destroyed him without resistance.[12]

Malte's is the discovery of that force too great for us, *impersonal death*, which is the excess of our strength, that which exceeds it, that which would make our strength prodigious if we succeeded in making it ours anew. He could not master this discovery, he could not make it the basis of his art. What happens, then?

> For some time yet I will still be able to write all this and bear witness to it. But the day will come when my hand will be far from me, and when I order it to write, it will trace words to which I will not have consented. The time of that other interpretation will come, when the words will come apart, when all meaning will dissolve like clouds and fall down like rain. Despite my fear, I am like someone on the brink of great things, and I remember that I used to feel such glimmers within myself when I was going to write. But this time I will be written. I am the impression that will be transformed. Just a little more and I could, ah! understand all this, acquiesce in everything. Only one step, and my profound misery would be happiness. But I cannot take this step; I have fallen and cannot get up because I am broken.

One might well say that the narrative ends here; this is its extreme dénouement, beyond which everything must fall silent, and yet, strangely, these pages are on the contrary only the beginning of the book, which not only continues, but bit by bit and in the entire second part moves steadily further from the immediate personal ordeal, no longer makes any allusion to it except with a prudent reserve, if we assume that Malte, when he speaks of the somber death of Charles the Fearless or of the King's madness, does so in order not to speak of his own death or of his madness. Everything conspires to suggest that Rilke hid the end of the book at the beginning, in order to demonstrate to himself that after this end something remains possible, that it is not the frightful final line after which there is nothing more to say. And we know that, nevertheless, the completion of *Malte* marked for its author the beginning of a crisis that lasted ten years. No doubt the crisis had

---

[12][Quotations from Rilke's correspondence are translated with an eye to Jane Bannard Green and M.D. Herter Norton's translation from the German, *Letters of Rainer Maria Rilke* (New York: Norton Press, 1945–48 — Trans.]

other deep levels, but Rilke himself always connected it with this book where he felt he had said everything and yet had hidden the essential, so that his hero, his double, still hovered about him, like an ill-buried dead man who kept wanting to find a dwelling in his gaze. "I am still convalescing from that book" (1912). "Can you understand that after that book I have been left behind just like a survivor, at a loss in the deepest region of myself, unoccupied, unoccupiable?" (1911). "In consistent despair, Malte has come up behind everything, to a certain extent behind death, so that nothing is possible for me any more, not even dying" (1910). We must retain this expression, which is rare in Rilke's experience and which shows the experience opened onto that nocturnal region where death no longer appears as possibility proper, but as the empty depths of the impossible, a region from which he most often turns aside, in which he will nonetheless wander ten years, called into it by the work and the work's demand.

He endures this ordeal with patience, a painful consternation, and the disquietude of a wanderer who has no relationships even to himself. It has been observed that in four and a half years he lives in fifty or so different locations. In 1919 he writes again to a friend, "My inner self has closed up steadily as if to protect itself; it has become inaccessible to me, and now I do not know whether in my heart there is still the strength to enter into world relationships and to realize them, or whether only the tomb of my former spirit has quietly remained there." Why these difficulties? They arise because the whole problem for him is to begin from the point at which the "vanished one" was destroyed. How can a beginning be made from the impossible? "For five years, ever since *Malte* was finished, I have been living like a rank beginner and in truth like someone who does not begin." Later, when his patience and his consent have extricated him from this "lost and desolate region" by permitting him to encounter his true poet's language, that of the *Elegies,* he will say concisely that in this new work, starting from the same givens which had made Malte's existence *impossible,* life becomes *possible* again, and he will say moreover that he has not found the way out by backing up, but on the contrary, by pushing further on upon the hard road.

2. Death's Space

In the Elegies, the affirmation of life and that of death are revealed as one. To admit of one without the other — we celebrate this discovery here — a limitation which in the end excludes all that is infinite. Death is the side of life which is not turned toward us, nor do we shed any light upon it. We must try to become as fully conscious as possible of our existence which is at home in both unbounded realms and is nourished forever by both. . . . The true form of life extends through both spheres, the blood of the mightiest circulation flows through both: there is neither a here nor a beyond but the great unity.

The fame which has greeted this letter to Hulewicz and made the thoughts by which Rilke tried to comment upon his poems better known than the poems shows how much we like to substitute interesting ideas for the pure poetic movement. And it is striking that the poet too is constantly tempted to unburden himself of the dark language, not by expressing it, but by understanding it — as if, in the anguish of words which he is called upon only to write and never to read, he wanted to persuade himself that in spite of everything he understands himself; he has the right to read and comprehend.

The Other Side

Rilke's reading has "raised" a part of his work to the level of ideas. It has translated his experience. Rilke rejects the Christian solution, this is well known. It is here below, "in a purely earthly consciousness, profoundly, blessedly terrestrial," that death is a beyond to be learned by us, recognized and welcomed — perhaps furthered. Death exists not only, then, at the moment of death; at all times we are its contemporaries. Why, therefore, can we not accede immediately to that other side, which is life itself but related otherwise, become other, the other relation? One might be content to recognize the definition of this region in its inaccessibility: it is "the side which is not turned toward us, nor do we shed light upon it." Thus it would be what essentially escapes, a kind of transcendence, but of which we cannot say that it has value and reality, about which we know only this: that we are turned away from it.

But why "turned away"? What makes us necessarily unable in our own fashion to turn back? Our limits, apparently: we are limited beings. When we look in front of us, we do not see what is behind. When we are here, it is on the condition that we renounce elsewhere. The limit retains us, contains us, thrusts us back toward what we are, turns us back toward ourselves, away from the other, makes of us averted beings. To accede to the other side would be thus to enter into the liberty of that which is free of limits. But are we not, in a way, beings freed from the here and now? I see, perhaps, only what is in front of me, but I can represent to myself what is behind. Thanks to consciousness, am I not at all times elsewhere from where I am, always master of the other and capable of something else? Yes, it is true, but this is also our sorrow. Through consciousness we escape what is present, but we are delivered to representation. Through representation we reintroduce into our intimacy with ourselves the constraints of the face-to-face encounter; we confront ourselves, even when we look despairingly outside of ourselves.

This is called destiny: being face to face
and nothing else, and always opposite.

Such is the human condition: to be able to relate only to things which turn us away from other things and, graver still, to be present to ourselves in everything and in this presence not to meet anything except head-on, separate from it by this vis-à-vis and separated from ourselves by this interposition of ourselves.

At this juncture one can say that what excludes us from the limitless is what makes us beings deprived of limits. We believe ourselves to be turned away by each finite thing from the infinitude of all things. But we are no less turned away from each thing by the way in which we grasp it, representing it to make it ours — to make of it an object, an objective reality, to establish it in our utilitarian world by withdrawing it from the purity of space. *"The other side"* is where we would cease to be turned away from a single thing by our way of looking at it, averted from it by our gaze.

With all its eyes the creature sees
the Open. Our eyes only are
as if reversed.

To accede to the other side would thus be to transform our way of having access. Rilke is very tempted to see consciousness, as his era conceived of it, as the principal difficulty. In a letter of February 25, 1926 he specifies that it is the low "degree of consciousness" which puts the animal at an advantage by permitting it to enter into reality without having to be the center of it. "By Open we do not mean the sky, the air, space — which for the observer are still objects, and thus opaque. The animal, the flower *is* all that without realizing it, and has thus before itself, beyond itself, that indescribably open freedom which, for us, has its extremely short-lived equivalents perhaps only in the first instants of love — when one being sees in the other, in the beloved, his own extension — or again in the outpouring to God."

It is clear that Rilke confronts here the idea of consciousness closed upon itself, inhabited by images. The animal is where it looks, and its look does not reflect it, nor does it reflect the thing, but opens the animal onto the thing. The other side, then, which Rilke also calls "the pure relation," is the purity of the relation: the fact of being, in this relation, outside oneself, in the thing itself, and not in a representation of the thing. Death in this sense would be the equivalent of what has been called intentionality. Because of death "we look out with a great animal gaze." Through death the eyes turn back, and this return is the other side, and the other side is the fact of living no longer turned away, but turned back, introduced into the intimacy of conversion, not deprived of consciousness but established by consciousness outside it, cast into the ecstasy of this movement.

Let us reflect upon the two obstacles. The first stems from the locality of beings, their temporal or spatial limit — from, that is, what could be called a "bad extension," where one thing necessarily supplants another, can't be seen except hiding the other, etc. The second difficulty comes from a *bad interiority*, that of consciousness, where we are no doubt free from the limits of the here and now, where in the matrix of our intimacy everything is at our disposal, but where we are also excluded by this closed intimacy from true access to everything — excluded, moreover, from things by the imperious, the violent way we master them, by the purposeful activity that makes us possessors, producers, concerned with results and avid for objects.

On the one hand, then, a bad space, on the other a bad "interior." On the one hand, nevertheless, reality and the force of the exterior; on the other, the profundity of intimacy, the freedom and silence of the invisible. Mightn't there be a point where space is at once intimacy and ex-teriority, a space which, outside, would in itself be spiritual intimacy? An intimacy which, in us, would be the reality of the outdoors, such that there we would be within ourselves outside in the intimacy and in the intimate vastness of that outside? This is what Rilke's experience — which had at first a "mystical" form (the one he encounters at Capri and at Duino),[13] then the form of the poetic experience — leads him to recognize, or at least to glimpse and sense, and perhaps to call forth by expressing it. He names it *Weltinnenraum*, the world's inner space, which is no less things' intimacy than ours, and the free communication from one to the other, the strong, unrestrained freedom where the pure force of the undetermined is affirmed.

Through all beings spreads the one space:
the world's inner space. Silently fly the birds
all through us. O I who want to grow,
I look outside, and it is in me that the tree grows![14]

The World's Inner Space

What can be said of it? What exactly is this interiority of the exterior, this extension within us where "the infinite," as Rilke says at the time of the Capri experience, "penetrates so intimately that it is as though the shining stars rested lightly in his breast"? Can we truly accede to this space? And how can we? For consciousness is our destiny; we cannot leave it; and in it we are never in space but in the vis-à-vis of representation where we are always busy, moreover — busy acting, doing and possessing. Rilke never departs from the decided affirmation of the Open, but his estimate of our power to approach it varies greatly. Sometimes it seems that man is always excluded from it. At other times Rilke allows a hope for the "great movements of love," when you go beyond the beloved, when you are true to the audacity of this movement which knows neither stop nor limit, neither wants nor is able to rest in the person sought, but destroys this person or sur-passes him in order that he not be the screen that would hide the outside. These are such grave conditions that they make us prefer failure. To love is always to love someone, to have someone before you, to look only at him and not beyond him — if not inadvertently, in the leap of passion that knows nothing of ends. And so love finally turns us away, rather than turning

[13]We find the narrative of this experience under the title *Adventure I, Adventure II* in *Prose Fragments.*
[14]Poem dated August 1914.

us back. Even the child, who is nearer the pure danger of immediate life,

> ... the young child, already
> we turn him around and force him to look backwards
> at the world of forms and not into the Open, which
> in the animal's face is so profound.

And even the animal, "whose Being is infinite for it, inconceivable, unreflective," even the animal which, "where we see the future, sees everything, and sees itself in everything and safe forever" — sometimes the animal too bears "the weight and the care of a great sadness," the uneasiness that comes of being separated from original bliss and as if removed from the intimacy of its own breath.

Thus one could say that the Open is absolutely uncertain and that never, upon any face or in any gaze, have we perceived its reflection, for all mirroring is already that of a figurative reality. "*Always it is the world and never a Nowhere without no.*" This uncertainty is essential: to approach the Open as something sure would surely be to miss it. What is striking, and characteristic of Rilke, is how much nevertheless he remains certain of the uncertain, how he tries to set aside its doubtfulness, to affirm it in hope rather than in anguish, with a confidence not unaware that the task is difficult but which constantly renews the glad forecast. It is as if he were sure that there is in us, on account of the very fact that we are "turned away," the possibility of turning back, the promise of an essential reconversion.

In fact, if we come back to the two obstacles which in life keep us turned toward a limited life, it seems that the principal obstacle — since we see animals, who are free of it, accede to what is closed for us — is the bad interiority which is our own. And it seems that this bad consciousness can, from the imprisoning or banishing power which it was, become the power of welcome and adherence: no longer that which separates us from real things, but that which restores them to us at the point where they escape divisible space and enter the essential extension. Our bad consciousness is bad, not because it is interior and because it is freedom outside objective limits, but because it is not interior enough and because it is by no means free. For in it, as in the bad outside, objects reign, along with the concern for results, the desire to have, the greed that links us to possession, the need for security and stability, the tendency to know in order to be sure, the tendency to "take account" which necessarily becomes an inclination to count and to reduce everything to accounts — the very destiny of the modern world.

If there is hope, then, for our turning back, it lies in our turning away always more, through a conversion of the consciousness. Instead of leading consciousness back toward that which we call the real but which is only the objective reality where we dwell in the security of stable forms and separate existences—instead, also, of maintaining consciousness at its own surface, in the world of representations which is only the double of objects—such a conversion would turn it away toward a profounder intimacy, toward the most interior and the most invisible, where we are no longer anxious to do and act, but free of ourselves and of real things and of phantoms of things, "abandoned, exposed upon the mountains of the heart," as close as possible to the point where "the interior and the exterior gather themselves together into a single continuous space."

Novalis had certainly expressed a similar aspiration when he said: "We dream of voyaging across the universe. Isn't the universe, then, in us? We do not know the depths of our mind. Toward the interior goes the mysterious road. Eternity with its worlds, past and future, is in us." Nor is there any doubt that Kierkegaard says something that Rilke understood when he awakens the deep reaches of subjectivity and wants to free it from general categories and possibilities so as to grasp it afresh in its singularity. However, Rilke's experience has its own particular features: it is foreign to the imperious and magic violence by which, in Novalis, the interior affirms and gives rise to the exterior. And it is no less foreign to all surpassing of the earthly: if the poet goes further and further inward, it is not in order to emerge in God, but in order to emerge outside and to be faithful to the earth, to the plenitude and the superabundance of earthly existence when it springs forth outside all limits, in its excessive force that surpasses all calculation. Moreover, Rilke's experience has its own tasks. They are essentially those of the poetic word. And it is in this that his thought rises to a greater height. Here the theistic temptations which encumber his ideas on death fade, as do his hypotheses on consciousness and even the idea of the Open, which sometimes tends to become an existing region and not existence itself in its demandingness, or the excessive, limitless intimacy of this demand.

Conversion: Transmutation into Invisibility

And yet what happens when, turning always further away from the exterior, we descend toward that imaginary space, the heart's intimacy?

One might suppose that consciousness is seeking unconsciousness as its solution; that it dreams of dissolving in an instinctive blindness where it would regain the great unknowing purity of the animal. This is not the case. Instead (except in the Third Elegy where the elemental speaks), Rilke experiences this interiorization as a transmutation of significations themselves. It is a matter — he says so in his letter to Hulewicz — of "becoming as fully conscious as possible of our existence." And he says in the same letter: "All the configurations of the here and now are to be used not in a time-bound way, but, as far as we are able, to be placed in those superior significances in which we have a share." The words "superior significances" indicate that this interiorization which reverses the consciousness's destiny by purifying it of everything it represents and produces, of everything that makes it a substitute for the objective real which we call the world (a conversion which cannot be compared to phenomenological reduction, but which nonetheless evokes it), does not go toward the void of unknowing, but toward higher or more demanding meanings — closer too, perhaps, to their source. Thus this more inner consciousness is also more conscious, which for Rilke means that "in it we are introduced into the givens of earthly existence independent of time and space" (it is only a matter, then, of a broader, more distended consciousness). But more conscious also means: more pure, closer to the demand that founds the consciousness and that makes it not the bad intimacy which closes us in, but the force of the surpassing where intimacy is the bursting and springing of the outside.

But how is this conversion possible? How is it accomplished? And what gives it authority and reality, if it is not to be reduced to the uncertainty of "extremely momentary" and perhaps always unreal states?

Through conversion everything is turned inward. This means that we turn ourselves, but that we also turn everything, all the things we have to do with. That is the essential point. Man is linked to things, he is in the midst of them, and if he renounces his realizing and representing activity, if he apparently withdraws into himself, it is not in order to dismiss everything which isn't he, the humble and outworn realities, but rather to take these with him, to make them participate in this interiorization where they lose their use value, their falsified nature, and lose also their narrow boundaries in order to penetrate into their true profundity. Thus does this conversion appear as an immense task of transmutation, in which things, all things, are transformed and interiorized by becoming interior in us and by becoming interior to themselves. This transformation of the visible into the invisible and of the invisible into the always more invisible takes place where the fact of being unrevealed does not express a simple privation, but access to the other side "which is not turned toward us nor do we *shed light* upon it." Rilke has repeated this in many ways, and these formulae are among the best known to the French reader: "We are the bees of the Invisible. We ardently suck the honey of the visible in order to accumulate it in the great golden hive of the Invisible." "Our task is to impregnate the provisional and perishable earth so profoundly in our mind, with so much patience and passion, that its essence can be reborn in us invisible."

Every man is called upon to take up again the mission of Noah. He must become the intimate and pure ark of all things, the refuge in which they take shelter, where they are not content to be kept as they are, as they imagine themselves to be — narrow, outworn, so many traps for life — but are transformed, lose their form, lose themselves to enter into the intimacy of their reserve, where they are as if preserved from themselves, untouched, intact, in the pure point of the undetermined. Yes, every man is Noah, but on closer inspection, he is Noah in a strange way, and his mission consists less in saving everything from the flood than, on the contrary, in plunging all things into a deeper flood where they disappear prematurely and radically. That, in fact, is what the human vocation amounts to. If it is necessary that everything visible become invisible, if this metamorphosis is the goal, our intervention is apparently quite superficial: the metamorphosis is accomplished perfectly of itself, for everything is perishable, for, says Rilke in the same letter, "the perishable is everywhere engulfed in a deep being." What have we then to do, we who are the least durable, the most prompt to disappear? What have we to offer in this task of salvation? Precisely that: our promptness at disappearing, our aptitude for perishing, our fragility, our exhaustion, our gift for death.

Death's Space and the Word's

Here again, then, is the truth of our condition and the weight of our problem. Rilke, at the end of the *Elegies*, uses this expression: "the infinitely dead." An ambiguous formula. But one can say of men that they are infinitely mortal, a little more than mortal. Everything is perishable, but we are the most perishable; all things pass, and are transformed, but we want transformation, we want to pass, and our will is this passing on, further. Hence the call: "Want change" ("Wolle die Wandlung"). We must not rest, but pass on. "Nowhere is there staying" ("Bleiben ist nirgends"). "Whatever closes itself into staying the same is already petrified." To live is always already to take leave, to be dismissed and to dismiss what is. But we can get ahead of this separation and, looking at it as though it were behind us, make of it the moment when, even now, we touch the abyss and accede to the deep of being.

Thus we see that conversion—the movement toward the most interior, a work in which we transform ourselves as we transform everything—has something to do with our end, and that this transformation, this fruition of the visible in the invisible for which we are responsible, is the very task of dying, which has until now been so difficult for us to recognize. It takes effort, yet effort evidently quite different from that which we put into making objects and projecting results. We even see now that it is the opposite of purposeful work, although similar in one point. For in both cases it is certainly a matter of "transformation." In the world things are *transformed* into objects in order to be grasped, utilized, made more certain in the distinct rigor of their limits and the affirmation of a homogeneous and divisible space. But in imaginary space things are *transformed* into that which cannot be grasped. Out of use, beyond wear, they are not in our possession but are the movement of dispossession which releases us both from them and from ourselves. They are not certain but are joined to the intimacy of the risk where neither they nor we are sheltered any more, but where we are, rather, introduced, utterly without reserve, into a place where nothing retains us at all.

In a poem, one of his last, Rilke says that interior space "translates things." It makes them pass from one language to another, from the foreign, exterior language into a language which is altogether interior and which is even the interior of language, where language names in silence and by silence, and makes of the name a silent reality. "*Space (which) exceeds us and translates things*" is thus the transfigurer, the translator par excellence. But this statement suggests more: is there not another translator, another space where things cease to be visible in order to dwell in their invisible intimacy? Certainly, and we can boldly give it its name. This essential translator is the poet, and this space is the poem's space, where no longer is anything present, where in the midst of absence everything speaks, everything returns into the spiritual accord which is open and not immobile but the center of the eternal movement.[15]

[15]To praise the poetry of Jacobsen, Rilke says, "One does not know where the verbal weave finishes or where the space begins."

If the metamorphosis of the visible into the invisible is our task, if it is the truth of conversion, then there is a point at which we see it through without losing it in the evanescence of "extremely momentary" states: this point is the word. To speak is essentially to transform the visible into the invisible; it is to enter a space which is not divisible, an intimacy which, however, exists outside oneself. To speak is to take one's position at the point where the word needs space to reverberate and be heard, and where space, becoming the word's very movement, becomes hearing's profundity, its vibration. "How," says Rilke, in a text written in French, "how could one sustain, how could one save the visible, if not by creating the language of absence, of the invisible?"

The Open is the poem. The space where everything returns to deep being, where there is infinite passage between the two domains, where everything dies but where death is the learned companion of life, where horror is ravishing joy, where celebration laments and lamentation praises—the very space toward which "all worlds hasten as toward their nearest and truest reality," the space of the mightiest circulation and of ceaseless metamorphosis—this is the poem's space. This is the Orphic space to which the poet doubtless has no access, where he can penetrate only to disappear, which he attains only when he is united with the intimacy of the breach that makes him a mouth unheard, just as it makes him who hears into the weight of silence. The Open is the work, but the work as origin.

Song as Origin: Orpheus

When Rilke exalts Orpheus, when he exalts the song which is being, he is not speaking of the ultimate perfection of a song which begins by being sung, or even of the fullness of song, but of song as origin and the origin of song. There is, it is true, an essential ambiguity in the figure of Orpheus. This ambiguity belongs to the myth which preserves the figure and is its reserve, but the ambiguity also stems from the uncertainty in Rilke's thoughts, from the way in which, little by little in the course of the experience, he dissolved the substance and reality of death. Orpheus is not like the Angel in whom the transformation is achieved, who is unaware of its risks but also of its protection and significance. Orpheus is the act of metamorphosis: not the Orpheus who has conquered death, but he who always dies, who is the demand that we disappear and who disappears in the anguish of this disappearance, an anguish which becomes song, a word which is the pure movement of dying. Orpheus dies a little more than we do, he is we ourselves bearing the anticipated knowledge of our death, knowledge which is dispersion's intimacy. If the poem could become a poet, Orpheus would be the poem: he is the ideal and the emblem of poetic plenitude. Yet he is at the same time not the completed poem, but something more mysterious and more demanding: the origin of the poem, the sacrificial point which is no longer the reconciliation of the two domains, but the abyss of the lost god, the infinite trace of absence, a moment to which Rilke comes closest perhaps in these three lines:

O you, lost god! You, infinite trace!
By dismembering you the hostile forces had to disperse you
To make of us now hearers and a mouth of Nature.

This ambiguity manifests itself in many ways. Sometimes it seems that, for Rilke, what makes the human word heavy, foreign to the purity of becoming, is also what makes it more expressive, more capable of its proper mission — the metamorphosis of the visible into invisibility where the Open is at hand. The world's inner space requires the restraint of human language in order truly to be affirmed. It is only pure and only true within the strict limitations of this word.

The one space through which birds plunge is not
the intimate space which sets off your face
. . . .
Space exceeds us and translates things:
That the tree's being may succeed for you,
cast around it the inner space, that space
which announces itself in you. Surround it with restraint.
It knows not how to limit itself. Only in taking form
from your renunciation does it truly become a tree.[16]

Here the task of the poet is that of a mediation which Hölderlin was first to express and celebrate.[17] The poet's destiny is to expose himself to the force of the undetermined and to the pure violence of being from which nothing can be made, to endure this force courageously, but also to contain it by imposing upon it restraint and the perfection of a form. This is a requirement full of risk:

[16]Poem dated June 1924.
[17]At least in the hymn, *So, on a festival day* . . .

Why must someone stand here like a shepherd,
Exposed thus to such excess of influence?

Yet it is a task which consists, not in surrendering to being's unresolvable ambiguity, but in giving it decisiveness, exactitude, and form, or, as he says, in "making things from anguish": in lifting the uncertainty of anguish to the resolution of an exact formulation. We know how much the concern to give expression to things, and to express them with the finite words that suit them, counted for Rilke. In this respect, the inexpressible seems beside the point to him. To speak is our task, to tell finite things in an accomplished fashion that excludes the infinite is our power, because we are ourselves finite beings, anxious to come to a finish and able, in the realm of the finite, to grasp completion. Here the Open closes under the constraint of a language so determined that, far from being the pure milieu where conversion to the interior and transmutation into invisibility are achieved, it transforms itself into a graspable thing, becomes the discourse of the world, a language where things are not transformed but immobilized, fixed in their visible aspect, as it sometimes happens in the Expressionist part of Rilke's work, the *Neue Gedichte*, a work of the eye and not of the heart, *Herzwerk*.[18]

Or, on the contrary, the poet turns toward the most inward as toward the source whose pure, silent surging must be preserved. Then the true poem is no longer the word that captures, the closed space of the telling word, but the breathing intimacy whereby the poet consumes himself in order to augment space and dissipates himself rhythmically: a pure inner burning around nothing.

Breathing, O invisible poem!
World's space which purely and always
exchanges itself for very being. Counterweight,
in which rhythmically I am achieved.
. . . .
A gain in space.

And in another sonnet:

To sing in truth is a different breath
A breath around nothing. A stirring in God. The wind.

[18]So he says to himself, after finishing the *Neue Gedichte:*
The work of vision is done
Now do the work of the heart.

"A breath around nothing." That is something like the truth of the poem when it is no longer anything but a silent intimacy, a pure expenditure in which our life is sacrificed — and not in view of any result, in order to conquer or acquire, but for nothing, in the pure relation to which the symbolic name of God is given here. *"To sing is a different breath"*: it is no longer the language which is graspable and grasping affirmation, covetousness and conquest, the breathing that is aspiration as much as respiration, which is always in quest of something, which is durable and wants duration. In the song, to speak is to pass on, to consent to the passage which is pure decline, and language is no longer anything but "that profound innocence of the human heart through which it is able to describe, in its irresistible fall all the way to its ruin, a pure line."

Metamorphosis, then, appears as the happy consumption of being when, without reserve, it enters into the movement where nothing is preserved, which does not realize, accomplish, or save anything, which is the pure felicity of descending, the joy of the fall, the jubilant word which one unique time gives voice to disappearance, before disappearing into it:

> Here, among those who pass, in the Kingdom of decline,
> Be the glass that rings and, in the brilliant resonance, is already broken.

But, one has immediately to add, Rilke also, and much more gladly, conceives of metamorphosis as an entrance into the eternal, and of imaginary space as liberation from time the destroyer. "It would seem to me almost wrong still to call time what was rather a state of liberty, in a very perceptible way a space, the environment of the Open, and not the act of passing."[19] Sometimes, in his last works, he seems to allude to a completed time which would hold still in a pure circle of time closed upon itself. But whether space is this time risen above the passing moment, or the space which "drinks absent presence" and changes duration into timelessness, it appears as the center where what is no longer still subsists. And our vocation, to establish things and ourselves in this space, is, not to disappear, but to perpetuate: to save things, yes, to make them invisible, but in order that they be reborn in their invisibility. And so death, that readier death which is our destiny, again becomes the promise of survival, and already the moment is at hand

[19]*Kein Vergehn:* Rilke opposes "space" here, and "the Open," to consumption by time, the fall toward the end.

when dying for Rilke will be to escape death — a strange volatization of his experience. What does it mean and how is it accomplished?

3. Death's Transmutation

It is in the Ninth Elegy that Rilke indicates the power which belongs to us — to us the most perishable of all beings — to save what will last longer than we.

> And these things whose life
> is decline understand that you praise them; fleeting,
> they lend us, us the most fleeting, the power to save.
> They want us to change them in the bottom of our invisible heart
> into — O infinite — into ourselves! whatsoever we may be in the end.

Such, then, is our privilege. Granted, it is linked to our gift for disappearing, but only because in this disappearance the power to conserve is also manifest, and because in this readier death resurrection is expressed, the joy of a transfigured life.

We are imperceptibly approaching the instant in Rilke's experience when dying will not be to die, but to transform the fact of death, and when the effort to teach us not to deny the extreme but to expose ourselves to the overpowering intimacy of our end will culminate in the peaceful affirmation that there is no death, that "close to death, one no longer sees death." The animal who lives in the Open is "free of death." But we, to the extent that ours is necessarily the perspective of a life which is limited and maintained between limits, "we see only death."

> Death, we see only death; the free animal
> always has its decline behind it,
> and before it God, and when it moves, it moves
> in Eternity, as springs flow.

Death, "to see only death," is thus the error of a limited life and of a poorly converted consciousness. Death is that very concern to delimit which we introduce into being; it is the result and perhaps the means of the bad transmutation by which we make of all thing objects — tightly closed, well-finished realities imbued with our preoccupation with the finish. Freedom must be liberation from death, the approach toward the point where death becomes transparent.

For close to death one no longer sees death,
and one stares outward, perhaps with a great animal gaze.

Thus we should say no longer now that death is the side of life from which we are turned away. It is only the error in this turning: aversion. Wherever we turn away, there is death, and what we call the moment of dying is only the crook of the turn, the extreme of its curvature, the end point beyond which everything reverses itself, everything turns back. This is so true that in the ordeal of conversion — that return inward by which we go into ourselves outside of ourselves — if we are somehow stolen from death it is because without even perceiving it we pass the instant of dying, having gone too far, inattentive and as if distracted, neglecting what we would have to have done to die (be afraid, hold onto the world, want to *do* something). And in this negligence death has become forgetfulness; we have forgotten to die. After the account of his two mystical experiences, Capri and Duino, where for the first time he seems to have felt what after 1914 he will call the world's inner space, Rilke, speaking of himself in the third person, adds:

> In fact he had been free for a long time, and if something prevented his dying, perhaps it was only this: that he had overlooked it once, somewhere, and that he didn't have, like others, to go on ahead in order to reach it, but on the contrary, to go back the other way. His action was already outside, in the confident things that children play with, and was perishing in them.[20]

The Intimacy of Invisible Death

It might seem surprising that he should be so little disturbed by this volatization of the experience to which he devotes himself. The explanation is that this very evanescence expresses the movement toward which he tends profoundly. Just as each thing must become invisible, likewise what makes death a thing, the brute fact of death, must become invisible. Death enters into its own invisibility, passes from its opacity to its transparency, from its terrifying reality to its ravishing unreality. It is in this passage its own conversion; through this conversion it is the ungraspable, the invisible — the source, however, of all invisibility. And suddenly we understand why Rilke always kept silent,

[20][Here I have compared Blanchot's French with G. Craig Houston's English translation of the German, *Selected Works,* (New York: New Directions, 1967), vol. 2 — Trans.]

even to himself, about the death of Malte. Not to perceive this death was to give it its one chance to be authentic. Ignorance made it not the fatal error of the terrible limit against which we are broken, but the bloom of the glad moment when, by interiorizing itself, it loses itself in its own intimacy. And likewise, in his last illness, he wanted not to know of what he was dying or that he was going to die: "Rilke's conversations with his doctor invariably reflect his desire that his pain be no one's . . . . Strange conversations," recounts Dr. Haemerli. "They always went right up to the point where the sick man would have had to pronounce the word death, but at which all at once he stopped prudently." This prudence is difficult to interpret. One doesn't know whether the desire "not to see death" expresses fear of seeing it, elusiveness and flight before the inconceivable, or, on the contrary, the profound intimacy which creates silence, imposes silence, and turns into ignorance in order not to stay within the boundaries of limited knowledge.

Thus we see more clearly how Rilke's thoughts have shifted since the days when he wished for a personal death. As before — although he no longer expresses the distinction in such a decisive fashion — he remains willing to speak of two deaths, to see in one sheer death, death's pure transparency, but in the other the opaque and impure. And as before — more precisely than before — he sees between these two deaths the difference made by an expenditure of effort, by a transmutation: either because bad death, the one that has the brutality of an event and of a random occurrence, remains an untransmuted death, a death not reintroduced into its essential secret, or because it becomes in true death the intimacy of transmutation.

Another aspect of his thought which gains precision is that this task of transmutation, which infinitely exceeds us and cannot result from our wordly aptitude for acting and doing, is only accomplished in us by death itself — as if, in us alone, death could purify, could interiorize itself and apply to its own reality that power of metamorphosis, that force of invisibility whose original profundity it is. And why is it in us, in humans, of all beings the most fragile, that death finds this perfection? It is because not only do we number among those who pass away, but in this kingdom of decline we are also those who consent to pass, who say yes to disappearance and in whom disappearance becomes speech, becomes word and song. Thus death is in us the purity of dying because it can reach the point where it sings, because it finds in us "that . . identity of absence and presence" which is manifest in the song, the extreme tip of fragility which at the moment of breaking resonates, whose vibration is the pure resonance of the very break. Rilke affirms that death is "der eigentliche Ja-sager," the authentic yea-sayer, it says only yes. But this only happens in the being that has the power to speak, just as speaking is not truly speech and essential word except in this absolute yes where the word gives voice to death's intimacy. Thus there is a secret identity between singing and dying, between death—the transmutation of the invisible by the invisible—and the song within which this transmutation is accomplished. We come back here to what Kafka, at least in the sentences we ascribed to him, seemed to seek to express: I write to die, to give death its essential possibility, through which it is essentially death, source of invisibility; but at the same time, I cannot write unless death writes in me, makes of me the void where the impersonal is affirmed.

No One's Death

The word *impersonal* which we introduce here indicates the difference between the outlooks of the early and the late Rilke. If death is the heart of the transparency where it infinitely transforms itself, there can no longer be any question of a personal death, where I would die in the affirmation of my own reality and my unique existence, a death such that I would be supremely invisible in it and it visible in me (with that monumental character which death has in Brigge the Chamberlain during his lifetime). And my prayer can no longer be:

Oh Lord, grant to each his own death,
the dying which truly evolves from this life
where he found love, meaning and distress

but rather: Grant me the death which is not mine, the death of no one, the dying which truly evolves from death, where I am not called upon to die, which is not an event—an event that would be proper to me, which would happen to me alone—but the unreality and the absence where nothing happens, where neither love nor meaning nor distress accompanies me, but the pure abandon of all that.

Rilke is doubtless unwilling to restore to death the lowly impersonality which would make of it something less than personal, something always improper. The impersonality toward which death tends in Rilke is ideal. It is above the person: not the brutality of a fact or the randomness of chance, but the volatization of the very fact of death, its transfiguration at its own center. Moreover, the ambiguity of the word *eigen (der eigene Tod,* "death proper"), which means "own," proper to me as well as authentic, is significant here. (Heidegger seems to dwell on this ambiguity when he speaks of death as the absolutely proper possibility, by which he means that death is the uttermost possibility, the most extreme thing that happens to the self, but also the "ownmost," the most personal event to befall the "I," the event where "I" affirm myself the most and the most authentically.) This ambiguity allows Rilke never to cease recognizing himself in his early prayer: Grant to each his own, his proper death, the death which is properly death, the essential death and the death which is essentially death; grant to me this essence which is also mine, since it is in me that it has been purified — that it has become, through inward conversion, through the consent and the intimacy of my song, pure death, the purification of death by death and thus my work, the work of art which is the passage of things into the heart of death's purity.

One must not forget, in fact, that this effort to raise death to itself, to make the point where it loses itself within itself coincide with the point at which I lose myself outside of myself, is not a simple internal affair, but implies an immense responsibility toward things and is possible only through their mediation — through the movement which is entrusted to me and which must raise things themselves to a point of greater reality and truth. This is essential in Rilke. It is through this double requirement that he preserves in poetic existence the tension without which it would perhaps fade into a rather pale ideality. One of the two domains must never be sacrificed to the other: the visible is necessary to the invisible; it is saved in the invisible, but it is also what saves the invisible. This "holy law of contrast" reestablishes between the two poles an equality of value:

> Being here below and being beyond, may both claim you
> Strangely, without distinction.

The Ecstatic Experience of Art

The hidden certitude that "beyond" is only another mode of being "here below" when I am no longer simply in myself but outside, close to the sincerity of things: this is what draws me constantly back toward their "sight," and turns me toward them so that the turning back may be accomplished in me. In a way, I save myself no less by seeing things than I save them by giving them access to the invisible. Everything hinges on the movement of seeing, when in it my gaze, ceasing to direct itself forward with the pull of time that attracts it to goals, turns back to look "as if over the shoulder, behind, toward things," in order to reach "their closed existence," which I see then as perfected, not crumbling or being altered by the wear of active life, but as it is in the innocence of being. I see things then with the disinterested and somewhat distant look of someone who has just left them.

This disinterested gaze, which has no future and seems to come from the heart of death, this look to which "all things give themselves at once more distantly and somehow more truly," is the gaze of the mystical Duino experience, but it is also the gaze of "art." And it is correct to say that the artist's experience is an ecstatic experience and that it is, like the Duino experience, an experience of death. To see properly is essentially to die. It is to introduce into sight the turning back again which is ecstasy and which is death. This does not mean that everything sinks into the void.[21] On the contrary, things then offer themselves in the inexhaustible fecundity of their meaning which our vision ordinarily misses — our vision which is only capable of one point of view. "A finch that was near him and whose blue gaze he had already met on other occasions, touched him now across a more spiritual distance, but with such an inexhaustible significance that it seemed nothing was hidden anymore."

Hence the unfailing fondness for things, the faithful abiding with them which Rilke advised at all periods of his life as that which can best bring us toward a form of authenticity. It might well be said that often when he thinks of the word *absence,* he thinks of what the *presence* of things is for him: he thinks of that being-a-thing, humble, silent, grave obedience to the pure gravity of forces which is repose in the web of influences and the balance of movements. Again, toward the end of his life he said: "My world begins next to things." "I have . . . the particular happiness of living by means of things."

There is not one thing in which I do not find myself;
It is not my voice alone that sings: everything resonates.

He considered with regret painting's tendency to depart from "the object." He sees there a reflection of war and a mutilation. Thus, speaking of Klee, he says:

[21]Although à propos of the Capri "experience," Rilke acknowledges the void: "extension"

During the war years I often thought I felt exactly this disappearance of "the object" (for the extent to which we accept one — and in addition aspire to express ourselves through it — is a matter of faith: broken beings are best expressed, then, by fragments and debris . . .). But now, reading this book by Hausenstein, so full of intelligence, I have been able to discover in myself an immense calm, and to understand, in spite of everything, how safe all things are for me. It takes the obstinacy of a city dweller (and Hausenstein is one), to dare claim that nothing exists any more. For myself, I can start afresh from your little cowslips. Really, nothing prevents me from finding all things inexhaustible and intact: where would art find its point of departure if not in this joy and this tension of an infinite beginning?[22]

This text not only reveals Rilke's preferences in an interesting way, but brings us back to the profound ambiguity of his experience. He says it himself: art takes its point of departure in things, but what things? Intact things — *unverbraucht* — when they are not being used and used up by their use in the world. Art must not, then, start from the hierarchically "ordered" things which our "ordinary" life proposes to us. In the world's order things have being according to their value; they have worth, and some are worth more than others. Art knows nothing of this order. It takes an interest in realities according to an absolute disinterestedness, that infinite distance which is death. If it starts then, from things, it starts from all things without distinction. It does not choose, it takes its point of departure in the very refusal to choose. If the artist prefers to look among things for "beautiful" ones, he betrays being, he betrays art. Rilke, on the contrary, refuses to "choose between the beautiful and the unbeautiful. Each is only a space, a possibility, and it is up to me to fill each perfectly or imperfectly." Not to choose, not to refuse anything access to vision and, in vision, to transmutation — to start from things, but from all things: this is a rule which always tormented him and which he learned perhaps from Hofmannsthal. The latter, in a 1907 essay, *The Poet and These Times,* said of the poet, "It is as if his eyes had no lids." He must not leave anything out of himself, he must not withold himself from any being, from any phantasm

---

is arranged in a way so little "human" that men "could only name it: emptiness."

[22][The English translation from the German which I compared to Blanchot's French is by Violet M. Macdonald (London: Methuen & Co. Ltd., 1951) — Trans.]

born of a human mind; he can reject no thought. Likewise in 1907 Rilke says with the same force in a letter to Clara Rilke: "No more than one choice is permitted. He who creates cannot turn away from any existence; a single failing anywhere at all snatches him from the state of grace, makes him faulty through and through." The poet, lest he betray himself by betraying being, must never "turn away." By this aversion he would surrender to bad death, the one that limits and delimits. He must in no way defend himself; he is essentially a man without defenses:

> A being with no shell, open to pain,
> Tormented by light, shaken by every sound.

Rilke often used the image of the little anemone he saw one day in Rome. "It had opened so wide during the day that it could not close up again at night." Thus, in an Orpheus sonnet, he exalts this gift for welcoming infinitely as a symbol of poetic openness: "*You, acceptance and force of so many worlds,*" he says, in a line where the word *Entschluss,* ("resolution"), echoing the word *erschliessen* ("to open"), reveals one of the sources of Heidegger's *Entschlossenheit* ("resolute acceptance"). So the artist must be, and so his life. But where is this life to be found?

> But when, in which of all the lives
> Are we at last beings who open and welcome?

If the poet is truly linked to this acceptance which doesn't choose and which seeks its starting point not in any particular thing but in all things and, more profoundly, in a region anterior to things, in the indeterminacy of being — if the poet must live at the intersection of infinite relations, in the place opened and as if void where foreign destinies cross — then he can well say joyfully that he takes his point of departure in things: what he calls "things" is no longer anything but the depth of the immediate and undetermined, and what he calls point of departure is the approach toward the point where nothing begins. It is "the tension of an infinite beginning," art itself as origin or again the experience of the Open, the search for a true dying.

The Secret of Double Death

So we have returned, now, to the center from which all the ambiguity of the movement radiates. To start off from things, yes, that is necessary. It is they that must be saved; it is in them, by turning authentically toward them, that we learn to turn toward the invisible, to feel the movement of transmutation and, in this movement, to transmute transmutation itself, to the point where it becomes the purity of death purified of dying, in the unique song where death says yes and which, in the fullness of this yes is song's very fullness and its perfection. This movement is certainly difficult, a long and patient experience. But at least it shows us clearly where we must begin. Are not things given us? "For my part, I can start afresh from your little cowslips; truly nothing prevents me from finding all things inexhaustible and intact." Yes, "nothing prevents me" — provided, however, that I be freed from every obstacle, from all limits. And this liberation will be illusory if, from the first step, it is not that radical turning back which alone makes me "him who is ready for everything, who excludes nothing," "a being with no shell." It is necessary, then, no longer to start from things in order to make possible the approach toward true death, but to start from the deep of death in order to turn toward the intimacy of things — to "see" them truly, with the disinterested gaze of him who does not cleave to himself, who cannot say "I," who is no one: impersonal death.

To start from death? But where, now, is death? One may judge that Rilke does much to "idealize" the ordeal of dying. He seeks to make it invisible to us, he wants to purify it of its brutality; he sees in it a promise of unity, the hope of a larger understanding. If death is the extreme, then it must be said that this is a very accommodating extreme, which takes such care not to threaten our faith in the oneness of being, our sense of the whole and even our fear of death, for this death disappears, discreetly, into itself. But this disappearance precisely, which has its reassuring side, also has a fearful one, which is like another form of its excessiveness, the image of what makes it an impure transcendence, that which we never meet, which we cannot grasp: the ungraspable; absolute indeterminacy. If death's true reality is not simply what from the outside we call quitting life — if death is something other than its worldly reality, and if it eludes us, turning always away — then this movement makes us sense not only its discretion and its essential intimacy but also its profound unreality: death as abyss, not that which founds but the absence and the loss of all foundation.

This is an impressive result of Rilke's experience, for it enlightens us in spite of him, as if through the mediation of his reassuring intentions it continued to speak to us in the harsh original language. When the force upon which he makes everything depend is detached from the moment when it has the reality of the last instant, it escapes him and escapes us constantly. It is inevitable but inaccessible death; it is the abyss of the present, time without a present, with which I have no rela-tionships; it is that toward which I cannot go forth, for in it *I* do not die, I have fallen from the power to die. In it *they* die; they do not cease, and they do not finish dying.

There is much to suggest that the movement by which he purifies death, by taking away its random character, forced Rilke to incorporate this randomness in its essence, to close it upon its absolute indeter-minacy, so that instead of being only an improper and untimely event, death becomes, at the heart of its invisibility, that which is not even an event, that which is not accomplished, yet which is there, the part of this event which its accomplishment cannot realize.

Rilke's assertion, which has had repercussions in philosophy, that there is something like a double death, two relations with death, one which we like to call authentic and the other inauthentic, only expresses the *doubleness* within which such an event withdraws as if to preserve the void of its secret. Inevitable, but inaccessible; certain, but un-graspable. That which produces meaning (nothingness as the power to negate, the force of the negative, the end starting from which man is the decision to be without being) is the risk that rejects being—is history, truth. It is death as the extreme of power, as my most proper possibility, but also the death which never comes to me, to which I can never say yes, with which there is no authentic relation possible. In-deed, I elude it when I think I master it through a resolute acceptance, for then I turn away from what makes it the essentially inauthentic and the essentially inessential. From this point of view, death admits of no "being *for* death"; it does not have the solidity which would sustain such a relation. It is that which happens to no one, the uncertainty and the indecision of what never happens. I cannot think about it seriously, for it is not serious. It is its own imposter; it is disintegration, vacant debilitation—not the term, but the interminable, not proper but featureless death, and not true death but, as Kafka says, "the sneer of its capital error."

Orphic Space

What is, moreover, very striking in Rilke's itinerary is the way the force of the poetic experience led him, and almost without his knowing it, from the search for a personal death—clearly it is with this kind of death that he feels most kinship—to an altogether different obligation. After hav-ing, at first, made art "the road toward myself," he feels increasingly that this road must lead to the point where, within myself, I belong to the outside. It leads me where I am no longer myself, where if I speak it is not I who speak, where I cannot speak. To encounter Orpheus is to encounter this voice which is not mine, this death which becomes song, but which is not my death, even though I must disappear in it more profoundly.

Once and for all,
It is Orpheus when there is song. He comes and he goes.

These words seem merely to echo the ancient idea according to which there is only one poet, a single superior power to speak which "now and again throughout time makes itself known in the souls that submit to it." This is what Plato called enthusiasm. Closer to Rilke, Novalis had affirmed it in his turn, in a way which the Orpheus verses seem to recall: "Klingsohr, eternal poet, does not die, remains in the world." But Orpheus, precisely, does die, and he does not remain: he comes and he goes. Orpheus does not symbolize the lofty transcendence of which the poet would be the vehicle and which would lead him to say: it is not I who speak but the god who speaks in me. Orpheus does not signify the eternity and the immutability of the poetic sphere, but, on the contrary, links the "poetic" to an immeasurable demand that we disappear. He is a call to die more profoundly, to turn toward a more extreme dying:

O seek to understand that he must disappear!
Even if the anguish of it dismay him.
While his word extends this world,
Already he is beyond where you may not accompany him.
. . . .
And he obeys by going beyond.

Through Orpheus we are reminded that speaking poetically and disappearing belong to the profundity of a single movement, that he who sings must jeopardize himself entirely and, in the end, perish, for he speaks only when the anticipated approach toward death, the premature separation, the adieu given in advance obliterate in him the false certitude of being, dissipate protective safeguards, deliver him to a limitless insecurity. Orpheus conveys all this, but he is also a more mysterious sign. He leads and attracts us toward the point where he himself, the eternal poem, enters into his own disappearance, where he identifies himself with the force that dismembers him and becomes "pure contradiction," the "lost god," the god's absence, the original void of which the first elegy speaks in connection with the myth of

Linos, and from which "the uninterrupted tidings formed of silence" propagate themselves through terrified space—the murmur of the interminable. Orpheus is the mysterious sign pointed toward the origin, where not only secure existence and the hope of truth and the gods are lacking, but also the poem; where the power to speak and the power to hear, undergoing their own lack, endure their impossibility.

This movement is "pure contradiction." It is linked to the infinitude of the transformation which leads us not only to death, but infinitely transmutes death itself, which makes of death the infinite movement of dying and of him who dies him who is infinitely dead, as if in death's intimacy it were for him a matter of dying always more, immeasurably—of continuing inside death to make possible the movement of transformation which must not cease, night of measureless excess, *Nacht aus Übermass*, where one has in nonbeing eternally to return to being.

Thus the rose becomes for Rilke the symbol both of poetic action and of death, when death is no one's sleep. The rose is like the perceptible presence of Orphic space, the space which is nothing but outerness and which is nothing but intimacy, superabundance where things do not limit or infringe upon each other, but in their common unfurling make room instead of taking it up, and constantly "transform the outside world . . . into a handful of Within."

Almost a being without boundaries and as if spared
and more purely inner and very strangely tender
and illuminating itself right up to the edge,
is such a thing known to us?

The poem—and in it the poet—is this intimacy opened to the world, unreservedly exposed to being. It is the world, things and being ceaselessly transformed into innerness. It is the intimacy of this transformation, an apparently tranquil and gentle movement, but which is the greatest danger, for then the word touches the deepest intimacy, demands not only the abandonment of all exterior assurance but risks its very self and introduces us into that point where nothing can be said of being, nothing made, where endlessly everything starts over and where dying itself is a task without end.

Rose, oh reiner Widerspruch, Lust
Niemandes Schlaf zu sein unter soviel
Lidern.

Rose, O pure contradiction, delight
Of being no one's sleep under so many
lids.

Rilke and Mallarmé

If we wanted to isolate the characteristic feature of Rilke's experience, the one which his poetry conserves above and beyond the images and forms, we would have to look for it in a particular relation to the negative: in the tension which is a consent, the patience which obeys but which nevertheless goes beyond ("He obeys by going beyond"), in the slow and practically invisible action without efficacy but not without authority, which he opposes to the active force of the world and which, in song, is secret attentiveness to death.

Rilke, like Mallarmé, makes poetry a relation to absence. How different, however, are the experiences of these two poets, apparently so close; how different the demands that occupied them within the same experience. While for Mallarmé absence remains the *force* of the negative — that which removes "the reality of things" and delivers us from their weight — for Rilke absence is also the presence of things, the intimacy of the being-a-thing where the desire to fall toward the center in a silent, immobile, endless fall is gathered. Mallarmé's poetry pronounces being with the brilliance of that which has the power to annihilate, to suspend beings and suspend itself by withdrawing into the dazzling vivacity of an instant. This poetry retains the decisiveness that makes of absence something active, of death an act and of voluntary death — where nothingness is entirely within our mastery — the poetic event par excellence, brought to light by the *Igitur* experiment. But Rilke, who also turns toward death as toward the origin of poetic possibility, seeks a deeper relation with death. He sees in voluntary death still only the symbol of a violent power and a spirit of strength upon which poetic truth cannot be founded. He sees there an offense against death itself, a failing with respect to its discreet essence and to the patience of its invisible force.

Absence is linked, in Mallarmé, to the suddenness of the *instant*. For an instant, at the moment when everything falls back into nothingness, the purity of being gleams. For an instant, universal absence becomes pure presence; and when everything disappears, disappearance appears. This is pure clarity apparent, the unique point where light is darkness shining, and it is day by night. Absence in Rilke is linked to the *space* which is itself perhaps freed from time, but which nonetheless, through the slow transmutation that consecrates it, is also like another time, a way of approaching a time which would be the very time of dying or the essence of death, a time very different from the impatient and violent agitation which is ours, as different as poetry's ineffectual action is from effective action.

In these times, when in the restlessness of the interminable and the stagnation of endless error we have to dwell outside of ourselves, outside of the world, and, it would seem, even die outside of death, Rilke wants to acknowledge a supreme possibility, one more movement, the approach to grace, to the poetic opening: a relation with the Open that is happy at last, the liberation of the Orphic word in which space is affirmed, space which is a "Nowhere without no." Then to speak is a glorious transparency. To speak is no longer to tell or to name. To speak is to celebrate, and to celebrate is to praise, to make of the word a pure radiant consumption which still speaks when there is no more to say, does not name what is nameless but welcomes it, invokes and glorifies it. This is the only language where night and silence are manifest without being interrupted or revealed:

> O tell me, poet, what you do.   — I praise.
> But the mortal and monstrous,
> how do you endure it, welcome it?   — I praise.
> But the nameless, the anonymous,
> how, poet, do you invoke it?   — I praise.
> Where do you derive the right to be true
> in all disguises, beneath every mask?   — I praise.
> And how does silence know you, and furor,
> as well as the star and the tempest?   — Because I praise.

Inspiration

The Outside, the Night

Whoever devotes himself to the work is drawn by it toward the point where it undergoes impossibility. This experience is purely nocturnal, it is the very experience of night.

In the night, everything has disappeared. This is the first night. Here absence approaches—silence, repose, night. Here death blots out Alexander's picture; here the sleeper does not know he sleeps, and he who dies goes to meet real dying. Here language completes and fulfills itself in the silent profundity which vouches for it as its meaning.

But when everything has disappeared in the night, "everything has disappeared" appears. This is the *other* night. Night is this apparition: "everything has disappeared." It is what we sense when dreams replace sleep, when the dead pass into the deep of the night, when night's deep appears in those who have disappeared. Apparitions, phantoms, and dreams are an allusion to this empty night. It is the night of Young, where the dark does not seem dark enough, or death ever dead enough. What appears in the night is the night that appears. And this eeriness does not simply come from something invisible, which would reveal itself under cover of dark and at the shadows' summons. Here the invisible is what one cannot cease to see; it is the incessant making itself seen. The "phantom" is meant to hide, to appease the phantom night. Those who think they see ghosts are those who do not want to see the night. They crowd it with the terror of little images, they occupy and distract it by immobilizing it—stopping the oscillation of eternal starting over. It is empty, it is not; but we dress it up as a kind of being; we enclose it, if possible, in a name, a story and a resemblance; we say, like Rilke at Duino, "It is Raimondine and Polyxène."

The first night is welcoming. Novalis addresses hymns to it. Of it one can say, *In* the night, as if it had an intimacy. We enter into the night and we rest there, sleeping and dying.

But the *other* night does not welcome, does not open. In it one is still outside. It does not close either; it is not the great Castle, near but unapproachable, impenetrable because the door is guarded. Night is inaccessible because to have access to it is to accede to the outside, to remain outside the night and to lose forever the possibility of emerging from it.

This night is never pure night. It is essentially impure. It is not that beautiful diamond, the void, which Mallarmé contemplates, a poetic sky beyond the sky. It is not true night, it is night without truth, which does not lie, however—which is not false. It is not our bewilderment when our senses deceive us. It is no mystery, but it cannot be demystified.

In the night one can die; we reach oblivion. But this *other* night is the death no one dies, the forgetfulness which gets forgotten. In the heart of oblivion it is memory without rest.

To Lie Down upon Nikita

In the night, to die, like to sleep,[1] is one more of the world's present moments, another of day's resources. It is the admirable last stroke which completes, the culminating moment, perfection. Every man seeks to die in the world, wishes to die of the world and for its sake. In this perspective, dying means setting forth to meet the freedom which frees me from being, that decisive separation which permits me to escape from being by pitting action, labor, and struggle against it—and thus permits me to move beyond myself toward the world of others.[2] I am, only because I have made nothingness my power: only because I am able not to be. Dying, then, marks the defining limit of this power; it is the grasp of this nothingness and, with this understanding, the affirmation that others come toward me through death. It is also the affirmation that freedom leads to death, sustains me even in death, makes of death my freely chosen death. It is as if I confused myself, in the end, with the world's ultimate finish. To die is thus to embrace the whole of time and to make of time a whole. It is a temporal ecstasy. One never dies now, one always dies later, in the future—in a future which is never

[1]See, in the Appendixes, a few pages entitled "Sleep, night."
[2]At least this is the case if others form a whole, a possible totality. If the whole, though, is no whole at all, the movement that goes from me toward others never comes back toward me. It remains the circle's broken call. Moreover, the movement does not even go from me toward others; no one answers me, because I do not call, because from "me" nothing originates.

an actuality, which cannot come except when everything will be over and done. And when everything is over, there will be no more present: the future will again be past. This leap by which the past catches up with the future, overstepping the present, is the sense of human death, death permeated with humanity.

This point of view is not simply one of hope's illusions; it is implicit in our life, and it is, so to speak, the truth of our death, at least of this first death which we find *in* the night. We want to die of this negation which operates in productive operations, which is the silence of our words and gives meaning to our voice, which makes of the world the future, the culmination of the world. Man dies alone, perhaps, but the solitude of his death is very different from the solitude of a person who lives alone. It is strangely prophetic. It is (in a sense) the solitude of a being who belongs, not to the past at all, but entirely to the future, who ceases to be in order to become solely he who will be, outside present limits and possibilities. He dies alone because he does not die now, where we are, but altogether in the future and at the extreme reach of the future, disengaged not only from his present existence but also from his present death. He dies alone because he dies as everyone; and this too makes for great solitude. From this we also see why death rarely seems to be achieved. To those who remain and surround the dying person, death comes as a death to be died still more. And it rests with them: they must preserve and prolong it until the moment when, time being at an end, everyone will die joyfully together. In this sense everyone is in agony till the end of the world.

Brekhounov, the rich merchant who has always succeeded in life, cannot believe that a man such as he should have to die all of a sudden simply because one evening he gets lost in the Russian snow. "It cannot be." He mounts his horse, abandons the sledge and his servant Nikita, who is already three-fourths frozen. He is decisive and enterprising, as always: he goes ahead. But already this activity is active no longer. He walks at random, and his step goes nowhere. It is the meandering false step which, like a labyrinth, draws him into the space where every move ahead is also a move back. Or he turns in circles, he obeys the fatality of the circle. Having set out at random, so he returns "at random," as far as the sledge, where the scantily clad Nikita, who for his part goes to no such lengths just to die, is sinking into the frigid cold of death. "Brekhounov," Tolstoy recounts, "paused for a few moments in silence; then, suddenly, with the same resolution with which he used to strike hands when making a good purchase, he took a step back and, turning

up his sleeves, began raking the snow off Nikita and out of the sledge."
Apparently nothing has changed: he is still the active merchant,
decisive and enterprising, who always finds something to do and always
succeeds in everything. "That's our way," says this man, pleased with
himself. Yes, he is always the best, and he belongs to the class of the
best men; he is alive and healthy. But at that instant something happens. While his hand moves upon the cold body, something breaks.
What he is doing breaks the limits, is no longer what takes place here
and now.

> To his great surprise he could say no more, for tears came to his
> eyes and his lower jaw began to quiver rapidly. He stopped speak-
> ing and only gulped down the risings in his throat. "Seems I was
> badly frightened and have gone quite weak," he thought. But this
> weakness was not only unpleasant, but gave him a peculiar joy
> such as he had never felt before.[3]

Later he was found dead, lying upon Nikita and embracing him tightly.

In this perspective to die is always to seek to lie down upon Nikita,
to stretch oneself out upon the whole world of Nikitas, to embrace all
other men and all of time. What is still represented to us here as a vir-
tuous conversion, an opening of the soul and a great fraternal emotion,
is not any of these things, however, not even for Tolstoy. To die is not to
become a good master, or even one's own servant; it is not a moral advance. The death of Brekhounov tells us nothing "good," and his
gesture — the movement which makes him lie down all at once upon a
frozen body — says nothing either. It is simple and natural; it is not
human, but inevitable. This is what had to happen. He could no more
escape it than he could avoid dying. To lie down upon Nikita: this is the
incomprehensible and necessary movement that death wrings from us.

It is a nocturnal gesture. It does not belong to the category of
habitual acts, it is not even an inhabitual action. Nothing is accomplished by it. The intention that first made him act — to warm
Nikita, to warm himself close to the sun of the Good — has evaporated.
The gesture is without purpose, without significance; it has no reality.
"He lies down to die." Brekhounov, the decisive, enterprising man,
even he can lie down only to die. It is death itself which all at once bends
this robust body and lays it down in the white night. And this night

---

[3][The English translation of Tolstoy quoted here is by Aylmer Maude, "Master and
Man," in *The Death of Ivan Ilytch and Other Stories* (New York: New American
Library, 1960) — Trans.]

does not frighten him; he does not refuse it or draw back from it. On the contrary, he hurries joyfully to meet it. But, as he lies down in the night, it is, all the same, upon Nikita that he lies, as if this night were still the hope and future of a human form, as if we could not die except by entrusting our death to someone else, to all the others, that it might await in them the icy depths of the future.

Night as Trap

The first night is another of day's constructions. Day makes the night; it builds up its strong points in the night. Night speaks only of day; it is the presentiment of day, day's reserve and its profundity. Everything ends in the night; that is why there is day. Day is linked to night because it would not be day if it did not begin and come to an end. That is the rule it goes by: it is beginning and end. Day arises, day is done. That is what makes it indefatigable, industrious, and creative; that is what makes day the incessant labor of the day. The more it expands, with the proud aim of becoming universal, the more the nocturnal element threatens to withdraw into the light itself: the more nocturnal is that which enlightens us, the more it is the uncertainty and immensity of the night.

This is an essential risk. It is one of day's possible moves. There are several. It may, for example, greet night as the edge of what is not to be ventured upon. Night, then, is accepted and acknowledged, but only as a limit and as the necessity of a limit: we must not go beyond. So says Greek moderation. Or, night is what day must finally dissolve: day works at its empire; it is its own conquest and elaboration; it tends toward the unlimited, although in the accomplishment of its tasks it only advances step by step and observes limit and barriers strictly. So says reason, the triumph of enlightenment which simply banishes darkness. Or again, night is what day wants not just to dissolve, but to appropriate: night is thus the essential, which must not be destroyed but conserved, and welcomed not as a limit but for itself. Night must pass into day. Night becoming day makes the light richer and gives to clarity's superficial sparkle a deep inner radiance. Then day is the whole of the day and the night, the great promise of the dialectic.

When we oppose night and day and the movements accomplished in each, it is still to the night of day that we allude, to the night that is day's night, the night of which we say that it is the true night, for it has day's truth just as it has day's laws, those which, precisely, assign it the duty of opposing itself to the day. Thus, for the Greeks, to submit to dark destiny is to assure balance: moderation is respect for the immoderate and thus exacts respect from it. That is why it is so necessary for the Greeks that the daughters of Night not be dishonored but that nonetheless they have their domain and keep there, that they not be errant or elusive, but checked and held to the oath of this restriction.

But the *other* night is always other. Only in the day does it seem comprehensible, ascertainable. In the day it is the secret which could be disclosed; it is something concealed that awaits its unveiling. Only the day can feel passion for the night. It is only in the day that death can be desired, planned, decided upon—reached. It is only in the day that the *other* night is revealed as love that breaks all ties, that wants the end and union with the abyss. But in the night it is what one never joins; it is repetition that will not leave off, satiety that has nothing, the sparkle of something baseless and without depth.

The trap, the *other* night, is the first night which we can penetrate, which we enter—granted, with anguish, and yet here anguish secludes us and insecurity becomes a shelter. In the first night it seems that we will go—by going further ahead—toward something essential. And this is correct, to the extent that the first night still belongs to the world and, through the world, to day's truth. To advance in this first night is not an easy movement though. It is evoked by the labors of Kafka's beast in *The Burrow*. There you assure yourself of solid defenses against the world above, but leave yourself open to the insecurity of the underneath. You build after day's fashion, but below ground, and what rises sinks, what is erected is swallowed up. The more the burrow seems solidly closed to the outside, the greater the danger that you be closed in with the outside, delivered to the peril without any means of escape. And when every foreign threat seems shut out of this perfectly closed intimacy, then it is intimacy that becomes menacing foreignness. Then the essence of danger is at hand.

There is always a moment when, in the night, the beast hears the other beast. This is the *other* night. And this is in no way terrifying; it says nothing extraordinary, it has nothing in common with ghosts and trances. It is only muffled whispering, a noise one can hardly distinguish from silence, the seeping sands of silence. Not even that. Only the sound of some activity, some foraging or burrowing—at first intermittent, but once perceived it won't go away. Kafka's story has no end. The last sentence opens onto this unending movement: "Everything continued without any change." One of the publishers adds that only a few pages are missing, those which describe the decisive combat in which the hero of the narrative was to succumb. This is a rather poor reading. There could be no decisive combat. Such a combat admits of no decision, of no fight either, but only of a wait, an approach, suspicions, the vicissitudes of an always more threatening threat. But this threat is infinite, it is indecisive; it is contained entirely in its very indecision. What the beast senses in the distance — that monstrous thing which eternally approaches it and works eternally at coming closer — is itself. And if the beast could ever come into this thing's presence, what it would encounter would be its own absence: itself, but itself become the other, which it would not recognize, which it would not meet. The *other* night is always the other, and he who senses it becomes the other. He who approaches it departs from himself, is no longer he who approaches but he who turns away, goes hither and yon. He who, having entered the first night, seeks intrepidly to go toward its profoundest intimacy, toward the essential, hears at a certain moment the *other* night — hears himself, hears the eternally reverberating echo of his own step, a step toward silence, toward the void. But the echo sends this step back to him as the whispering immensity, and the void is now a presence coming toward him.

Whoever senses the approach of the *other* night has the impression that he is approaching the heart of the night, the essential night which he seeks. And no doubt it is "at that moment" that he gives himself up to the inessential and loses all possibility. Thus it is that moment which he must avoid, just as the traveler is advised to avoid the point where the desert becomes seductive mirage. But such prudence is useless here. There is no exact moment at which one would pass from night to the *other* night, no limit at which to stop and come back in the other direction. Midnight never falls at midnight. Midnight falls when the dice are cast, but they cannot be cast till Midnight.

Therefore one must turn away from the first night. That at least is possible. One must live in the day and labor for its sake. Yes, one has to do that. But to labor for the day is to find, in the end, the night; it is thus to make night the job of the day, to make night a task and an abode. It is to construct the burrow. And to construct the burrow is to open night to the *other* night.

The risk of surrendering to the inessential is itself essential. To flee it is to be pursued by it. It becomes the shadow which always follows you and always precedes you. To seek it methodically is also to misconstrue it. Not to know of it makes life easier and tasks more feasible, but in ignorance it still lies concealed; forgetfulness is the depth of its remembrance. And whoever senses it can no longer escape. Whoever has approached it, even if he has recognized in it the risk of the inessential, regards this approach as essential, sacrifices to it all of truth, all the important concerns to which he nevertheless still feels attached.

Why is this? Is it the power of error? Is it night's fascination? But it has no power, it does not call, it attracts only by negligence. Whoever believes he is attracted finds himself profoundly neglected. Whoever claims to be in the thrall of an irresistible vocation, is only dominated by his own weakness. He calls irresistible the fact that there is nothing to resist; he calls vocation that which does not call him, and he has to shoulder his nothingness for a yoke. Why is this? Why do some embark upon works in order to escape this risk — to elude rather than respond to "inspiration," constructing their work as a burrow where they want to think they are sheltered from the void and which they only build, precisely, by hollowing and deepening the void, creating a void all around them? Why do others, so many others, knowing that they betray the world and the truth of purposeful activities, have only one concern: to deceive themselves by imagining that they still serve the world in which they only seek refuge and assurance? In this way they no longer betray only the movement of true endeavors; with their bad conscience — which they assuage with honors, services, with the feeling of accomplishing all the while a mission, of being guardians of culture, the oracles of a people — they are traitors to the error of their idleness. And perhaps others neglect even to construct the burrow, for fear that by protecting them this shelter would protect in them that which they must surrender, would bolster their presence too much and thus avert the approach of that point of uncertainty toward which they slip, "the decisive combat" with indecision. No one hears tell of these. They leave no account of their journey, they have no name, they are anonymous in the anonymous crowd because they do not distinguish themselves, because they have entered into the realm of the indistinct.

Why? Why this move? Why this hopeless movement toward what is without importance?

Orpheus's Gaze

When Orpheus descends toward Eurydice, art is the power by which night opens. Because of art's strength, night welcomes him; it becomes welcoming intimacy, the harmony and accord of the first night. But it is toward Eurydice that Orpheus has descended. For him Eurydice is the furthest that art can reach. Under a name that hides her and a veil that covers her, she is the profoundly obscure point toward which art and desire, death and night, seem to tend. She is the instant when the essence of night approaches as the *other* night.

However, Orpheus's work does not consist in ensuring this point's approach by descending into the depths. His *work* is to bring it back to the light of day and to give it form, shape, and reality in the day. Orpheus is capable of everything, except of looking this point in the face, except of looking at the center of night in the night. He can descend toward it; he can — and this is still stronger an ability — draw it to him and lead it with him upward, but only by turning away from it. This turning away is the only way it can be approached. This is what concealment means when it reveals itself in the night. But Orpheus, in the movement of his migration, forgets the work he is to achieve, and he forgets it necessarily, for the ultimate demand which his movement makes is not that there be a work, but that someone face this point, grasp its essence, grasp it where it appears, where it is essential and essentially appearance: at the heart of night.

The Greek myth says: a work can be produced only if the measureless experience of the deep — which the Greeks recognized as necessary to the work and where the work endures its measurelessness — is not pursued for its own sake. The deep does not reveal itself directly; it is only disclosed hidden in the work. This is an essential, an inexorable answer. But the myth shows nonetheless that Orpheus's destiny is not to submit to this ultimate law. And, of course, by turning toward Eurydice, Orpheus ruins the work, which is immediately undone, and Eurydice returns among the shades. When he looks back, the essence of night is revealed as the inessential. Thus he betrays the work, and Eurydice, and the night. But not to turn toward Eurydice would be no less untrue. Not to look would be infidelity to the measureless, imprudent force of his movement, which does not want Eurydice in her daytime truth and her everyday appeal, but wants her in her nocturnal obscurity, in her distance, with her closed body and sealed face — wants to see her not when she is visible, but when she is invisible, and not as the intimacy of a familiar life, but as the foreignness of what excludes all intimacy, and wants, not to make her live, but to have living in her the plenitude of her death.

That alone is what Orpheus came to seek in the Underworld. All the glory of his work, all the power of his art, and even the desire for a happy life in the lovely, clear light of day are sacrificed to this sole aim: to look in the night at what night hides, the *other* night, the dissimulation that appears.

This is an infinitely problematic movement, which day condemns as a form of unjustifiable madness, or as exonerating immoderation. From day's perspective, the descent into the Underworld, the movement down into vain depths, is in itself excessive. It is inevitable that Orpheus transgress the law which forbids him to "turn back," for he already violated it with his first steps toward the shades. This remark implies that Orpheus has in fact never ceased to be turned toward Eurydice: he saw her invisible, he touched her intact, in her shadowy absence, in that veiled presence which did not hide her absence, which was the presence of her infinite absence. Had he not looked at her, he would not have drawn her toward him; and doubtless she is not there, but in this glance back he himself is absent. He is no less dead than she — dead, not of that tranquil worldly death which is rest, silence, and end, but of that other death which is death without end, the ordeal of the end's absence.

Day, judging Orpheus's undertaking, also reproaches him with having proved impatient. Orpheus's error seems then to lie in the desire which moves him to see and to possess Eurydice, he whose destiny is only to sing of her. He is Orpheus only in the song: he cannot have any relation to Eurydice except within the hymn. He has life and truth only after the poem and because of it, and Eurydice represents nothing other than this magic dependence which outside the song makes him a shade and renders him free, alive, and sovereign only in the Orphic space, according to Orphic measure. Yes, this is true: only in the song does Orpheus have power over Eurydice. But in the song too, Eurydice is already lost, and Orpheus himself is the dispersed Orpheus; the song immediately makes him "infinitely dead." He loses Eurydice because he desires her beyond the measured limits of the song, and he loses himself, but this desire, and Eurydice lost, and Orpheus dispersed are necessary to the song, just as the ordeal of eternal inertia is necessary to the work.

Orpheus is guilty of impatience. His error is to want to exhaust the infinite, to put a term to the interminable, not endlessly to sustain the very movement of his error. Impatience is the failing of one who wants to withdraw from the absence of time; patience is the ruse which seeks to master this absence by making of it another time, measured otherwise. But true patience does not exclude impatience. It is intimacy with impatience — impatience suffered and endured endlessly. Orpheus's impatience is thus at the same time a proper movement: in it begins what will become his own passion, his highest patience, his infinite sojourn in death.

Inspiration

If the world judges Orpheus, the work does not. It sheds no light on his faults. The work says nothing. And everything proceeds as if, by disobeying the law, by looking at Eurydice, Orpheus had only obeyed the deep demand of the work — as if, by this inspired movement, he had indeed captured from Hell the obscure shade and had, unknowingly, led it back into the broad daylight of the work.

To look at Eurydice, without regard for the song, in the impatience and imprudence of desire which forgets the law: *that* is *inspiration*. Would inspiration, then, transform night's beauty into the unreality of the void? Would it make Eurydice a shade and render Orpheus "infinitely dead"? Is inspiration, then, that critical moment when the essence of night becomes the inessential, and the first night's welcoming intimacy becomes the deceptive trap, the *other* night? We cannot say otherwise. From inspiration we sense only failure, we recognize only confused violence. But if inspiration pronounces Orpheus's failure and declares Eurydice lost twice over — if it expresses the insignificance and the void of the night — it turns Orpheus and it propels him toward that failure and that insignificance irresistibly, as if to renounce failure were much graver than to renounce success, as if what we call the insignificant, the inessential, error, could, to one who accepts the risk and surrenders to it without restraint, reveal itself as the source of all authenticity.

The inspired and forbidden gaze destines Orpheus to lose everything: not only himself, not only day's reality; but night's essence. This is certain, unexceptionable. Inspiration pronounces Orpheus's ruin and the certainty of his ruin, and it does not promise, as compensation, the work's success any more than it affirms in the work the ideal triumph of Orpheus or the survival of Eurydice. The work, through inspiration, is no less compromised than Orpheus is threatened. It reaches, in that instant, its point of extreme uncertainty. That is why it resists so often and so strongly that which inspires it. That is also why it protects itself by saying to Orpheus: You will keep me only if you keep from looking at *her*. But that forbidden movement is precisely what Orpheus must accomplish in order to carry the work beyond what assures it. It is what he cannot accomplish except by forgetting the work, seduced by a desire that comes to him from the night, and that is linked to night as to its origin. In this gaze, the work is lost. This look is the only moment in which the work is lost absolutely. Something more important than the work, more bereft of importance than the work, announces and affirms itself. The work is everything to Orpheus except that desired look where it is lost. Thus it is only in that look that the work can surpass itself, be united with its origin and consecrated in impossibility.

Orpheus's gaze is Orpheus's ultimate gift to the work. It is a gift whereby he refuses, whereby he sacrifices the work, bearing himself toward the origin according to desire's measureless movement — and whereby unknowingly he still moves toward the work, toward the origin of the work.

Then for Orpheus everything collapses into the certainty of failure where there remains only, as compensation, the work's uncertainty, for is there ever a work? Before the most convincing masterpiece, where the brilliance and resolution of the beginning shine, it can also happen that we confront something extinguished: a work suddenly become invisible again, which is no longer there, has never been there. This sudden eclipse is the distant memory of Orpheus's gaze; it is the nostalgic return to the uncertainty of the origin.

The Gift and the Sacrifice

Were we to insist upon what such a moment seems to say of inspiration, we would have to state: it links inspiration to *desire*. It introduces into concern for the work the movement of *unconcern* in which the work is sacrificed: the work's ultimate law is broken; the work is betrayed in favor of Eurydice, in favor of the shade. Insouciance is the movement of sacrifice — a sacrifice which can only be light and insouciant. Perhaps it is sin. Indeed, it is immediately expiated as sin, but its substance is all levity, unconcern, innocence. This is a sacrifice without ceremony, where the sacred itself, night in its unapproachable profundity, is given back — through the insouciant look which is not even a sacrilege, which by no means has the weight or the gravity of a profanation — to the inessential, which is not the profane but less than any such category.

Granted, the essential night which, before his insouciant look, follows Orpheus — the sacred night which he captures in the song's fascination and which, then, is maintained within the song's limits and its measured space — this night is certainly richer, more august than the empty futility which it becomes after he looks. The sacred night encloses Eurydice; it encloses within the song what surpasses the song. But it is itself also enclosed. It is bound, it follows, it is the sacred mastered by the force of rites, which is to say order, rectitude, law, the way of the Tao, and the axis of the Dharma. The look of Orpheus unbinds it, breaks the limits, breaks the law that contained and that restrained essence. His gaze is thus the extreme moment of liberty, the moment when he frees himself from himself and, still more important, frees the work from his concern, frees the sacred contained in the work, *gives* the sacred to itself, to the freedom of its essence, to its essence which is freedom. (This is why inspiration is the gift par excellence.) Everything is risked, then, in the decision to look. It is in this decision that the origin is approached by the force of the gaze that unbinds night's essence, lifts concern, interrupts the incessant by discovering it. This is a moment of desire, of insouciance and of authority.

Orpheus's look links inspiration to *desire*. *Impatience* links desire to *insouciance*. Whoever is not impatient will never come to insouciance, to the instant when concern is united with its own transparency.

But whoever is merely impatient will never be capable of the insouciant, weightless gaze of Orpheus. That is why impatience must be the core of profound patience, the pure flash which an infinite waiting, which the silence and reserve of this attention cause to spring from its center not only as the spark which extreme tension ignites, but as the brilliant point which has escaped this mindful wait—the glad accident, insouciance.

The Leap

Writing begins with Orpheus's gaze. And this gaze is the movement of desire that shatters the song's destiny, that disrupts concern for it, and in this inspired and careless decision reaches the origin, consecrates the song. But in order to descend toward this instant, Orpheus has to possess the power of art already. This is to say: one writes only if one reaches that instant which nevertheless one can only approach in the space opened by the movement of writing. To write, one has to write already. In this contradiction are situated the essence of writing, the snag in the experience, and inspiration's leap.

Inspiration,
Lack
of Inspiration

The leap is inspiration's form or movement. This form or this movement makes inspiration unjustifiable. But in this form or movement inspiration also comes into its own: its principal characteristic is affirmed in this inspiration which is at the same time and from the same point of view lack of inspiration — creative force and aridity intimately confounded. Hölderlin undergoes the rigors of this condition when he endures poetic time as the time of distress, when the gods are lacking but where God's default helps us: Gottes Fehl hilft. Mallarmé, whom sterility tormented and who shut himself into it with heroic resolve, also recognized that this deprivation did not express a simple personal failing, did not signify that he was deprived of the work, but announced his encounter with the work, the threatening intimacy of this encounter.

Automatic Writing

In our time — and in a form which misunderstandings and facile interpretations have impoverished but also preserved — this essential aspect of inspiration was rediscovered by surrealism. André Breton sustained it by persevering in his affirmation of automatic writing's value. What did this discovery contribute? Apparently the opposite of what it signified: an easy method, an instrument always at hand and always effective, poetry brought well within everyone's reach, the glad presence, after all, of the immediate. Anybody at all was immediately a perfect poet. Better still, the poem, unwavering and absolute, passed from being to being and wrote itself all by itself in each.

So it seemed: an attractive myth in any event, which was well worth investigating. But in reality, where the most facile means were being proposed, there hid behind this facility an extreme demand; and behind this certitude—this gift offered to everyone and disclosed in each without regard to talent or degree of culture—was concealed the insecurity of the inaccessible, the infinite experience of that which cannot even be sought, a probing of what never is in evidence, the exacting demands of a search which is no search at all and of a presence which is never granted. Nothing is closer to us, it seems, than the poetry of automatic writing, since it turns us toward the immediate. But the immediate is not close; it is not close to what is close to us. It staggers us; it is, just as Hölderlin said, the terrible upheaval.

In the *Entretiens*, Breton stresses the difficulty of such a spontaneity.

On this occasion I won't abstain, in passing, from dealing with the accusation of *laziness* which is periodically brought against those who devote or have devoted themselves with more or less perseverance to writing or to any other form of automatic activity. In order to be truly automatic, this writing must in effect have succeeded in placing itself in a condition of detachment with respect to the solicitations of the exterior world as well as with respect to individual preoccupations of a utilitarian, or sentimental, or other similar order. It still seems to me today incomparably more simple, less troubling, to satisfy the demands of reflective thought than to make this thought utterly available, so that one no longer has an ear for anything except *what the shadow mouth says*.[4]

It is natural that what was initially apparent in this conjunction of poetry and unreflective writing was the decision to escape constraints. Reason supervises us, the critical intellect restrains us, we speak according to customs and conventions. Automatic writing reveals to us a way of writing apart from these powers, in the daylight but as if outside the day in a nocturnal fashion, free from the everyday and from its inhibiting scrutiny. Hence the fact that in the history of surrealism the freedoms of writing are linked to "sleep experiences," and are like calmer, less hazardous versions of these. Each of Breton's friends sought night naïvely in a premeditated sleep; each slipped out of his customary self and believed himself freer, master of a greater space. This produced disorders which had to be stopped for "considerations of elementary mental hygiene." It might be said that prudence is out of place here. But imprudence did not lead very far. It led Desnos, for example, not to lose himself, not to wander astray, far from himself, but, Breton said, "to want to concentrate attention upon himself."

4*Entretiens*, 1913–1952.

Automatic writing tended to suppress constraints, suspend intermediaries, reject all mediation. It put the hand that writes in contact with something original; it made of this active hand a sovereign passivity, no longer a means of livelihood, an instrument, a servile tool, but an independent power, over which no one had authority any more, which belonged to no one and which could not, which knew not how to do anything—but write: a dead hand analogous to that hand of glory which magic speaks of (magic whose error lay, precisely, in wanting to make use of it).

This hand seems to put the depths of language at our command. But in reality, we cannot use this language at all, any more than we can use this hand, which is as foreign to us as if it had forsaken us or as if it were drawing us into the very milieu of forsakenness, where there are no more resources, where there is no more support, no more grasp or limit.

This is what automatic writing initially reminds us: the language whose approach it ensures is not a power—is not power to speak. In it I can do nothing and "I" never speak.

And yet, is it not a stroke of good fortune as well? Does it not also guarantee us the freedom to say all? Does it not establish the artist as if at the center of everything and exempt him from the judgments of the other powers—aesthetic, moral, or legal? The artist seems to bear no responsibility for a limitless passion which opens him to all and reveals all to him. Everywhere is his country, and everything his affair; and he has the right to see into everything. This is attractive and overwhelming.

The right not to choose is a privilege, but an exhausting one. The right not to choose is also the refusal to choose, the duty not to consent to any choice, the necessity to elude the choices which the natural order of the world—which is the order we live in—proposes to us (or which any order expressed by a law, transcendent or immanent, proposes to us). It is not, moreover, a matter of refusing to choose in a sort of moral decision, through an inverse ascetic discipline, but rather of reaching the moment where it is no longer possible to choose. It is a matter of reaching the point where to speak is to say all and where the poet becomes the one who cannot withdraw from anything, who turns away from nothing, but is yielded up, without any protection whatever, to the foreignness and the measureless excess of being.

Automatic writing, then, in which people have generally been content to discern the invention of a very particular diversion, does nothing other than give form to the initial poetic demand: the one by which we have seen Rilke infinitely tormented, the one which Hugo von Hofmannsthal, seeking to return to poetry the keys of its kingdom, is also led to express when, in his 1907 essay, *The Poet and These Times,* he says of the inspired person:

> He is there, silently changing places, nothing but eye, but ear, and receiving his color only from the things upon which he alights. He is a spectator; no, he is the hidden companion, the silent brother of all things, and the change of his colors is an intimate torment for him, for he suffers from all things, and he delights in them at the same time that he suffers. This power of painful joy is the whole content of his life. He suffers from feeling things so much, he suffers from each and from all together, he suffers from their singularity and from the coherence that unites them, he suffers from what is elevated in them, valueless, sublime, vulgar; he suffers from their moods and their thoughts . . . . He cannot neglect anything. Upon no being, no thing, no phantom — upon no phantasm born of human brain has he permission to close his eyes. It is as if his eyes had no lids. He hasn't the right to banish any of the thoughts that press upon him by claiming that he belongs to another order, for, in the order which is his, each thing must find its place. In him everything must and everything wants to meet . . . . Such is the unique law to which he submits: not to forbid a single thing access to his soul.[5]

And Hofmannsthal alludes to the other aspect of inspiration which we are attempting to show — its not lacking when it lacks, but its expressing, in this lack as well, the profundity, the profusion and the mystery of its presence:

> It is not that the poet thinks ceaselessly of all the things in the world; they think of him. They are in him, they dominate him.

[5]In a letter, Keats expresses himself in almost the same way: "As to the poetical Character itself (I mean that sort of which, if I am anything, I am a Member . . .): it is not itself — it has no self — it is everything and nothing — It has no character — it enjoys light and shade; it lives in gusto, be it foul or fair, high or low, rich or poor, mean or elevated. . . . A Poet is the most unpoetical of any thing in existence; because he has no Identity — he is continuingly in for — and filling some other body — The Sun, the Moon, the Sea, and Men and Women, who are creatures of impulse, are poetical, and have about them an unchangeable attribute — the poet has none; no identity — he is certainly the most unpoetical of all God's Creatures. If, then, he has no self, and if I am a Poet, where is the Wonder that I should say I would write no more?" [From *The Letters of John Keats,* ed. Hyder Edward Rolling (Cambridge, Mass.: Harvard Univ. Press, 1958), 1: 386–387 — Trans.]

Even his arid hours, his depressions, his dismay are impersonal moods; they correspond to the jags on a seismograph, and a profound enough gaze could read in them secrets still more mysterious than in the poems themselves.

The Murmur's Inexhaustibility

When the poet is told, as André Breton put it sumptuously in *The First Manifesto:* "Keep on as much as you like. Trust in the murmur's inexhaustibility," it seems that only the infinite wealth of poetic inspiration is thereby conveyed to us. Inspiration's primary characteristic is to be inexhaustible, for it is the approach of the uninterrupted. Whoever is inspired—whoever thinks he is—has the feeling that he is going to speak forever, write forever. Rilke remarks that when he was writing *The Book of Hours,* he felt as though he could no longer stop writing. And Van Gogh says he cannot stop working. Yes, it is endless, it speaks, it does not cease speaking, a language with no silence, for in it silence is spoken. Automatic writing is the affirmation of this language without silence, of this infinite murmur opened near us, underneath our common utterances, which seems an eternal spring. To the writer it says: I give you the key to all words. A marvelous promise, which each writer hastens to interpret as if what was said were: All words will be yours. But it is still more than that which is promised him: not only the whole of language, but language as origin, the pure springing of the origin, where speaking precedes not one or another utterance but its possibility—where speaking always precedes itself.

The ambiguity of this movement lies in the fact that at first the point toward which inspiration or automatic writing turns us—this language all gathered up together to which we have access, which opens an access for itself through us by annihilating us, by changing us into no one—at first this language does not seem to be one with which nothing can be done. It seems, on the contrary, that if you maintain contact with it, everything will be able to be said and that everything said will partake of the purity of the origin. It seems possible to be both he who manipulates everyday words—with more or less talent, more or fewer resources—and he who touches that moment of language when it is not manipulable, when what approaches is the neutral, indistinct word which is speaking's being, the idled word with which nothing can be done. And because the writer thinks he remains both one and the other—both the man who manipulates words and the place where the unmanipulable which language is escapes every division and is pure indeterminacy—the illusion comes over him that he can manipulate the unmanipulable and in this original speech say everything and give voice and expression to everything.

But is it an illusion? If it is, it holds sway, not like a mirage which would afford the poet an effortless vision, but like a temptation which entices him off the sure roads and leads him toward the most difficult and the most remote. Then inspiration appears little by little in its true light: it is powerful, but on the condition that he who welcomes it become very weak. It has no need of the world's resources, or of personal talent, but one has therefore to have renounced these resources, to have no longer any means of support in the world and to be free of oneself. It is, they say, magic; it works instantly, without time's long approaches, without intermediary. That is to say: one has to waste time, surrender the right to act and the power to produce.

The purer the inspiration, the more dispossessed is he who enters the space where it draws him, where he hears the origin's closer call. It is as if the wealth he comes into, that superabundance of the source, were also extreme poverty, were indeed refusal's superabundance, and made of him the one who does not produce, who wanders astray within an infinite idleness. Common sense is wrong, then, to think that the arid state to which the most inspired of artists are a prey means that inspiration—this grace which is given and taken away—suddenly fails them. One ought rather say that there is a point where inspiration and the lack of inspiration are confounded, an extreme point where inspiration, this movement outside of tasks, of acquired forms and proven expressions, takes the name aridity and becomes the absence of power, the impossibility which the artist questions in vain, which is a nocturnal state, at once marvelous and desperate. There he lingers, in search of an errant word—he who has not been able to resist the excessively pure force of inspiration.

Lord Chandos

In *Lord Chandos's Letter*, Hugo von Hofmannsthal described this standstill, this state of suspense when inspiration has the same countenance as sterility, when it is the enchantment that immobilizes words and banishes thoughts. Lord Chandos tries to convey to Francis

Bacon why he has renounced all literary preoccupations. "I have," he explains, "completely lost the ability to treat coherently, by thought or word, any subject whatever." Before the most general and the most lofty words, he feels an uneasiness: not a simple doubt about their value or a hesitation as to their legitimacy, but the impression of a reality coming apart, of a thing rotting and crumbling into dust. It is not that he lacks words, but that they are transformed before his eyes. They cease to be signs and become gazes, an empty light, attractive and fascinating. They are no longer words but the being of words, that fundamental passivity with which automatic writing seeks to put us in contact. "Isolated words swam around me; they congealed and became eyes fixed on me. And I in my turn was forced to stare at them. They were whirlpools, dizzying when the gaze plunged into them, which turned ceaselessly, and beyond them was the void." At the same time, Lord Chandos describes another aspect of this transformation: words lose all coherence, objects become useless, but, in the shelter of this lack, a new contact forms with things' intimacy, a presentiment of unknown relations, of another language, capable of expressing the infinite acceptance which the poet is when he becomes the refusal to choose — capable also of enclosing the silence that lies in the deepest recesses of things. Hofmannsthal gives this experience the slightly flaccid character of his harmonious melancholy, but he finds at least one striking expression to communicate the demand from which no artist can escape. This demand assigns to the artist — to the most irresponsible of men — the responsibility for what he cannot accomplish, and makes him guilty for what he cannot say, for what cannot be said. Hofmannsthal writes:

> At that moment I felt, with a certainty which did not cease to hurt, that neither next year, nor the next after that nor in any year of my life will I write any book, either in Latin or in English, for a strange and painful reason . . . . I mean that the language in which it might have been given me not only to write but to think is neither Latin nor English, nor Italian nor Spanish, but a language of which I know not a word. It is the language which mute things speak to me and in which I will perhaps one day, from the depths of the tomb, have to justify myself before an unknown judge.

Max Brod reports that Kafka read *Lord Chandos's Letter* as a kindred text. And certainly Kafka, when he wrote, felt judged from deep down in his words by that unknown tongue of which he was not the master, but for which he was responsible, and which, with torments and preposterous accusations, removed him more and more from the authority to write—separated him from that gay and somewhat mannered talent which was his at first—and condemned him to a language whose understanding was refused him but whose justification was required of him. We are drawn, by too strong a movement, into a space where truth lacks, where limits have disappeared, where we are delivered to the immeasurable. And yet it is there that we are required to maintain an even step, not to lose a sense of proportion and to seek a true language by going all the way down into the deep of error.

One has to defend against this movement if one wants nevertheless to produce. It is as if one couldn't escape sterility except by escaping the omnipotence of inspiration, as if one couldn't write except—since one must write—by resisting the pure need to write, by avoiding the approach of what is to be written, that word without beginning or end which we cannot express except by silencing it. This is the magic torment which is linked to the call of inspiration. One necessarily betrays it: and not because books are only the degraded echo of a sublime word, but because one only writes them by silencing what inspires them, by failing the movement they claim to recall, by interrupting "the murmur."

Whoever wants to write and to produce has ceaselessly to put this exaltation to sleep within himself. Mastery presupposes this sleep by which the creator pacifies and deceives the power that leads him on. He is creative and capable, according to the capability which leaves its trace upon the world, only because he has placed between his activity and the center from which shines the original word, the interval, the thickness of sleep. His lucidity is made of this sleep. One would be deceived, then, about surrealist experiments, and these would deceive us about the place where inspiration is situated, if they invited us to see in inspiration an event like sleep. In fact one sleeps, in a way, to evade it. Kafka repeatedly says to Gustav Janouch, "If it weren't for these terrible nights of insomnia, in general I wouldn't write." He must be understood profoundly: inspiration, that errant word which cannot come to an end, is *the long night of insomnia*. And it is in order to defend himself against it, by turning away from it, that the writer actually comes to write. Writing is an activity that returns him to the world where he can sleep. That is also why surrealism does not put its trust in sleep when it entrusts itself to the dream. If there is a relation between "inspiration" and dream, this is because the dream is an allusion to a refusal to sleep within sleep—an allusion to the impossibility of sleeping which sleep becomes in the dream. The adepts of the first surrealist hypnoses believed they were abandoning themselves to sleep. Hypnosis, however, consists not in putting to sleep, but in preventing sleep. It maintains within concentrated night a passive, obedient light, the point of light which is unable to go out: paralyzed lucidity. The power that fascinates has come into contact with this point, which it touches in the separated place where everything becomes image. Inspiration pushes us gently or impetuously out of the world, and in this outside there is no sleep, any more than there is rest. Perhaps it must be called night, but night—the essence of night—does not, precisely, let us sleep. In it there is no refuge to be found in sleep. Sleep is a way out through which we seek to escape, not the day, but the night, from which there is no way out.

The Work: A Road toward Inspiration

The failures of automatic writing do not discourage André Breton. In his eyes they do not in the least diminish the demand it represents. And if he continues to hope for an absolute success from it, and even to ask of it something like a means toward its own purification, this hope is analogous to the one which protects the artist when, wanting to produce a work, but not wanting to betray what inspires it, he seeks to reconcile the irreconcilable and to find the work where he must expose himself to the essential lack of work, the essential inertia. This is a harrowing experience, which can be pursued only under the veil of failure. And yet, while the experience is the infinitely hazardous movement which cannot succeed, we call what issues from it success. This torment we call happiness, and this arid poverty becomes the bountifulness of inspiration. This laborious, this indefatigable despair is the sheer good fortune or the grace of a gift that requires no effort. One artist tells us what all of them encounter within the experience: "My paintings are valueless." "As a painter I will never amount to anything important, I feel this absolutely." That is the truth of the experience. The artist must persevere in the realm of this "valuelessness"; he has to maintain the will to achieve and the claim on perfection while suffering the distress of an irredeemable failure. And yet for us this failure is called Van Gogh. And this distress becomes a flaming torch, the very essence of color.

The essential thing to be said about this experience is perhaps as follows: for a long time works went through it, but unknowingly. Or they gave it a name that hid it. That was when art wanted to make the gods present or to represent men. Today it is different. The work is no longer innocent; it knows whence it comes. Or at least it knows how to seek, and in this seeking how to approach always nearer to the origin, and in this approach how to keep without fail to the path where possibility is gambled, where the risk is essential and failure threatens. This is what the work seems to ask, this is where it pushes the artist: away from itself and from its realization. This experience has become so grave that the artist pursues it endlessly. Despairing of success yet at the same time concerned for the essential, he produces this experience in the broad daylight. He seeks to express it directly or, in other words, *to make of the work a road toward inspiration* — that which protects and preserves the purity of inspiration — *and not of inspiration a road toward the work.*

It makes no difference that this process is logically erroneous. For it is precisely the necessity of this error, the fact that it apparently precludes any outcome and that nonetheless it is the extreme demand — it is precisely this quality as requirement ruling out result — which obliges the artist not to turn away from it and mysteriously to sustain the inordinateness of it. But there is another difficulty which puts him even more profoundly in the wrong. Rilke alludes to it in a letter to Clara Rilke:

> This shows you incontrovertibly that we must submit to the most extreme ordeals, but also, it seems, that we are not to breathe a word about them before plunging into our work. We are not to lessen them by communicating them. For the unique — that which no one else would understand or have the right to understand, that sort of disorder which is proper to us — must enter into our work to become valid and to reveal its law, which is an original design that only the transparency of art renders visible . . . . I imagine sometimes what folly — and what an error — Van Gogh would have committed if he had had to communicate to anyone at all the nature of his vision, if he had had to consider with other people the motifs from which he was going to extract his paintings.

Van Gogh's call to Gauguin is born of this desire for an immediate communication. Gauguin comes. "Hardly was he there, the friend so much desired, his other self, than Van Gogh, from despair, shaved off his ears."

Perhaps, in effect, the experience is wrecked from the instant it breaks with its intimacy and seeks to reveal itself. Perhaps it seeks disclosure only in order to become bearable, to lighten and "lessen" itself. To such a perhaps, each responds for himself alone: one cuts off his ear, but he makes no painting of it; another wanders, makes disturbances in the streets—and it is the beginning of *Aurelia*, which ends under the snow, rue de la Vieille-Lanterne. It suffices to point out here that automatic writing is another answer to this question. It says intrepidly: only the moment of the experience counts; all that matters is the anonymous, visible trace of an absence without reserve. Everything must become public. The secret must be violated. The dark must enter into the day, it must dawn. What cannot be said must nevertheless be heard: Quidquid latet apparebit. Everything hidden: *that* is what must appear. And not with the anxiety of a guilty conscience, but with the insouciance of happy lips. — What, without risks or perils? With the ease of a word that escapes, of an unconscious, ignorant liberty? Not without risks and never in the calm of an indifferent spontaneity. Automatic writing is passive; this also means that it places itself in the imprudence and the temerity of a movement of pure passion. It is the word become *desire*, trusting to desire to bring it back to its source. And what it tirelessly affirms, what it cannot silence, what it can neither begin nor finish expressing, is what René Char echoes when he says, *"The poem is the realized love of desire still desiring."* And André Breton: *"Desire, yes, always."*

Communication
and the
Work
VI

Reading

Reading: in the writer's logbook we are not surprised to come upon confessions of this sort: "Always this anguish when I go to write . . . ." And when Lomazzo tells us of the fright that seized Leonardo every time he wished to paint, we understand this too, or we feel that we could understand.

But were someone to confide in us, "Always anxious when I go to read," or were a person unable to read except at rare, privileged moments, or were he to overturn his whole life, renounce the world with its activities and all its happiness just to make his way toward a few minutes of reading — doubtless we would assign him a spot beside that patient of Pierre Janet's who did not like to read because, she said, "a book one reads becomes dirty."

Listening to music makes a musician of him who merely enjoys listening. Likewise looking at a painting. Music and painting are worlds entered by those who hold the key. The key is apparently the "gift," and the gift would seem to be the delight and the intelligence of a certain taste. Amateurs of music and of painting are recognizable types who bear their penchant openly, with pride, like a delicious pain which sets them apart. The others modestly acknowledge that they have no ear. One has to be gifted to hear and to see. The gift is a closed space — concert hall, museum — into which one retires in order to enjoy a clandestine pleasure. Those who do not have the gift remain outside; those who do, go in and out as they please. Naturally, music is loved on Sundays only; this divinity is no more demanding than another.

Reading requires no gifts at all and shows this appeal to a natural distinction for what it is. No one is gifted, be he author or reader, and whoever feels that he is feels primarily that he is not — feels infinitely ill equipped, absent from the power attributed to him. And just as to be an "artist" is not to know that art already exists, that there is already a world, so reading, seeing, hearing the work of art demands more ignorance than knowledge. It requires a knowledge endowed with an immense ignorance and a gift which is not given ahead of time, which has each time to be received and acquired in forgetfulness of it, and also lost. Each painting, each piece of music makes us a present of the organ we need to welcome it; each one "gives" us the eye and the ear we need to see and hear it. Nonmusicians are those who make up their minds in advance to refuse this possibility of hearing; they evade it as though it were a threat or a hindrance which they guard against suspiciously. André Breton repudiates music, because he wants to preserve in himself the right to hear the discordant essence of language, his unmusical music. And Kafka, who never ceases to acknowledge that he is deafer to music than anyone else in the world, does not fail to discover in this weak point one of his strengths: "I am strong, really. I have a certain strength, and, to characterize it briefly and not very clearly, it is my unmusicalness."

Generally speaking, he who does not love music cannot stand it, just as the person who rejects a painting by Picasso thrusts it from him with a violent hatred, as if he felt directly threatened. That he may not even have looked at the painting says nothing against his good faith. It is not in his power to look at it. Not to look at it does not put him in the wrong; it is a form of his sincerity, an accurate premonition of the force that closes his eyes. "I refuse to look at that." "I couldn't live with that in sight." These clichés bring out the hidden reality of the work of art, its absolute intolerance, more forcefully than does the amateur's suspect self-satisfaction. It is quite true that one cannot live with a painting in plain sight.

The plastic arts have this advantage over writing: they manifest more directly the exclusive void within which the work seems to want to dwell, far from every gaze. *The Kiss* by Rodin lets itself be gazed at and even enjoys being thus regarded, but the *Balzac* goes without a look, it is a closed and sleeping thing, absorbed in itself to the point of disappearing. The book seems to lack this decisive separation, which sculpture makes its element and which places in the center of space another, rebel space—an inaccessible space both evident and withdrawn, perhaps immutable, perhaps ever restless, the contained violence in the face of which we always feel in excess. The statue one digs up and presents for the public's admiration does not expect anything from this and does not receive anything; it seems, rather, torn from its place. But the book which one recovers, the manuscript that leaves its drawer to enter the broad daylight of reading: is it not, by impressive good fortune, born again? What is a book no one reads? Something that is not yet written. It would seem, then, that to read is not to write the book again, but to allow the book to *be*: written — this time all by itself, without the intermediary of the writer, without anyone's writing it. The reader does not add himself to the book, but tends primarily to relieve it of an author. And all the alacrity in his approach (in this shadow which passes so vainly over the pages and leaves them intact) — everything that lends reading its superfluous appearance, including even paltry attention and lack of grave interest: all the reader's infinite lightness, then, affirms the new lightness of the book, which has become a book without an author. Now it is a book relieved of the seriousness, the effort, the heavy anguish, the weight of a whole life that was spilled out into it. It has become a book minus the sometimes terrible, the always formidable experience which the reader effaces and, with his providential unconcern, considers as nothing.

The reader, without knowing it, is engaged in a profound struggle with the author. Whatever intimacy may subsist today between the book and the writer, and however sharply the figure, the presence, the history of the author may be brought into focus by the circumstances of the book's circulation (circumstances which, while not arbitrary, are perhaps already somewhat anachronistic) — despite all this, every reading where consideration of the writer seems to play so great a role is an attack which annihilates him in order to give the work back to itself: back to its anonymous presence, to the violent, impersonal affirmation that it is. The reader is himself always fundamentally anonymous. He is any reader, none in particular, unique but transparent. He does not add his name to the book (as our fathers did long ago); rather, he erases every name from it by his nameless presence, his modest, passive gaze, interchangeable and insignificant, under whose light pressure the book appears written, separate from everything and everyone.

Reading makes of the book what the sea and the wind make of objects fashioned by men: a smoother stone, a fragment fallen from the sky without a past, without a future, the sight of which silences questions. Reading gives to the book the abrupt existence which the statue "seems" to get from the chisel alone. From its reading the book acquires the isolation which witholds the statue from the eyes that see it — the haughty remove, the orphan wisdom which dismisses the sculptor along with the gaze wishing to sculpt it still. Somehow the book needs the reader in order to become a statue. It needs the reader if it is to declare itself a thing without an author and hence without a reader. It is not primarily a more human truth that reading brings to the book; but neither does reading make the book something inhuman — an "object," a pure compact presence, the fruit of the deep which our sun did not ripen. Reading simply "makes" the book, the work, become a work beyond the man who produced it, the experience that is expressed in it and even beyond all the artistic resources which tradition has made available. The singular property of reading demonstrates the singular sense of the verb "to make" in the expression "it makes the work become a work." The word *make* here does not designate a productive activity. Reading does not produce anything, does not add anything. It lets be what is. It is freedom: not the freedom that produces being or grasps it, but freedom that welcomes, consents, says yes, can say only yes, and, in the space opened by this yes, lets the work's overwhelming decisiveness affirm itself, lets be its affirmation that it is — and nothing more.

"Lazare, Veni Foras"

A reading which takes the work for what it is, and thus disencumbers it of its author, does not consist in introducing, in his place, a reader — a person firmly rooted in existence, having a history, a profession, a religion, and even reading experience, who, based upon all that, would begin a dialogue with the other person who wrote the book. Reading is not a conversation; it does not discuss, it does not question. It never asks of the book, and still less of the author: "What did you mean exactly? What truth, then, do you bring me?" A genuine reading never puts the genuine book into question. But neither does it submit to the "text." Only the nonliterary book is presented as a tightly woven net of determined significations, a set of real affirmations. Before being read by anyone, the nonliterary book has already been read by all, and it is this prior reading that guarantees it a solid existence. But the book which has its origin in art has no guarantee in the world, and when it is read, it has never been read before. It does not come into its presence as a work except in the space opened by this unique reading, each time the first and each time the only.

Hence the strange liberty of which reading — literary reading — gives us the prime example: a movement which is free insofar as it does not submit to, does not brace itself upon anything already present. The book, doubtless, is there, and not only its paper and ink reality but also its essence. It is there as a web of stable meanings, as the assertiveness which it owes to a preestablished language, and as the enclosure, too, formed around it by the community of all readers, among whom I, who have not read it, already have a place. And this enclosure is also that of all books which, like angels with intertwined wings, keep close watch over this unknown volume. For a single book imperiled makes a dangerous gap in the universal library. The book is there, then, but the work is still hidden. It is absent, perhaps radically so; in any case it is concealed, obfuscated by the evident presence of the book, behind which it awaits the liberating decision, the "Lazare, veni foras."

To make this stone fall seems to be reading's mission: to render it transparent, to dissolve it with the penetrating force of the gaze which unimpeded moves beyond. There is in reading, at least at reading's point of departure, something vertiginous that resembles the movement by which, going against reason, we want to open onto life eyes already closed. This movement is linked to desire which, like inspiration, is a leap, an infinite leap: I want to *read* what is, however, not written. But there is more; and what makes the "miracle" of reading still more singular — what perhaps enlightens us as to the sense of all thaumaturgies — is that here the stone and the tomb do not only withhold the cadaverous void which is to be animated; they constitute the presence, though dissimulated, of what is to appear. To roll back the stone, to obliterate it, is certainly something marvelous, but it is something we achieve at every moment in everyday language. At every moment we converse with Lazarus, dead for three days — or dead, perhaps, since always. In his well-woven winding sheet, sustained by the most elegant conventions, he answers us and speaks to us within ourselves. But what answers the call of literary reading is not a door falling open or becoming transparent or even getting a bit thinner. It is, rather, a ruder stone, better sealed, a crushing weight, an immense avalanche that causes earth and sky to shudder.

Such is the nature of the "opening" that reading is made of: nothing opens but that which is closed tighter; only what belongs to the greatest opacity is transparent; nothing consents to enter into the levity of a free and happy yes except what has been borne as the crushing weight of a no, devoid of substance. And this is not to say that the poetic work seeks out obscurity in order to disconcert everyday comprehension. We are simply situating, between the book which is there and the work which is never there in advance — between the book which is the hidden work and the work which can only be affirmed in the palpable thickness of this manifest concealment — a violent rupture: the passage, that is, from the world where everything has more or less meaning, where there is obscurity and clarity, into a space where, properly speaking, nothing has meaning yet, toward which nevertheless everything which does have meaning returns as toward its origin.

But these remarks too could easily deceive us if we took them to mean that reading blazes a trail from one language to another, or that it is a bold démarche, a conquest requiring initiative and persistence. Reading's approach is perhaps a difficult happiness, but, still, reading is the easiest thing. It is effortless liberty, a pure yes that blossoms in immediacy.

The Light, Innocent Yes of Reading

Reading, in the literary sense, is not even a pure movement of comprehension. It is not the interpretation that keeps meaning alive by pursuing it. Reading is situated beyond or before comprehension. Nor is to read exactly to send out a call so that the unique work, which is to be revealed in the reading, might disclose itself behind the appearance of ordinary language, behind the book that belongs to everyone in general. Doubtless there is a sort of call, but it can only come from the work itself. It is a silent call, which amidst the general noise imposes silence, and which only reaches the reader's ear because he answers it. This call turns him away from ordinary relations and toward the space in whose proximity the reading, by abiding there, becomes the approach to the work and an utterly joyful welcome to the work's generosity. And this welcome lifts the book to the work which it is; and this transport is the same as the one which lifts the work to being and makes of the welcome the sheer delight whereby the work proclaims itself. The reading is this abiding, and it has the simplicity of the light and transparent yes which this sojourn is. Even if it demands of the reader that he enter a zone where he can scarcely breathe and where the ground slips out from under his feet — and even if, leaving aside these stormy approaches, reading still seems to be participation in that open violence, the work — nonetheless, in itself it is tranquil and silent presence, the calm center of measureless excess, the silent yes at the eye of every storm.

The freedom of this present yes, this utterly happy and transparent consent, is the essence of reading. It sets reading in diametrical opposition to the work. For the work, through the experience of creation, touches upon absence, upon the torments of the infinite; it reaches the empty depths of that which never begins or ends—the movement which exposes the creator to the threat of the essential solitude and delivers him to the interminable.

In this sense reading is more positive than creation: more creative, although it produces nothing. For it partakes of decisiveness; it has the lightness, the irresponsibility, and the innocence of resolution. It does nothing, and everything is accomplished. The anguish, the unfinished narratives, the torment of a wasted life and of a mission betrayed; each day, moreover, turned into exile, each night an exile from sleep and finally the conviction that "*The Metamorphosis* is unreadable, a radical failure"—all that is for Kafka. But for the reader of Kafka the anguish becomes ease and contentment, the torment of guilt is transformed into innocence, and for every shred of text there is the joy of plenitude, the sure evidence of complete success, the revelation of the unique work: inevitable, unforeseeable. Such is the essence of reading, of the weightless yes. Much more than the creator's somber struggle, much more than the artist's battle to master chaos by disappearing therein, it evokes the divine aspect of creation.

Hence the fact that many complaints of authors against readers seem out of place. Montesquieu writes: "I ask a favor which I fear will not be granted me: it is that I not be judged for twenty years' work by a reading that takes one minute; and that the whole book, not a few sentences, be approved or condemned." He asks for what artists often regret not obtaining when bitterly they picture to themselves the offhand reading, the distracted glance, and the negligent ear that greets their works. So many efforts, sacrifices, cares, calculations, a life of solitude, centuries of meditation and research all evaluated, judged, and suppressed by the ignorant decision of the first-come, according to the mood he chances to feel. And perhaps Valéry is right to be concerned about the uncultivated reader of today who expects to be helped along in his reading by the facile character of the text itself. But the scrupulous attention of an almost religiously devoted reader whose cultivated reading even becomes a kind of cult would make no difference. It would entail even graver perils. For if the lightness of the light reader who dances once quickly round the text is doubtless not a true lightness, it is harmless, and it even holds a certain promise: it announces the happiness and innocence of reading, which is perhaps in fact a dance with an invisible partner in a separated space—a helplessly joyful dance with the "tomb." One must not wish upon such lightness the movement of a graver concern, for where levity is given us, gravity does not lack.

Communication

What most threatens reading is this: the reader's reality, his personality, his immodesty, his stubborn insistence upon remaining himself in the face of what he reads — a man who knows in general how to read. To read a poem is not to read yet another poem; it is not even to enter, via this poem, into the essence of poetry. The reading of a poem is the poem itself, affirming itself in the reading as a work. It is the poem giving birth, in the space held open by the reader, to the reading that welcomes it; it is the poem becoming power to read, becoming communication opened between *power* and *impossibility*, between the power linked to the moment of reading and the impossibility linked to the moment of writing.

Communication of the work lies not in the fact that it has become communicable, through reading, to a reader. The work is itself communication. It is intimacy shared in struggle by reading's demand and writing's: by the work as form and measure, constituting itself as power, and the same work's measureless excess, tending toward impossibility. It is intimate strife shared moreover by the form where the work takes its shape and the limitlessness where it is all refusal, by the resolution which is the being of beginning and the indecision which is the being of beginning over. This violence lasts as long as the work is a work. It is violence that is never pacified, but it is also the calm of an accord; it is rivalry, and also the reconciliation — an understanding. But it breaks off as soon as it ceases to be the approach toward what rules out any understanding.

To read is thus not to obtain communication from the work, but to "make" the work communicate itself. And, if we may employ an inadequate image, to read is to be one of the two poles between which, through mutual attraction and repulsion, the illuminating violence of communication erupts — one of the two poles between which that event comes to pass and which it constitutes by the very passage. But of course this comparison is inadequate. At most it indicates that the antagonism, which in the work opposes its two moments, reading and writing (or, more exactly, which makes of the work a tension where its moments seem to oppose each other two by two), opens the work by means of this radical disjunction to the freedom of its communication. But we should not so simply represent this antagonism as that of fixed poles opposing each other like two powers determined once and for all, called reading and writing. It must at least be added that this antagonistic exaltation, which eventually takes the personified form of the reader and the author, has never ceased to develop in the course of the work's genesis. Although, in the end, the work seems to have become a dialogue between two persons in whom two stabilized demands have been incarnated, this "dialogue" is primarily the more original combat of more indistinct demands, the torn intimacy of irreconcilable and inseparable moments which we call measure and measurelessness, form and infinitude, resolution and indecision. Beneath their successive oppositions, these moments steadily give reality to the same violence. To the violence, that is, of what tends to open and tends to close, tends to cohere in the contours of a clear figure that limits, and yet tends to err without end, to lose itself in an ever restless migration, that of the *other* night which never comes but comes back again. In this communication it is obscurity that must reveal itself and night that must dawn. This is revelation where nothing appears, but where concealment becomes appearance.

The Reader Yet to Come

It is sometimes said that every author writes in the presence of some reader or that he writes in order to be read. This is a rather careless way of speaking. One ought to say that the reader's role, or that which will become, once the work is complete, the power or the possibility of reading, is already present, in changing forms, in the genesis of the work. To the extent that to write is to snatch oneself back from the impossibility where writing becomes possible, writing assumes the characteristics of reading's demand, and the writer becomes the nascent intimacy of the still infinitely future reader. But it goes without saying that this power is nonetheless power to write, only because of the opposition to itself which it becomes in the experience of impossibility.

There is not power on one side, impossibility on the other; there is no such clash of these contraries. There is, in the event of the fact of writing, the tension which, through the intimacy into which the writing gathers them, demands of the opposites what they are in their extreme opposition, but demands also that they come into their own by quitting themselves, by detaining each other together outside themselves in the restless unity of their common belonging. The power in question is power only by comparison with impossibility, the impossibility which is affirmed as power.

The writer, inasmuch as he remains a real person and believes himself to be this real person who is writing, also believes that he willingly shelters in himself the reader of what he writes. He feels within himself, vital and demanding, the role of the reader still to be born. And very often, through a usurpation which he barely escapes, it is the reader, prematurely and falsely engendered, who begins to write in him. (Hence, to give only a simplistic example, those choice passages, those fine phrases which come to the surface and which cannot be said to have been written, but only to be readable.) This illusion, as we can now understand, comes from the fact that the moments which prefigure reading's demand pass through the writer in the course of the work's genesis. But these moments must, precisely, fall outside of him when they are gathered together in the final decisiveness of the reading — in the liberty of the welcome and of the sojourn near the work which alone constitutes an authentic reading.

The writer can never read his work for the very same reason which gives him the illusion that he does. "He is," says René Char, "the genesis of being who projects and of a being who contains." But in order for the "being who contains" — the being who gives form and measure, the form-giver, the "Beginner" — to attain the ultimate metamorphosis which would turn him into "the reader," the finished work has to escape from him. It has to escape from the one who makes it, complete itself by putting him at a distance, culminate in this "distancing" which dispossesses him conclusively, this distancing which then, precisely, takes the form of the reading (and in which the reading takes form).

The moment when that which is glorified in the work *is* the work, when the work ceases in some way to have been made, to refer back to someone who made it, but gathers all the essence of the work in the fact that now there is a work — a beginning and initial decision — this moment which cancels the author is also the moment when, as the book opens to itself, the reading finds its origin in this opening.

Reading is born, therefore, at this moment when the work's distance from itself changes its sign. In the course of the book's genesis this "void" marked the work's unfinished quality, but also the intimacy of its progression, the first precipitous advances of the "being who projects." This emptiness changes its sign, and the reading is born at the moment when the distance of the work with respect to itself no longer indicates incompletion but perfection, no longer signifies that the work is not yet done, but that it never needed to be done.

In general the reader, unlike the writer, naïvely feels superfluous. He does not think that he fashions the work. Even if the work overwhelms him, and all the more so if it becomes his sole concern, he feels that he does not exhaust it, that it remains altogether outside his most intimate approach. He does not penetrate it; it is free of him, and this freedom makes for the profundity of his relation to the work, the intimacy of his yes. But in this very yes, the work's freedom still keeps him at a distance. It reestablishes the distance which alone assures the freedom of the welcome and which is constantly reborn from the passion of the reading that abolishes it.

This distance is what perfects the work — if, that is, the reader keeps it pure, and inasmuch as it is, moreover, the measure of his intimacy with the work. For he is close to the work to the degree that he recognizes it as a work regardless of him. By removing it from any author and from all consideration of having been made, this distance gives the work for what it is. And so it would seem that reading's effacement, which renders it innocent of the work's making and exempts it from this responsibility, is, for that very reason, nearer to the accomplished work, to the essence of its creation, than is the author who always believes himself to have made everything and created all.

Abhorrence of a Vacuum

But this *distance,* which evokes the yes of the finished work (given as complete in the moment when, for the movement that completed it, is substituted the affirmation that it is) — this distance of the work with respect to itself, to the reader, to the world's doings, to other works — this distance which, precisely, constitutes reading's innocence also defines its responsibility and its risk. It seems to be very difficult to preserve such an interval. Here the natural abhorrence of a vacuum is expressed in the need to fill it up with a judgment of value. The work is said to be good or bad with respect to morality, laws, various systems of values, etc. It is declared to be successful or not with respect to rules (very precarious at present) which may constitute instances of an esthetic, that is to say the simple impressions of a more or less refined taste or of a more or less vigorous absence of taste. The work is judged to be rich or poor with respect to culture, which compares it to other works, which does or does not draw from it an increase in knowledge, which adds it to the national, to the human treasury or yet again sees in it only a pretext to talk or to teach.

It is possible that the more a work is esteemed, the more it is imperiled. For when it is designated as a good work, it is assigned a place on the side of the good which uses it, rendering it utilitarian. A work which is judged bad sometimes finds room in this judgment to preserve itself. It is put aside, condemned to the nether regions of libraries, or burned, or forgotten; but in a sense this exile, this disappearance in the midst of flames or in tepid forgetfulness also extends the proper distance of the work. It corresponds to the force of the work's remove. This does not mean that a century later the work will necessarily find the readers it lacked. Posterity is promised to no one, and no book would consider it a happy ending. The work does not endure over the ages; it is. This being can inaugurate a new age, for it is an appeal to the beginning, recalling that nothing is affirmed except through the fecundity of an initial decisiveness. But the work's very coming to be is revealed by the flash of its disappearance at least as well as by the false light shed by survival from mere habit. The feeling that works escape time originates in the work's "distance," and expresses, by disguising it, the remove which always comes from the work's presence. Our impression that works are ageless expresses, by forgetting it, what makes the work always accede to presence for the first time in its reading — its unique reading, each time the first and each time the only.

The risk which this reading entails, however, is no mere matter of chance. If the work's "void," which is its presence to itself in its reading, is difficult to preserve, this is not only because it is in itself hard to sustain, but also because it remembers, as it were, the void which, in the course of the work's genesis, marked the incompletion of the work and was the tension of its antagonist moments. That is why reading draws whoever reads the work into the remembrance of that profound genesis. Not that the reader necessarily perceives afresh the manner in which the work was produced — not that he is in attendance at the real experience of its creation. But he partakes of the work as the unfolding of something in the making, the intimacy of the void which comes to be. If this progression takes on the aspect of a temporal unfolding, it founds the essence of the literary genre called the novel.

This kind of reading — this presence to the work as a genesis — changes, and thus produces the critical reading: the reader, now the specialist, interrogates the work in order to know how it was fashioned. He asks it the secrets and the conditions of its creation, and examines it closely to see whether it answers adequately to these conditions, etc. The reader, having become the specialist, becomes an author in reverse. The true reader does not rewrite the book, but he is apt to return, drawn by an imperceptible pull, toward the various prefigurations of the reader which have caused him to be present in advance at the hazardous experience of the book. It ceases, then, to appear necessary to him and again becomes a possibility among others. It regains the indecisiveness of something uncertain, something altogether still to be achieved. And the work thus regains its disquietude, the wealth of its indigence, the insecurity of its void, while reading, joining in this disquietude and espousing this poverty, comes to resemble the desire, the anguish, and the levity of a movement of passion.

All these metamorphoses belong to the authentic essence of reading. Its task is to keep what we call the work's distance pure, but no less to keep it alive: to make it communicate with the work's intimacy, to keep this intimacy from congealing and protecting itself in the vain solitude of the ideal. The "vacuum" which, in the course of the work's genesis, belongs to the torn intimacy of the work, seems, in the end, to fall out of it. While opening it altogether to itself, rendering it absolutely present, the emptiness seems nevertheless to make of this presence the remove which preserves its approach, giving us the impression that the painting is always behind the painting and also that the poem, the temple, and the statue escape the vicissitudes of time, whose mark, however, they bear.

It is as if this divisive void which, in the course of the genesis, is now the abyss where the work subsides, now the soaring energy by which it comes to light, now that empty violence where everything repeats eternally but then again the search from which everything begins — it is as if this "distant interior," as Michaux calls it, passed, at the moment of completion, altogether outside, isolating the work, forming around it that halo of absence so characteristic of the presence of masterpieces, which is like their aura of glory and which shelters them beneath a veil of empty majesty, unexpressive indifference. Thus are works immobilized in a lifeless distance. Isolated, preserved by a void which is no longer a reading but a cult of admiration, they cease to be works. The work of art is never connected to repose, it has nothing to do with the tranquil certitude which makes masterpieces familiar; it does not take shelter in museums. In this sense it never is. And if, clumsily transposing the idea that it is not an object someone has perfected, we say of it that its perfection is everlasting, at least this reminds us that the work never ceases to be related to its origin: that the incessant experience of the origin is the condition of its being, and also that the antagonistic violence due to which it was, in the course of its genesis, the opposition of its contrary moments, is not just a feature of this genesis, but belongs to the character of agonistic struggle which is the character of the work's very being. The work is the *violent liberty* by which it is communicated, and by which the *origin* — the empty and indecisive depth of the origin — is *communicated* through the work to form the brimming resolution, the definiteness of the beginning. That is why the work tends ever increasingly to manifest the experience of the work: the experience which is not exactly that of its creation and which is not that of its technical fashioning either. This experience leads the work ceaselessly back from the clarity of the beginning to the obscurity of the origin and subjects its brilliant apparition, the moment of its opening, to the disquietude of the dissimulation into which it withdraws.

The reading which takes form in the work's distance — the reading which is the form of this void and the moment when it seems to fall out of the work — must thus also be a profound return to its intimacy, to what seems its eternal birth. Reading is not an angel flying about the work and, with winged feet, making this sphere turn. It is not the look which from without, from behind the window, captures what is happening within a foreign world. It is connected to the life of the work. It is present at all the work's moments. It is one of them, and it is by turns and at the same time each of them. It is not only their remembrance, their ultimate transfiguration; it retains in itself everything that is really at stake in the work. That is why in the end it alone bears all the weight of communication.

The Work and History

It is not surprising then, that, strengthened by such intimacy, reading, incarnated in the reader, should naturally proceed to take over the work, wanting to "grasp" it, reducing and eliminating all distance from it. Nor is it surprising that reading should make of this distance, this sign of the work's completion, the principle of a new genesis: the realization of the work's historical destiny. In the world of culture, the work becomes the guarantor of truths and the repository of meaning. None of this is surprising; this movement is inevitable. But it does not simply mean that the artistic work follows the course of works in general and obeys the law that moves them through their successive transformations. For this movement is also encouraged by the work's own nature. It comes from the profound distance of the work from itself, the remove due to which it always escapes what it is — seems, for example, definitively finished and yet incomplete; seems, in the restlessness that steals it from every grasp, to enter into complicity with the infinite variations of becoming. The distance which puts the work beyond our reach and beyond time's — where it perishes in glorious immobility — also exposes it to all the contingencies of time, showing it ceaselessly in search of a new form, of another culmination, acquiescing in all the metamorphoses which, attaching it to history, seem to make of its remove the promise of an unlimited future.

Thus the reading which initially projected itself into the intimacy of the work, only to fall out of it the better to maintain it and to fix it in a monumental immobility, finally projects itself outside and makes of the work's intimate life something which can no longer be realized unless it is displayed in the world and filled with the world's life and with history's.

This transformation is produced to the extent that the "empty" movement takes on content, while the work, momentarily or definitively losing the force and the intimacy of its constant genesis, unfolds as a newborn world where values are at stake and where these values call for arbitration by some criterion or contribute to the advent of such a standard, such a truth.

So: that which, in the work, was communication of the work to itself, *the origin blossoming into a beginning*, becomes the communication of a given thing. That which, opening it, made the work the advent and the brilliance of what opens becomes an opened place, in the image of this world of stable things and in imitation of this subsisting reality where, from a need to subsist, we live. And that which had neither sense nor truth nor value, but in which everything seemed to take on sense, becomes the language which says true things, says false things, and which one reads for instruction, for increased self-knowledge, or to cultivate the mind.

Through this realization then, the work is realized outside of itself and also on the model of exterior things, at their invitation. Through this movement — determined, so to speak, by gravity — instead of being the force of the beginning, the work becomes a thing beginning. Instead of getting all its reality from the pure, contentless affirmation that it is, it becomes an enduring reality, containing many meanings which it acquires from the movement of time or which are perceived variously according to culture's forms and the exigencies of history. And through all this, through all that makes it graspable — makes of it no longer the being of the work but the work functioning in the productive fashion of works of the world — it puts itself at the reader's service. It takes part in the public dialogue. It expresses or it refutes what is generally said; it consoles, it entertains, it bores, not by virtue of itself or by virtue of a relation with the void and the cutting edge of its being, but via its content, and then finally thanks to its reflection of the common language and the current truth. At this juncture what is read is surely no longer the work; rather, these are the thoughts of everyone rethought, our common habits rendered more habitual still, everyday routines continuing to weave the fabric of our days. And this movement is in itself very important, one which it is not fitting to discredit. But neither the work of art nor its reading is present here.

This transformation is not definitive; it is not even an evil or a good for the work. Disappearance, even when it is disguised as useful presence, belongs to the work's essence; and we should add that it is also related to the dialectic of art. This movement leads from the hymn — where the work, art, and the world are absent — to the work where men and the world seek to make themselves present, and from there to the work where the very experience of the work — art, the communication of the origin as a beginning — is affirmed in a presence which is also disappearance.

It is sometimes said regretfully that the work of art will never again speak the language it spoke when it was born, the language of its birth, which only those who belonged to the same world heard and received. Never again will the Eumenides speak to the Greeks, and we will never know what was said in that language. This is true. But it is also true that the Eumenides have still never spoken, and that each time they speak it is the unique birth of their language that they announce. Long ago they spoke as enraged and appeased divinities before withdrawing into the temple of night — and this is unknown to us and will ever remain foreign. Later they spoke as symbols of the dark forces that must be combated in order for there to be justice and culture — and this is only too well known to us. Finally, one day, perhaps they will speak as the work in which language is always original, in which it is the language of the origin. And this is unknown to us, but not foreign. And notwithstanding all this, reading and vision each time recollect, from the weight of a given content and along the ramifications of an evolving world, the unique intimacy of the work, the wonder of its constant genesis and the swell of its unfurling.

Literature
and the
Original
Experience

VII

The
Future
and the Question
of Art

A sound response puts down roots in the question. The question is its sustenance. Common sense believes that it does away with the question. Indeed, in the so-called happy eras, only the answers seem alive. But this affirmative contentment soon dies off. The authentic answer is always the question's vitality. It can close in around the question, but it does so in order to preserve the question by keeping it open.

"What is art, and what can be said of literature?" Doubtless this kind of question is peculiarly ours, central to our times. However, since each time an answer is given, the question manages to be asked anew, as though it were indifferent to these answers, we can hardly avoid seeing in the "anew" a particularly surprising insistence. It may be that the question is only seeking peace in the repetition where what has once been said lapses into mere recitation. But perhaps by this harassment the question means above all to remain open. To remain in suspense? No. If we maintain oppositions, if we let them clash in the sterile space where what opposes itself never meets with itself, we altogether miss the liveliness of the question. We must, then, set aside that contrariness which tires problems out, and on the contrary, firmly keep literature separate from the debates where it divides without being able to return to itself as if to the origin of this divide.

The work: insofar as we locate all the seriousness of art in this one notion, we ought, it seems, to reconcile those who are naïvely anxious to glorify art and those who, since what they value in artistic activity is what makes it an activity and not a useless passion, wish to see it collaborate in the overall work of humanity. Both are prepared to acknowledge in man the excellence of a power and in the artist the exercise of a form of this power — requiring effort, discipline, study. Both say of human power that it has worth because it edifies — that is, builds. And does so not in some atemporal place, out of this world, but here and now, according to the limits which are properly ours and in conformity with the laws of all action to which it submits, just as it acquiesces in the ultimate goal: the completion of a work — an edifice in this world or, better, the edifice which is the true world to come where only freedom shall dwell.

Doubtless there subsists in this agreement a great disagreement. Art certainly aims to build, but according to itself and without welcoming anything of the clear light of day except what is proper to its particular task. Granted, art has as its goal something real: an object. But a beautiful object. Which is to say, an object of contemplation, not of use, which, moreover, will be sufficient to itself, will rest in itself, refer to nothing else, and be its own end (in the two senses of this term). True. And yet, points out the other side of this thinking, the goal of art *is* an object — a real, that is, an effective one. Not a momentary dream, a pure inner smile, but a realized action which is itself activating, which informs or deforms others, appeals to them, affects them, moves them — toward other actions which, most often, do not return to art but belong to the course of the world. They contribute to history and thus are lost, perhaps, in history. But there they will ultimately be regained, in the concrete work which freedom will have become: the world, the world realized as its very wholeness.

This is a strong and important answer. Art, as we see in Mallarmé, and then, in a different light, in Valéry, appears to vouch for Hegel's saying: man is what he makes. If there is anyone who is to be judged by his works, it is the artist. He is, so they say, the creator: the creator of a new reality, which opens in the world a wider perspective, a possibility by no means closed but such, on the contrary, that reality in all its forms is enlarged because of it. He is, moreover, the creator of himself in what he creates. He is a richer artist because of the trials he undergoes for the sake of his works. He is other than he was thanks to this process, and if sometimes he is exhausted and dying in the work, *it* is thereby only the more alive.

Art is real in the work. And the work is real in the world, because it is realized there (in harmony with the world, even in the upheaval and the rupture), for it contributes to the world's realization and has no sense, will have no rest except in the world where man will be all he can be, man par excellence. But what is the result of this? Within the overall human undertaking, where the tasks conforming to the universal will for production and emancipation are necessarily the most immediately important, art can only follow. It can at most feign ignorance of this general destiny by considering that in the universe which bears it along it revolves according to its own little laws. But ultimately, even according to its own little laws which make of the *work* its only measure, art will collaborate as consciously and rigorously as possible in mankind's overall work, and for the sake of a universal day.

Is Art a Thing of the Past?

But what else results from this? Whoever acknowledges effective action in the thick of history as his essential task cannot prefer artistic action. Art acts poorly and little. It is clear that if Marx had followed the dreams of his youth and written the most beautiful novels in the world, he would have enchanted the world, but he would not have shaken it. Thus it is *Capital* that must be written and not *War and Peace*. We must not depict the murder of Caesar; we must be Brutus. These associations, these comparisons will appear absurd to contemplative minds. But as soon as art measures itself against action, immediate and pressing action can only put it in the wrong. It suffices to remember what Hölderlin wrote — Hölderlin about whom it would not be enough to say that his fate was linked to poetry's, for he had no existence at all except in and for poetry. And yet, in 1799, speaking of the revolution which he saw imperiled, he wrote to his brother, "And if the kingdom of darkness erupts after all in *full force*, then let us throw our pens under the table and go in God's name where the need is greatest and our presence the most useful."

Artistic *activity*, for him indeed who has chosen it, proves insufficient at the decisive hours — those hours that ring every hour — when "the poet must complete his message by renouncing himself." Formerly, art was able to coexist with other absolute demands. Painting served the gods, poetry made them speak. For these powers were not of this world, and, reigning outside of time, they did not measure the value of services rendered them in terms of temporal effectiveness. Art was also at the service of politics, but politics did not serve action only, and action had not yet become conscious of itself as the universal requirement. As long as the world has not yet come altogether into its own, art can probably reserve a place for itself there. But it is the artist himself who condemns this preserve if, having recognized in the *work* the essence of art, he thereby acknowledges the priority of *the overall work of humanity*. The place reserved for him in the world permits him to act in his work. But the work is nothing more, then, than the action of this reserve. It is simply a reservation, and therefore nonactivating. It is pure and simple reticence with respect to the historical undertaking which does not call for reserve, but for immediate, active, and orderly participation in generalized action. Thus, faithful to the law of the day, the artist finds himself in a position where not only does he subordinate the artistic work but renounces it and, out of fidelity, renounces himself. One hundred and forty years later another poet echoes Hölderlin — the poet most worthy in our time to answer him:

> In certain periods man's condition undergoes the icy assult of an evil sustained by the most dishonorable features of human nature. At the center of this hurricane, the poet will complete the sense of his message by renouncing himself, then will join the side of those who, having lifted from suffering its mask of legitimacy, assure the eternal return of the stubborn burden-bearer, the smuggler of justice. [René Char]

No one can easily consider himself exempt from this "renunciation," this abdication in favor of liberating action which the "self," the artistic self, impedes or only aids insufficiently. In 1934 André Gide wrote, "For a long time now, works of art will be out of the question."[1] And the fact that Hegel, a century earlier, at the beginning of his monumental course on esthetics, pronounced this sentence, "Art is for us a thing of the past," constitutes a judgment upon which art must reflect and which it will by no means consider refuted simply because since that date literature, the plastic arts, and music have produced substantial works. For at the moment Hegel spoke, he knew full well that Goethe was still alive and that all the arts in the West had experienced a renewal called Romanticism. What did he mean then, he who never spoke "lightly"? This, precisely: that since the day when the absolute consciously became the active process which is history, art has no longer been able to satisfy the need for an absolute. Relegated within us, it has lost its reality and its necessity; everything that was authentically true and alive in it now belongs to the world and to real, purposeful activity in the world.

---

[1]"For a long time now, works of art will be out of the question. In order to lend an ear to new, indistinct harmonies, one would have to be not deafened by lamentation. There is practically nothing in me any more that does not suffer sympathetically.

The Romantic Genius

"Relegated within us," Hegel says. Art is consigned to represent us to ourselves, and thus it has become esthetic enjoyment, the pleasure and pastime of an intimacy which is reduced to itself alone. It is, however, "within us" that art has sought to regain its sovereignty, its "value which cannot be evaluated" (René Char). The entire modern period is marked by this double movement which is already perceptible in Descartes: a perpetual play of exchange between an existence that becomes an increasingly pure, subjective intimacy and the ever more active and objective conquest of the world according to the aims of the realizing mind and the productive will. Hegel was the first to account fully for this double movement; and thereby, joined to Marx, he made its culmination possible.

Art too plays its part in this destiny, and sometimes it becomes artistic *activity*; but this activity is always reserved, and for that reason it is ultimately called upon to give way before the forthright truth of unreserved, immediate action. Sometimes it encloses itself in the affirmation of an inner sovereignty which accepts no law and repudiates all power. The stages of this proud vindication are well known. The artistic ego affirms that it is the sole judge of itself, the only justification for what it does and what it seeks. Romanticism's notion of genius strengthens this royal subject which is not only beyond ordinary rules but foreign to the law of achievement and success on its own terrain as well. Art, useless to the world where only effectiveness counts, is also useless to itself. If it succeeds, either this happens outside the realm of measured undertakings and limited tasks, in the boundless movement of life, or else it happens inasmuch as art withdraws into the most invisible and the most interior — into the empty point of existence where it shelters its sovereignty in refusal and the superabundance of refusal.

This demand, that art be ineffective, is by no means a vain flight which there would be no need to take seriously. Nothing is more important than this absolute autonomy which is refusal and than this refusal which, through a change in sign, is also the most prodigious affirmation. For it is the gift, the creative gift, that dispenses without restraint and without justification, that never can be justified yet upon which

---

Wherever my gaze turns, I see around me only distress. He who remains contemplative today demonstrates an inhuman philosophy, or monstrous blindness" (*Journals*, July 25, 1934).

justice can be founded. And if art, relegated within us, has not been appeased by the small contentment of esthetic pleasure, it is thanks to this
demand. Why, instead of dissipating itself in pure satisfaction, the joy
afforded by lovely objects, or in the frivolous vanity of an escapist ego,
has the passion of art, whether it be in Van Gogh or in Kafka, become
absolutely serious? Why has it become passion for the absolute? Why
are Hölderlin, Mallarmé, Rilke, Breton, René Char names signifying
that in the poem a possibility subsists for which neither culture nor
historical effectiveness nor even the pleasure of beautiful language can
account? Why do these names tell us that a possibility capable of
nothing persists as the sign in man of his own ascendency? This is not an easy
question to answer; perhaps it cannot yet be perceived in its true light.

At the very least we must bring out the difficulties which this demand or this passion encounters. The greatest difficulty does not lie in
the threat which it brings to bear upon the future of masterpieces. It is
true that art, in this perspective, no longer identifies itself entirely with
the work; it is not the same as its product. It is no longer on the side of
the real; it no longer seeks its proof in the presence of a finished object.
It affirms itself without proof in the deep of sovereign existence, prouder of
an indecipherable Goya sketch than of the whole history of painting. When
Goethe's Prometheus — when the Goethe of the Titanic affirmation — cries:
*"Have you not alone accomplished everything, sacred burning of the
heart?,"* this "accomplished everything" is the passionate demonstra-
tion with which intimacy responds to the reproaches of the purposeful
temperament. This sovereignty, then, has no kingdom. It burns in the
solitude of the sacred. The heart's passion alone accomplishes all, for it
is exposed to the fire which is the essence and the movement of All.

It is this omnipotence, symbolized by the Titans banished in the
depths of Tartarus because their insatiable desire is the torment and the
burning wheel of repetition, not the active negativity of time and productive action — it is this Titanic omnipotence that keeps watch at this
point over art. Art is the subjective passion which no longer wants any
part of the world. Here in the world subordination reigns: subordination to ends, to measured proportion, to seriousness and order. On one
front science, technology, the state; on another, significance, stable
values, the ideal of the Good and the True. Art is "the world turned up-
side down": insubordination, disproportion, frivolity, ignorance, evil,
non-sense. All this belongs to art: a wide domain, and one to which art
lays claim. What entitles it to do so? It has no title, nor can it have
any, for nothing authorizes it. It speaks of the heart, of irreducible

existence, it designates the sovereignty of the "subject." Strikingly enough, scarcely had Descartes opened the world to the Cogito's advance than Pascal closed the Cogito upon a more hidden intimacy which denounces it as "useless, uncertain and painful." But no less strikingly, this heart also has a logic, and this logic is not indifferent to reason, for it wants to be reason's principle. It only says that it is more certain, more substantial, more apt. "And it is upon this awareness, which is the heart's and instinct's, that reason must be based, and there its whole discourse must be founded." With a single stroke the sovereign power which haughtily dismisses science, which overturns useful into useless and cannot "pardon Descartes," is firmly established. But, with the same stroke, sovereignty is made to serve what it dominates. It becomes the auxiliary and the instrument of purposeful activity; it becomes useful to the world and even to numbers, to the rigor of mathematics.[2] A memorable reversal. Pascal is finally still a Cartesian. If he discloses the profundity of pure inner life, if he restores its richness, its free movement, it is Descartes he enriches and fortifies. For it is based upon the self that Descartes founds objectivity. And the more this self becomes deep, insatiable, and empty, the more powerful is the advance of the human will, which already in the heart's intimacy (but with a still unperceived intention) has posed the world as a set of objects that can be produced and are destined to usefulness.

The artist who thinks he sovereignly opposes all values and protects within himself through his art the source of all-powerful negation submits to the universal destiny no less than the artist who produces "useful" works. Perhaps he submits more. It is no accident that he cannot define art except with reference to the world. Art is the world overturned. But this overturning is also simply the "sly" means by which the world becomes more stable and more real. This tactic is of course limited, and only important at certain moments; history rejects it later on when, having itself clearly become negativity in action, it finds the dialectical vitality which assures it of its goal in the development of technical prowess.

The Question of Art

"What is art, and what can we say of literature?" Is art, then, for us a thing of the past? But why this question? It seems that art was once the

---

[2]"The heart feels that there are three dimensions and that numbers are infinite."

language of the gods; it seems, the gods having disappeared, that art remains the language in which their absence speaks—their lack, the hesitancy which has not yet decided their fate. It seems, as this absence grows deeper—becomes its own absence and forgetfulness of itself—that art seeks to become the presence of art, but that it does so initially by offering to man a means of self-recognition, of self-fulfillment. At this stage, art is what we call humanistic. It oscillates between the modesty of its useful manifestations (literature tends increasingly toward effective, interesting prose), and useless pride in being pure essence. This pride is most often expressed by the triumph of subjective states: art becomes a condition of the soul, it is "criticism of life," it is useless passion. Poetic here means subjective. Art appears as the artist and the artist as man—as man in the most general sense. Art is expressed to the extent that the artist *represents* humanity: represents, that is, the human being he is regardless of his particular being as an artist.

One might think at first that art's "humanism" lies principally in imitation or in the human preoccupations which it embraces. Thus it would seem that in order to become autonomous or essential again, art need only disengage itself from this subordinate role. But realist imitation is only the most apparent side of "humanistic" art. Just as Cartesian representation contains in itself the power of science (the power of conquest, the ability to conquer reality by negating and transforming it), so the artist becomes he who by representing transforms. He becomes the one who creates, the creator, but always, nonetheless, man the creator—creation at the level of man, of man understood as the ability to produce and to act, as the will to exert power, whose true nature is revealed by commitment to goals, by thought's need of objects in order to find its way. The fact that art is glorified in the creative artist is indicative of a great change in art. Art accepts subordination to him who practices it, consenting to be no more than he.

Clearly art's profound disquietude (most evident in literature which, through culture and the forms of language opens immediately to the development of historical action)—clearly the alienation which makes art seek itself by glorifying values that can only subordinate it—is symptomatic of the artist's malaise in a world where he perceives himself to be unjustified. The importance which attaches to the notion of the creator is very revealing in this regard. The ambiguity of this idea has made it rather versatile. For sometimes it has allowed art to take shelter in the inactive depths of subjectivity, the intensity of genius, the heart Pascal evokes when he says to Descartes and to his methodical task, "All that is ridiculous, not worth a single hour of effort." Sometimes, on the other hand, it gives art the right to compete for power and authority in the world, by defining the artist as the realizer, the superlative maker whom it claims, moreover, to protect against the anonymity of collective tasks by assuring him that he remains the exemplary individual, or man on a grand scale. For the creator is always unique; he aims to remain what he is irreducibly within himself, a treasure which cannot be compared even to the greatest action.

There is more that must be said. As we constantly hear it expressed in the most naïve or the most subtle ways, the artist claims the name creator because he thinks that thus he takes the place left vacant by the absence of the gods. This is a strangely deceptive ambition. It is an illusion, causing him to think he will become divine if he assumes the least divine of the god's functions, the one which is not sacred, which makes of God a laborer six days of the week, the demiurge, the "jack of all trades." This illusion, moreover, veils the emptiness upon which art must close, which it must in a certain way preserve as if this absence were its profound truth, the form in which it is properly to present art itself as its own essence.

Creativity does not become the divine attribute par excellence until the dawn of the accelerated period of history, when man becomes pure selfhood, but also effective action bent upon real ends, the expectation of an objective accomplishment. The artist who calls himself creator does not receive the heritage of the sacred, but only introduces into this heritage the preeminent principle of its subordination.

The New Search for Art

However, through another movement no less remarkable, art — man's presence to himself — does not manage to be satisfied with this humanist avatar which history reserves for it. It has to become its own presence. What it wants to affirm is art. What it seeks, what it attempts to achieve is the essence of art. This is striking in painting when, as Malraux has shown, it becomes apparent as one whole, but emerges also as its essence, destined to itself, no longer subordinated to values which it is supposed to celebrate or express, but in its own service alone, devoted to an absolute which neither living forms nor the tasks of men nor even formal esthetic concerns can name, so that it cannot be called anything but painting. This is a tendency which can be interpreted in many different ways, but it forcefully reveals a movement which, in varying degrees and along diverse paths, draws all the arts toward themselves, concentrates them upon the concern for their own essence, renders them present and essential. This is true for the poem (for literature "in general"),[3] for the plastic arts; perhaps it is true for Schoenberg.

Why this tendency? Why, when history subordinates it, contests it, does art become essential presence? Why Mallarmé and why Cézanne? Why, at the very moment when the absolute tends to take the form of history, when the times have concerns and interests no longer in harmony with the sovereignty of art, when the poet yields to the belletrist and he to the chronicler of the day-to-day—why, at the moment when through the force of the times art disappears, does it appear for the first time as a search in which something essential is at stake, where what counts is no longer the artist or active labor or any of the values upon which the world is built or even any of the other values upon which formerly the beyond opened? And why is this search nonetheless precise, rigorous, bent upon culminating in a work, in a work which *is*, and nothing more?

This is a remarkable phenomenon, difficult to grasp, more difficult still to interpret. But perhaps, before attempting any interpretation, we should go back to the insufficient reflections which have permitted us up to this point to discern the notion of the work.

[3]The fact that literary forms, that genres no longer have any genuine significance—that, for example, it would be absurd to ask whether *Finnegans Wake* is a prose work or not, or whether it can be called a novel—indicates the profound labor of literature which seeks to affirm itself in its essence by ruining distinctions and limits.

Characteristics
of the
Work of Art

Clearly the work of art has characteristics of its own. To distinguish itself from other forms of the human undertaking and from activity in general is its intent. Perhaps it does no more than pretend to this distinction. Or does what the work aims to be express the truth of what it is? In any case, we must try to describe it in the claims it makes too, which should enlighten us, if not about the work itself, at least about the questions it raises.

"Impersonified, the Volume"

The work of art does not refer immediately back to the person who presumably made it. When we know nothing at all about the circumstances that contributed to its production, about the history of its creation — when we do not even know the name of the person who made it possible — it is then that the work comes closest to itself. This is its true direction; it is this characteristic which is expressed in that superlative phenomenon, the masterpiece. Perfection, in the sense given this word by estheticians, is not what distinguishes the masterpiece, nor is the mastery which belongs to the artist and not to the work. Valéry is right to say that mastery is what permits one never to finish what one does. Only the artisan's mastery culminates in the object he fashions. For the artist the work is always infinite, unfinished. And thus the fact that the work is, the singular event of its being absolutely, is disclosed as not belonging to the mastery we associate with achievement. It belongs to another order.

Nor is the masterpiece defined by the long life which is promised it, though this seems to be the most envied privilege — at least in our late Occident — of artistic production. When we are confronted with *Les Chants de Maldoror*, we by no means suppose that they will be immortal.

That which assures their being absolutely, would not prevent them from disappearing absolutely. That which has placed them before us, the affirmation which they bring us, is not to be measured against historical duration; it asks neither for survival in this world nor for promotion to culture's paradise.

It is Mallarme who had the strongest awareness of this aspect of the work. "Impersonified, the volume, to the degree that one parts with it as author, solicits the approach of no reader. As such, be it known, between human accessories it takes place all alone: done, being." And his defiance of chance is a transposition of this "takes place all alone," a symbolic attempt to achieve "the elocutionary disappearance of the poet" — an experiment, finally, at grasping, as though at its source, not that which makes the work real, but the "impersonified" reality in it: that which makes it be, far more or still less than any reality.

But: does an object fashioned by an artisan or with a machine refer to its maker any more than the work of art does? It too is impersonal, anonymous. It does not bear any author's name.

Yes, this is true; it does not refer to the person who presumably made it, but neither does it refer to itself. As has often been observed, it disappears altogether into its uses. It refers to all it does, to its utilitarian value. The object never announces that it is, but how it serves. It does not appear. In order that it appear — this too has often been said — a break in the circuit of usage, a gap, an anomaly has to make it leave the world, leave its senses. And it seems then that, no longer there, it becomes its appearance, its image — what it was before being a useful thing or a significant value. This is also when it becomes, for Jean-Paul Richter and for André Breton, a veritable work of art.

That the work *is* marks the explosive brilliance of a unique event which comprehension can then take over, to which it feels it owes itself as if this event were its beginning, but which it initially understands only as that which escapes it. This event is incomprehensible because it happens in that anterior region which we cannot designate except under the veil of no. Our question continues to be the search for this region.

For the moment, let us simply acknowledge that the brilliance, the explosive decision — this presence or "lightning moment" (to use the expression to which Mallarmé and all those who resemble him since Heraclitus have always returned in order to express this event, the work) — let us acknowledge that such a dazzling affirmation arises neither from the assurance of stable truths nor from the clarity of the day which we have conquered and where living and being are accomplished in actions whose limits are familiar to us. The work brings neither certitude nor clarity. It assures us of nothing, nor does it shed any light upon itself. It is not solid, it does not furnish us with anything indestructible or indubitable upon which to brace ourselves. These values belong to Descartes and to the world where we succeed in living. Just as every strong work abducts us from ourselves, from our accustomed strength, makes us weak and as if annihilated, so the work is not strong with respect to what it is. It has no power, it is impotent: not because it is simply the obverse of possibility's various forms, but rather because it designates a region where impossibility is no longer deprivation, but affirmation.

The Statue Glorifies the Marble

The obscurity of this presence which escapes comprehension, which is unascertainable yet brilliant, explosive, and which, at the same time that it is an event, seems the silent repose of a closed thing — all this we try to bear in mind and define appropriately by saying: the work *is* eminently *what* it is made of. It is what makes its nature and its matter visible or present, it is the glorification of its reality: verbal rhythm in the poem, sound in music, light become color in painting, space become stone in the house.

By saying this we are still attempting to indicate what distinguishes the work from the object and from productive undertakings in general. For in the usual object (this much we know), matter itself is of no particular interest; and the more the matter that made it made it right for its use — the more the material is appropriate — the more it nears nothingness. And eventually all objects become immaterial, a volatile force in the swift circuit of exchange, the evaporated support of action which is itself pure becoming. This is evoked perfectly by the various transformations of money — from the heavy metal to that ungraspable vibration by which all the realities of the world, reduced to objects, are themselves transformed in the movement of the market place and volatilized into unreal moments in constant displacement.

The work makes what disappears in the object appear. The statue glorifies the marble. The painting is not made from material ingredients added to a canvas; it is the presence of this matter, which without it would remain hidden to us. And the poem likewise is not made with ideas, or with words; it is the point from which words begin to become their appearance, and the *elemental depth* upon which this appearance is opened while at the same time it closes.

This last remark in itself suggests that the emphasis we have placed on the material character of the work cannot result in a satisfactory definition; the work is not adequately accounted for by this thingly realness which it seems to place before us. This description is still only a sound comparison. It is, nevertheless, important, for it shows us that if the sculptor uses stone, and if the road builder also uses stone, the first uses it in such a way that it is not used, consumed, negated by usage, but affirmed, revealed in its obscurity, as a road which leads only to itself.

"Shifting Earth, Horrible, Exquisite"

Thus the work points us toward the deep of obscurity which we do not think we have designated by calling it elemental. Certainly it is not nature, for nature is always affirmed as already born and formed. Probably René Char is calling to this deep when he addresses the "shifting earth, horrible, exquisite"; Hölderlin calls it Mother Earth, the earth closed upon its silence, the subterranean earth that withdraws into its shadow. Rilke speaks to it thus: "Earth, is this not what you want, to be reborn invisible in us?" And Van Gogh shows it to us more forcefully still by saying, "I am attached to the earth." But these mythic names, powerful in themselves, remain foreign to what they name.

Here, however, where we seek only to take cognizance of the principal features of the work, let us remember that it is turned toward the elemental deep, toward that element which would seem to be the depth and shadow of the elemental. We know that objects do not allude to this deep, but that all the arts, in the appearance of *being* which they give to the *matter* out of which, afterwards, we say that their products are *made*, bring it forth among us in the unique event of the work.

Still, even from the point of view of description, we feel how inadequate this analysis is. For when the work takes place, certainly the elemental is illuminated and the deep is as if present, as if attracted toward the daylight (even though the work also pushes this deep down deeper by resting its full weight there). But with this compact emergence, this presence of "matter" in itself, not only does the matter proper to a particular form of art seem to be affirmed: it is not the stone alone and only the marble that the Temple of Eupalinos evokes, or the earth upon which it is built, but, by the force of the upheaval, the clear sky as well is more so to our eyes, and the sea it overlooks is nearer to itself, the night closer to night. Such, says Valéry, are the edifices which "sing."

When Hölderlin, in the first conversations with Sinclair on madness — conversations which probably date from 1804 — says of every work of art that it is a unique rhythm, he designates this same region, where everything is outer but as if impenetrable and closed.

When rhythm has become the sole and unique mode of thought's expression, it is then only that there is poetry. In order for mind to become poetry, it must bear in itself the mystery of an innate rhythm. It is in this rhythm alone that it can live and become visible. And every work of art is but one and the same rhythm. Everything is simply rhythm. The destiny of man is a single celestial rhythm, as every work of art is a unique rhythm.

We must also call to mind these words of Mallarmé, written with a view to reaffirming "the old genius of verse":

Thus launched independently, the principle which is none — but Verse! — attracts no less than disengages for its unfurling (the instant they shine there and die in a swift flower, upon some transparency like ether's) the thousand elements of beauty hastening to press near and to order themselves in the essential value. Sign! in the central abyss of a spiritual impossibility that anything be exclusive of everything, the divine numerator of our apotheosis, some supreme mold which does not take place as any object that exists: but it borrows all the scattered ores, unknown and floating according to some richness, to quicken there a seal, and to forge them.

This is an imposing text. For it assembles most of the work's claims: presence, the fact of being, which does not relate to historical duration and of which Rilke is probably speaking when, opposing Cézanne to impressionistic painting, he says: "They painted: I love this thing, instead of painting: here it is." This presence is not spiritual, or ideal, for it *attracts* to it the thousand *elements*, it borrows *all the scattered ores unknown and floating*, ("shifting earth, horrible, exquisite," says Char). Yet these ores, the elemental night of rhythm, the profundity which the name "elements" designates as materiality — all this the work attracts, but to *disengage* it, to reveal it in its *essence*, an essence which is the elemental obscurity. And in this obscurity thus rendered essentially present, not dissipated but disengaged, rendered visible *upon some transparency like ether's*, the work becomes that which unfurls, that which *quickens*, the *blossoming* of the apotheosis.

The Work, "Exalting Alliance of Contraries"

We see defining itself here another of the work's characteristic requirements. The work is not the deadened unity of repose. It is the intimacy and the violence of contrary movements which are never reconciled and never appeased — never, at least, as long as the work is a work. The work is the intimate confrontation with itself of an opposition between contraries, neither of which, though they are irreconcilable, has coherence except in the contest that opposes them one to the other. The work is this torn intimacy inasmuch as it is the "unfurling" of that which nevertheless hides and remains closed — a light shining on the dark, a light bright from the clarity of this darkness, which abducts and ravishes the dark in the first light of the unfurling, but also disappears into the absolutely obscure whose essence is to close in upon whatever would reveal it, to attract this disclosure into itself and swallow it up. René Char is alluding to this "exalting alliance of contraries" when he says, "The poet is the genesis of a being who projects and of a being who contains." The duality of content and form, of word and idea, is the commonest attempt, based upon the world and the language of the world, to understand the work in the violence which unifies it as the unique event of an essential discord within which only what is in struggle can be grasped and qualified.

Rilke, in the twenty-sixth sonnet (the first part), speaks thus of Orpheus, of the lost and dismembered god:

O you, lost god! you infinite trace!
By dismembering you the hostile forces had to disperse you
To make of us now hearers and a mouth of nature.

The work is Orpheus, but it is also the adverse power which tears it and divides Orpheus. And thus, in the intimacy of this rip, he who produces the work (the creator) originates as he who consecrates, who preserves it by listening to it (the reader). Hearing, speaking are determined in the work at the breach, in the torn unity which alone founds dialogue. The poet only speaks by listening. For he lives in the *separation* where the still wordless rhythm and the voice that says nothing but does not cease to speak must become power to name in him alone who hears it, who is nothing but attunement to it, a mediator capable of informing it. Likewise, he who listens, the "reader," is he by whom the work is spoken anew. Not respoken in an interminable repetition, but maintained in its decisiveness as a new, an initial word.

Hence the dependence of the artist with regard to the work. The strange character of inspiration is linked to this essential anteriority of the poem with respect to the poet. He feels, both in his life and in his work, that he is still to come, still absent when faced with the work which is itself altogether future, the presence and celebration of the future. This dependence is essential. The poet exists only poetically, as the possibility of the poem. And, in this sense, he only exists after it, although he stands uniquely before it. Inspiration is not the gift of the poem to someone existing already, but the gift of existence to someone who does not yet exist. And this existence is manifest as that which keeps steadfastly and altogether outside (hence the *separation* named above), in the permanent leave of absence granted to the self, to every subjective certainty and to the world's truth.

To say that the poet only exists after the poem means that he receives his "reality" from the poem, but that he does not dispose of this reality except in order to make the poem possible. In this sense he does not survive the creation of the work. He lives by dying in it. This also means that the finished poem regards him with indifference; it does not refer to him. He is by no means entitled to be cited and glorified by the poem as its origin. For what is glorified by the work is the work, or art, which the work holds concentrated in itself. And the creator is the one who from then on is dismissed, whose name is erased and whose memory fades. This also means that the creator has no power over his work, that he is dispossessed by it, that in it he is dispossessed of himself. He does not hold its meaning, its privileged secret. It is not incumbent upon him to "read" the poem — that is, to pronounce it anew, to speak it each time as new.

Author and reader are equals with respect to the work and in it. Both are unique. Neither has any existence except through this work and based upon it. The author is not the author in general of various poems, nor is the reader a reader who has a taste for poetry and understands all the great poetic works one after the other. Rather, both are unique. This means that the reader is no less "unique" than the author. For he as well is the one who, each time, speaks the poem as if afresh, not as an echo of the already spoken and already understood.

The Work Says: Beginning

The work, which we identify as the reciprocity in struggle of "the being who projects and the being who contains" (he who hears and he who speaks it), bears within itself the principle that so determines it. This principle lies in the work's torn intimacy: it is the first day of all and yet that very dawn always recaptured by the opaque profundity. This presence of being, the work, is an event. This event does not come to pass outside of time any more than the work is simply spiritual. Rather, through the work there takes place in time another time, and in the world of beings that exist and of things which subsist there comes, as presence, not another world, but the other of all worlds, that which is always other than the world.

It is in view of this claim that the question of the work and its historical duration can be approached. The work is a thing among others, which men use, in which they take interest, of which they make a means and an object of knowledge, of culture and even of vanity. In this capacity the work has a history, and scholars, cultivated men of taste consider it important. They study it, its history, and the history of art which it represents. But in this capacity it is also nothing more than an object, which finally has no value except to our concern for achievements, whose knowledge is a mere form.

The work is not a work when it is only an interesting object of study, a product among other products. In this sense, it has no history. The work is not history's business; rather, history makes it the business of professionals. And yet the work is history; it is an event, *the* event of history itself, and this is because its most steadfast claim is to give to the word *beginning* all its force. Malraux writes, "The work speaks on one day a language it will never speak again, that of its birth." But we must add this: what it says is not only what it is at the moment of being born, when it begins. Always it says, in one guise or another: beginning. It is thus that history belongs to it and that nevertheless it escapes history. In the world where it emerges to proclaim that now there is a work — in the usual time, that is, of current truths — it emerges as the unaccustomed, the unwonted, that which has no relation to this world or with this time. Never is it affirmed on the basis of familiar, present reality. It takes away what is most familiar to us. And always it is in excess: it is the superfluity of what always lacks. We have called this excess poverty the superabundance of refusal.

The work says this word, beginning, and what it claims to give to history is initiative, the possibility of a point of departure. But for its own part it does not begin. It is always anterior to any beginning, it is always already finished. As soon as the truth one thinks one draws from it comes to light, becomes the life and the action of daytime's clarity, the work closes in on itself as if it were a foreigner to this truth and without significance. For the work seems a stranger not only with respect to truths already known and certain; it is not only the scandal of the monstrous and of the nontrue; it always refutes the true, whatever it may be. Even if truth be drawn from the work, the work overturns it, takes it back into itself to bury and hide it. And yet the work says the work *beginning* and it matters greatly to the day. It is the dawning light that precedes the day. It initiates, it enthrones. *"Mystery which enthrones,"* says Char. But in itself it remains mysterious, excluded from the initiation and exiled from the clear truth.

In this sense the work is always original and at all moments a beginning. It is thus that it appears ever new, the mirage of the future's inaccessible truth. And it is new "now," it renews this "now" which it seems to initiate, to render more immediate. And finally it is very old, frightfully ancient, lost in the night of time. It is the origin which always precedes us and is always given before us, for it is the approach of what allows us to depart — a thing of the past, in a different sense from what Hegel said.

The Dialectic of the Work

Only if it is torn unity, always in struggle, never pacified, is the work a work. And only when it becomes light shining from the dark, the unfurling of that which remains closed, is it this torn intimacy. He who, as creator, produces the work by making it present, and the other who, as reader, abides with it to re-produce it, form one aspect of this opposition. But already they elaborate upon it, and they also stabilize it, by subsituting for the exalting contradiction the certainty of separated powers, always ready to forget that they are real only in the exaltation that unites by tearing them asunder. Because it cannot sustain within itself the antagonism which unifies by splitting, the work bears the principle of its ruin. And what ruins it is that it *seems* true. For from this semblance of truth is drawn an active truth and an inactive illusion which is called the beautiful. From this disjunction on, the work becomes a more or less effective reality and an esthetic object.

The reader who is not only a reader but lives and pursues a livelihood in a world where the clear daytime truth is a necessity believes that the work holds the moment of truth within it. But with respect to the truth attributed to it, the work is always what precedes. And it is in this regard always the nontrue, the no in which the true originates. The reader sees in the marvelous clarity of the work, not that which is brought to light by the darkness that withholds it and that hides in it, but that which is clear in itself—meaning: that which is understood and can be taken from the work, separated from it to be enjoyed and used. Thus the reader's dialogue with the work consists increasingly in "raising" it to truth, in transforming it into ordinary language, effective formulae, useful values. The dilettante and the critic, on the other hand, devote themselves to the "beauties" of the work, to its esthetic value; and they believe, as they busy themselves about this empty shell which they consider a disinterested object of interest, that they still partake of the work's reserve.

This transformation is necessarily accomplished at the moment when history becomes purposeful action through and through, commitment to a realized goal.

The Work and the Sacred

But one can also see why it is that in the periods when man is not yet present to himself and when it is the inhuman, the nonpresent, the divine that is present and activating, the work is very close to fulfillment of its requirements, and yet is also hidden and as if unrecognized. When art is the language of the gods, when the temple is the house where the god dwells, the work is invisible and art unknown. The poem names the sacred, and men hear the sacred, not the poem. And yet the poem names the sacred as unnamable; in this silence it speaks the unspeakable. "The branch of the first sun" is wrapped and hidden in the song. The poet transmits it veiled, so that "the fire not seen, undecomposable," might become our common origin (René Char). The poem is thus the veil which makes the fire visible, which reveals it precisely by veiling and concealing it. The poem shows, then; it discloses, but by concealing, because it detains in the dark that which can only be revealed in the light of darkness and keeps this mystery dark even in the light which the dark makes the first dawn of all. The poem is effaced before the sacred which it names; it is the silence that brings to the word the god that speaks in silence—but since the divine is unspeakable and ever speechless, the poem, through the silence of the god which it encloses in language, is also that which speaks as poem, and shows itself, as a work, at the same time that it remains hidden.

The work is thus both hidden in the god's profound presence and visible through the absence and obscurity of the divine. And thus it is the torn intimacy of its own essence. And what it says, when it names the sacred, is the battle of subterranean divinities—the Furies, the "dishonored daughters of Night"—against the gods of light who, in men's name, become guardians of justice. This combat is the struggle of the work's essence itself. And if, through the centuries, art returns from time to time to such myths, this is because it is present there and because there it is present alone, under the veil of the divine.

It seems that there is, with the passage of time, something like a "dialectic" of the work and a transformation of the sense of art. This movement does not correspond to determined historical periods, but it is nevertheless related to different historical forms. Limiting ourselves to a rather imprecise outline, we could say that it is according to this dialectic that the work moves from the erected stone, from the rhythmic and hymnlike cry where it announces the divine and makes the gods real, to the statue where it gives them form, to the productions in which it represents men, before becoming a figure of itself.

Concern for the Origin

The work moves thus from gods to men. It contributes to this movement; for always it pronounces the word *beginning* in a way which is more original than are the worlds, the powers which borrow that word in order to become manifest or to act. Even its alliance with the gods, to whom the work seems so close, is ruinous for the gods. In the work they speak, in the temple they dwell, but the work is also the silence of the gods; it is the oracle where the mystery of the god's silence becomes a mysterious language and the mystery of language. And in the temple the god dwells, but dwells hidden, absent with an impressive absence whose sacred space, manifested by the work—itself at once visible and invisible—is an ambiguous affirmation. The work bespeaks the divine, but only inasmuch as the divine is unspeakable. The work is the presence of the god's absence, and in this absence it tends to make itself present: to become, not Zeus any more, but statue, and no longer the real combat of the Furies and the gods of light, but inspired tragedy. And when the gods are overthrown, the temple does not disappear with them, but, rather, begins to appear. It reveals itself by continuing to be what it was from the first only unknowingly: *the abode of the gods' absence*.

The work is no less dangerous for man. Having subtracted from it the prestige and the immensity of the sacred, he wants to maintain it at his own level, and to affirm *himself* in it as mastery, success, the happy and reasoned accomplishment of purposeful activity. It soon appears that the work of art is by no means mastered by mastery, that it has to do no less with failure than with success, that it is not a thing one can achieve by perseverance, that effort is not honored in it, even when it demands effort, but profoundly denatured. In the work man speaks, but the work gives voice in man to what does not speak: to the unnamable, the inhuman, to what is devoid of truth, bereft of justice, without rights. Here man does not recognize himself; he does not feel justified. No longer is he present, either as man for himself, or before God, or as a god before himself.

Each time the work communicates, behind the gods or in men's name, it is as if to announce a greater beginning. If the gods seem to hold the keys of the origin, if they appear to be the primordial powers from which all emanates, the work, at the same time that it gives them voice, says something more original than they, says their default which is their Destiny—says, before Destiny, the shadow where it subsists making no sign and powerless.

The work was once the language of the gods, their absence's speech; subsequently it was the just, the balanced language of men, and then the language of men in their diversity. Then again it was the language of disinherited men, of those who do not speak. And then it was the language of what does not speak in men, of the secret, of despair or ravishment. What is left now for the work to say? What has always eluded its language? Itself. When all has been said, when the world comes into its own as the truth of the whole, when history wants to culminate in the conclusion of discourse—when the work has nothing more to say and disappears—it is then that it tends to become the language of the work. In the work that has disappeared the work wants to speak, and the experience of the work becomes the search for its essence, the affirmation of art, concern for the origin.

Here again, then, we come to grips with the question that art asks of us today; but we also grasp what is dangerous and precarious in this tendency to come directly into the daylight, this inclination of the work to emerge and make itself visible and present not only in itself but in the experience from which it is born. For what has the outline we have used shown us? What has this grid made visible? Only this: that art is constantly invisible to us. That it is always anterior to what it speaks of and to itself. Nothing is more striking than this movement which always hides the work and makes it all the more powerful in that it is less manifest. It is as if a secret law required of the work that it always be concealed in what it shows and thus that it only show what must remain concealed, and that finally it only show what must stay hidden by concealing it. Why is art so intimately allied with the sacred? It is because in the relation between art and the sacred, between that which shows itself and that which does not — in the movement whereby disclosure and dissimulation change places without cease, appealing and reaching to each other where, nevertheless, they are realized only as the approach of the unreachable — the work finds the profound *reserve* which it needs. It is hidden and preserved by the presence of the god, manifest and apparent through the obscurity of the divine, and again kept safe in reserve by this obscurity and this distance which constitutes its space and to which it gives rise as though thus to come into the light. It is this remove that permits the work to address the world and at the same time to reserve comment, to be the ever reserved beginning of every story. That is why, when the gods depart, it is not only the sense of what made it speak which threatens to fail the work but something much more important: the intimacy of its reserve, the remove which today it cannot locate elsewhere, as it did before the modern age, in nature's secrets, in the obscurity of the world still incompletely explored, not yet altogether explicit.

What will become now of art, now that the gods and even their absence are gone, and now that man's presence offers no support? For at present man no longer belongs to art, committed as he is to self-realization, which is to say to freeing himself from nature and from being through productive undertakings and effective action. And where will art find, elsewhere than in the divine, elsewhere than in the world, the space in which to base and to withhold itself? This too is the question which awakens the work to the experience of its origin, as if, in the search for art, whose essence has become its concern, it hoped henceforth to find its basis and its remove.

The
Original
Experience

Investigations on the subject of art such as those the esthetician pursues bear no relation to the concern for the work of which we speak. Esthetics talks about art, makes of it an object of reflection and of knowledge. Esthetics explains art by reducing it or then again exalts by elucidating it, but in all events art for the esthetician is a present reality around which he constructs plausible thoughts at no risk.

The work is deeply concerned for art. This is to say that for the work, art is never a given, and that the work can find art only by continuing toward its own completion in radical uncertainty, for it cannot know in advance whether art is what it is. As long as the work can serve art by serving other values, these permit the work to find art without having to seek it, and indeed allow that the finding not even be an issue. A work inspired by faith need not (and should not) trouble about itself. It bears witness to this faith, and if it does so poorly, if it fails, faith is not affected. Today the work has no faith other than itself. And this faith is absolute passion for that which depends upon the work alone to give it life. Yet the work by itself can discover only the absence of art. Perhaps the work has the power to present art, but only if it hides from itself that it is seeking by seeking art where the impossible preserves it. And because of this, when the work takes itself to be the task of grasping art in its essence, the impossible is its task, and the work is only realized as an infinite searching. For the characteristic most proper to the origin is to be always veiled by that of which it is the origin.

In advance of a particular work, does art not exist in other works which have already provided illustrious examples? Did Cézanne not think he encountered it in the Venetian paintings at the Louvre? If Rilke honors Hölderlin, does he not count on him for the certainty that the poem, that poetry exists? Perhaps Cézanne knows that art dwells in Venice, but the work of Cézanne does not know this. Cézanne spoke of *realization*, the supreme quality, and believed that thus he represented to himself the essence of Venetian art. But his work cannot hold this "realization" to be essential except by achieving it.

Doubtless one can conceive of such seeking, and describe it and trace the successive steps in what seems to us to be artistic creation. Malraux, for example, has shown that the artist becomes aware of his future work by living in that embodied consciousness of art, so to speak, which the Museum is for him, and which is art, not immobilized in its particular manifestations, but perceived in the changes which make of given works moments in an actual duration, and of art the always incomplete sense of such a movement. This is a significant idea, but mainly it helps us to understand or to imagine how the work is always lacking with respect to itself. For the implication is that, without the collection of all the works which incarnate it in time, art does not exist, yet that art is "true" only in the work always still to come.

The habits of thought which we owe to the commonplaces of subjective art lead us to believe that the artist or writer seeks to express himself and that for him what is missing from the Museum and from literature is he. What torments him, what he strives to fashion into a work, is said to be this expression of himself which he forms by means of an artistic technique.

Is Cézanne's concern to express himself, to give to art, that is, one more artist? He "swore to die painting." Was that just in order to live on? Does he sacrifice himself in this passion which knows no happiness simply so that his paintings might give form to the singular weather of his soul? This much no one can doubt: what he seeks has only one name. Painting. But painting can be found only in the work currently in progress, which demands that he himself exist only in it, and of which all his canvases are only traces, along an infinite road yet to be discovered.

Leonardo da Vinci is another example of this passion which wants to raise the work to the essence of art and which finally perceives in each work only an inconclusive step along the path of a search which we too recognize in the unfinished canvases, the pictures which seem open: this path is now the only essential work. We would certainly misconstrue Leonardo's destiny if we saw him as a painter who did not put his art above everything. He made painting an absolute. Yet it is not his judgments that reveal this to us, not even when he defines painting as "the greatest spiritual process." It is rather his anguish, that fright which seized him each time he put himself in front of a canvas. Because of conditions proper to the Renaissance, the search led Leonardo out of painting. But his was a search for art and art alone. The terror of having to realize the unrealizable, the anguish of painting, caused the search to evolve into forgetfulness of what was sought and into the exploration of a pure, useless knowledge in order that the frightful moment of realization become always more distant until the day when, in his notes, this revealing assertion was inscribed: "One must not desire the impossible." But why is the impossible what the work desires when it has become concern for its own origin?

Risk

In one of Rilke's letters, addressed to Clara Rilke, we find this answer: "Works of art are always the products of a danger incurred, of an experience pursued to the end, to the point where man can no longer continue." The work of art is linked to a risk; it is the affirmation of an extreme experience. But what is this risk? What is the nature of the bond that unites the work to risk?

From the point of view of the work (from the point of view of the requirements which characterize it and which we have described), we clearly see that it demands a sacrifice of him who makes it possible. The poet belongs to the poem; he belongs to it only insofar as he keeps to this free belonging. This relation is not simply the formal devotion which nineteenth-century writers stress. When it is said of the writer that he must live only in order to write well, or of the artist that he must sacrifice everything to the demands of his art, the perilous urgency, the prodigality of the risk which informs the artist's relation to the work is not expressed at all. The scholar too gives himself entirely to his scholarly task. And morality in general, the call of duty, pronounce the same fanatical decree, ultimately calling upon the individual to sacrifice himself and to perish. But the work is not such an unambiguous value demanding of us that we exhaust ourselves for its sake, for love of it, or out of fidelity to the goal it represents to us. If the artist runs a risk, it is because the work itself is essentially a risk. By belonging to the work, it is likewise to risk that he belongs.

In one of the *Sonnets to Orpheus*, Rilke summons us with these words:

We, we infinitely risked.

Why infinitely? Man is the most precarious of all beings, for he jeopardizes himself. The construction of a world, the transformation of nature through productive activity, only succeeds because of a daring challenge in the course of which everything easy is discounted. However, the goal of a protected, a satisfied and secure life also finds expression in this audacity. Precise tasks and reasonable obligations also speak. Man risks his life, but he does so under the protection of the familiar light of day, in view of the useful, the beneficial, and the true. Sometimes, in revolution, in war, under the pressure of history's development he risks his world, but he always does so in the name of a greater possibility, in order to reduce what exceeds his grasp, protect what he is, ensure the values to which his power is attached — in a word, to domesticate the day and extend it or verify it insofar as is possible.

What is the risk proper to the work when the work has the essence of art for its task? But is such a question not surprising in itself? Doesn't the artist appear to be free of life's burdens, and to bear no responsibility for what he creates? Does he not seem to live at his pleasure in the imaginary where, were he to run a risk, it would still be nothing but an image?

Exile

This is true. When Saint-Jean Perse named one of his poems *Exile*, he named the poetic condition as well. The poet is in exile; he is exiled from the city, from regular occupations and limited obligations, from everything connected to results, substantive reality, power. The outward aspect of the risk to which the work exposes him is precisely its inoffensive appearance. The poem is inoffensive, which is to say that whoever submits to it is deprived of himself as power, consents to be cast out from his own capability and from all forms of possibility.

The poem is exile, and the poet who belongs to it belongs to the dissatisfaction of exile. He is always lost to himself, outside, far from home; he belongs to the foreign, to the outside which knows no intimacy or limit, and to the separation which Hölderlin names when in his madness he sees rhythm's infinite space.

Exile, the poem then, makes the poet a wanderer, the one always astray, he to whom the stability of presence is not granted and who is deprived of a true abode. And this must be understood in the gravest sense: the artist does not belong to truth because the work is itself what escapes the movement of the true. For always, whatever our perspective upon it, it revokes the true, eludes signification, designating that region where nothing subsists, where what takes place has nevertheless not taken place, where what begins over has never begun. It points into the realm of the most dangerous indecision, toward the confusion from which nothing emerges. This eternal outside is quite well evoked by the image of the *exterior* darkness where man withstands that which the true must negate in order to become possibility and progress.

Error is the risk which awaits the poet and which, behind him, awaits every man who writes dependent upon an essential work. Error means wandering, the inability to abide and stay. For where the wanderer is, the conditions of a definitive here are lacking. In this absence of here and now what happens does not clearly come to pass as an event based upon which something solid could be achieved. Consequently, what happens does not happen, but does not pass either, into the past; it is never passed. It happens and recurs without cease; it is the horror and the confusion and the uncertainty of eternal repetition. It is not one truth or another that lacks, or truth in general; nor is it doubt that leads us on or despair that immobilizes us. The wanderer's country is not truth, but exile; he lives outside, on the other side which is by no means a beyond, rather the contrary. He remains separated, where the deep of dissimulation reigns, that elemental obscurity through which no way can be made and which because of that makes its awful way through him.

What man risks when he belongs to the work and when the work is the search for art is, then, the most extreme thing he could risk: not just his life, not only the world where he dwells, but his essence, his right to truth, and, even more, his right to death. He departs; he becomes, as Hölderlin calls him, the migrator—he who, like the priests of Dionysos, wanders from country to country in the sacred night. This errant migration can sometimes lead him to insignificance, to the facile contentment of a life crowned with approval, the platitudes of honorific irresponsibility. Sometimes it leads him into wretched vagrancy which is only the instability of a life bereft of a work. And sometimes it takes him to the deep where everything wavers, where everything meaningful is undermined, destabilized, where this upheaval ruins the work and hides in forgetfulness.

In the poem it is not any particular individual who risks himself alone, or a particular mind that is exposed to the touch and the burn of darkness. The risk is more essential. It is the danger of dangers by which, each time, the essence of language is radically placed in doubt. To risk language: this is one of the forms of this risk. To risk being—the word uttered when absence is spoken, and which the work pronounces by pronouncing the word *beginning* — this is the other form of the risk. In the work of art, being is risked. For whereas in the world where beings repel it in order to be, being is always concealed, negated, and denied (and thus protected too), in dissimulation's realm that which is concealed tends, on the contrary, to emerge, deep down in appearance, and that which is negated becomes the excess in affirmation. But this appearance reveals nothing, nothing is affirmed by this affirmation which is only the unstable position from which, if the work succeeds in containing it, the true will be able to take *place*.

The work draws light from the dark; it is a relation with what admits of no relations; it encounters being before the encounter is possible and where truth lacks. This is the essential risk. Here we reach the abyss. Here we bind ourselves, with a bond which cannot be too strong, to the nontrue, and to it we seek to bind an essential form of authenticity. This is what Nietzsche suggests when he says, "We have art so as not to go under [touch the bottom] on account of truth."[4]

He does not mean, as a superficial interpretation would have it, that art is the illusion which protects us against the mortal truth. He says with more certainty: we have art in order that what makes us go all the way to the bottom not belong to the domain of truth. The very bottom, the bottomless abyss belongs to art. And art is that deep which is *sometimes* the absence of profundity, of the foundation, the pure void bereft of importance, and *sometimes* that upon which a foundation can be given, but it is also *always at the same time* one and the other, the intertwining of the Yes and of the No, the ebb and flow of the essential ambiguity. And that is why all works of art and all literary works seem to leave comprehension behind and yet seem never to reach it, so that it must be said of them that they are always understood too much and always too little.

Let us try to investigate with more precision what happens to us because "we have art." And what is necessary in order that we have art? What is the meaning of this possibility? We still barely glimpse the implications of such questions, which have arisen in the work only since it has had art's essence for its task. And do we have art? The question remains undecided from the moment, precisely, when what must speak in the work is its origin.

4"Wir haben die Kunst, damit wir nicht an der Wahrheit zu Grunde gehen."

The Radical Reversal

When a contemporary philosopher names death as man's extreme possibility, the possibility absolutely proper to him, he shows that the origin of possibility is linked in man to the fact that he *can* die, that for him death is yet one possibility more, that the event by which man departs from the possible and belongs to the impossible is nevertheless within his mastery, that it is the extreme moment of his possibility. (And this the philosopher expresses precisely by saying of death that it is "the possibility of impossibility.")[5] Hegel had already seen action, language, liberty, and death to be aspects of one and the same movement; he had shown that only man's constant and resolute proximity to death allows him to become active nothingness capable of negating and transforming natural reality — of combating, of laboring, of knowing, and of being historical. This is a magical force: it is the absolute power of the negative which becomes the action of truth in the world. It brings negation to reality, form to the formless, definition to the indefinite. We want to draw these limits, mark these ends, come to the finish. That is the principle behind civilization's demands, the essence of the purposeful will which seeks achievement, which demands accomplishment and attains universal mastery. Existence is authentic when it is capable of enduring possibility right up to its extreme point, able to stride toward death as toward possibility par excellence. It is to this movement that the essence of man in Western history owes its having become action, value, future, labor and truth. The affirmation that in man all is possibility requires that death itself be possible: death itself, without which man would not be able to form the notion of an "all" or to exist in view of a totality, must be what makes all — what makes totality — possible.

But what is art, and what can we say of literature? The question returns now with a particular violence. If we have art — which is exile from truth, which is the risk of an inoffensive game, which affirms man's belonging to the limitless outside where intimacy is unknown, where he is banished from his capability and from all forms of possibility — how does this come about? How, if he is altogether possibility, can man allow himself anything resembling art? If he has art, does this not mean that, contrary to his apparently authentic definition — the requirement

---

[5]Emmanuel Levinas is the first to have brought out what was at stake in this expression (*Time and the Other*).

which is in harmony with the law of the day — he entertains with death a relation which is not that of possibility, which does not lead to mastery or to understanding or to the progressive achievements of time, but exposes him to a radical reversal? *This reversal*: would it not seem to be the *original experience* which the work must touch, upon which it closes and which constantly threatens to close in upon art and withhold it? The end, in this perspective, would no longer be that which gives man the power to end — to limit, separate, and thus to grasp — but the infinite: the dreadful infinitude on account of which the end can never be overcome. Death, then, would not be "the possibility absolutely proper to man," my own death, that unique event which answers Rilke's prayer: "O Lord, grant to each his own death," but on the contrary, that which never happens to me, so that never do I die, but rather "they die." Men die always other than themselves, at the level of the neutrality and the impersonality of the eternal They.

The characteristics of this reversal can only be recalled briefly here.

They die: this is not a reassuring formula designed to put off the fearsome moment. *They die*: he who dies is anonymous, and anonymity is the guise in which the ungraspable, the unlimited, the unsituated is most dangerously affirmed among us. Whoever experiences this suffers an anonymous, impersonal force, the force of an event which, being the dissolution of every event, is starting over not only now, but was in its very beginning a beginning again. And in its domain everything that happens happens over again. From the instant "they die," the instant is revoked. When someone dies, "when" designates not a particular date but no matter what date. Likewise there is a level of this experience at which death reveals its nature by appearing no longer as the demise of a particular person, or as death in general, but in this neutral form: someone or other's death. Death is always nondescript. Hence the feeling that the special signs of affection which those who were close to a person recently departed still show him are out of place. For now there is no more distinction to be made between close and distant. The only appropriate tears are impersonal ones, the general sadness of official mourners delegated by the indifference of the They. Death is public. If this does not mean that it is the sheer exteriorization which the spectacular side of death as ceremony expresses, one feels nonetheless at such spectacles how much death becomes indistinct and unmasterable *error*, the shifty point from which indetermination condemns time to the exhausting futility of repetition.

The Experience of Art

To the poet, to the artist this summons makes itself heard: "Be dead evermore in Eurydice."[6] This dramatic command apparently implies a reassuring other half: Be dead evermore in Eurydice so as to be alive in Orpheus. Art brings duplicity with it. This duplicity allows it to escape its own risk. It can always extricate itself by transforming the risk into security. Then it partakes of the world — of the world's successes and advantages — without incurring its obligations. Thus does art plunge into the other risk, the one which is without danger, which signifies only the unperceived loss of art, brilliant insignificance, tranquil talk wreathed in honors.

The duplicity cannot be outdone. But it must be suffered in all its depth. The duplicity of the happy dream which invites us to die sadly in Eurydice so as to survive gloriously in Orpheus is concealment concealing itself; it is forgetfulness profoundly forgotten. Yet behind this facile forgetting which arranges for us to obtain the satisfactions of glory, the fundamental duplicity is at work as well. It detaches us from all power. Now the happy dream is not so happy: it turns into a nightmare, it falls away in confusion and misery. The inessential, the complacent lightness becomes the unbearable loss of essence; beauty withers into error, error opens onto exile — onto migration outside, where there is neither intimacy nor rest. *Be dead evermore in Eurydice.* Yes, such is the call, such the command. But deep in this order "dead evermore" is echoed by "alive forever," and here "alive" does not signify life, but — in the guise of a reassuring ambiguity — the loss of the power to die, the loss of death as power and possibility. It signifies the essential sacrifice: the radical reversal which Rilke, who perhaps always sought to outwit it, expresses without grasping all the implications of what he writes, in a letter of January 6, 1923. He asks to see no longer in death something negative, but "das Wort Tod ohne Negation zu lesen." To read the word death *without* negation is to withdraw from it the cutting edge of decision and the power to negate; it is to cut oneself off from possibility and the true, but also from death as true event. It is to surrender to the indistinct and the undetermined, to the emptiness anterior to events, where the end has all the heaviness of starting over.

This experience is the experience of art. Art — as images, as words, and as rhythm — indicates the menacing proximity of a vague and vacant

[7]Rilke, *Sonnets to Orpheus*, XII, Pt. 2.

outside, a neutral existence, nil and limitless; art points into a sordid absence, a suffocating condensation where being ceaselessly perpetuates itself as nothingness.

Art is originally linked to this fund of impotence where everything falls back when the possible is attenuated. In the world, decisive affirmation dependably serves truth as a basis and foundation, as the place from which it can arise. By comparison, art originally represents the scandalous intimation of absolute error: the premonition of something not true but whose "not" does not have the decisive character of a limit, for it is, rather, brimming and endless indeterminacy with which the true cannot communicate. Nor does truth by any means have the power to reconquer it. The true cannot define itself vis-à-vis this "not" except by becoming the violence of the negative.

If the essential task of the true is to negate, this is because error *affirms* in the profuse plenitude which is its preserve outside of time and in all times. This affirmation is the perpetuity of what admits neither of beginning nor of end. It is neither productive nor destructive but stagnant; it is that which has never come, which is neither staunched nor spurting forth but coming back — the eternal lapping of return. It is in this sense that in art's milieu there is a pact contracted with death, with repetition, and with failure. Beginning again, repetition, the fatal return — everything evoked by experiences where estrangement is allied with the strangely familiar, where the irremediable takes the form of an endless repetition, where the same is posed in the dizziness of redoubling, where there is no cognition but only *re*cognition — all this alludes to that initial error which might be expressed as follows: what is first is not beginning, but beginning over, and being is precisely the *impossibility* of being for the first time.

One could bring this movement more sharply into focus — but not explain it — by evoking those forms and those crises called "complexes." Their essence is that at the moment they come about they have already done so: they only ever return. This is their characteristic feature. They are the experience of beginning again. "Again, again!" is the cry of anguish struggling with the irremediable, with being. Again, again, such is the closed wound of the complex. It takes place again, it recurs, yet another time. The basis of failure lies, not in the fact that an experience meets with no success, but in its beginning all over again. Everything begins again always — yes, one more time, again, again.

Some time ago now, Freud, surprised by the tendency to repeat, the powerful call of the anterior, recognized in it the call of death itself.

But perhaps what must finally come out is this: he who seeks in death the meaning of repetition is also led to ruin death as possibility—to bind it in repetition's spell. Yes, we are tied to disaster, but when failure returns, it must be understood as nothing but the return. The power that begins everything over again is older than the beginning: this is the error of our death.

A Return to the Question

We come here to the point where the question which has been asked of us makes the contradiction, to which every answer returns, emerge in all its force. What the work says is the word *beginning*. But today the work is the work of art: art is its starting point. And it says "the beginning" when it says "art," which is its origin and whose essence has become its task. But where has art led us? To a time before the world, before the beginning. It has cast us out of our power to begin and to end; it has turned us toward the outside where there is no intimacy, no place to rest. It has led us into the infinite migration of error. For we seek art's essence, and it lies where the nontrue admits of nothing essential. We appeal to art's sovereignty: it ruins the kingdom. It ruins the origin by returning to it the errant immensity of directionless eternity. The work says the word *beginning* from a starting point—art—which is complicit with the futility of starting over. The work declares being—and says choice, mastery, form—by announcing art which says the fatality of being, says passivity and formless prolixity. At the very moment of the choice art still holds us back in a primordial Yes and No. There, before any beginning, the somber ebb and flow of dissimulation rumbles.

Such is the question. It asks not to be overcome. That the work is able to pronounce the work *beginning* precisely because the origin attracts it to the place where it risks utter ruin, and because, precisely, it must escape *with a leap* the implacable insistence of something having neither beginning nor end: this might well be said. And likewise this: that the work is this leap and that it immobilizes itself mysteriously between the truth which does not belong to it and the prolixity of the unrevealable which would prevent it from belonging to itself—that it hovers between death as the possibility of understanding and death as the horror of impossibility. Moreover, the work's successful completion so close to the indefinite and the formless glorifies the proportion in it and makes its coherence, exactitude, and limit all the more impressive. Indeed, all this can be said. And it would all form the elements of an answer. But what does the answer mean as long as in it there remains this question: Do we have art? To this query there can be no decisive answer, at least not to the extent that the work's origin is its concern and that its task is the essence of what verges on the inessential.

We asked ourselves: "Why, when history contests it, does art tend to become essential presence?" What does this presence mean? Is it only the artistic form of what contests art, the affirmation of art's poverty reversed? Or does the desolate voice which asks, "What use are poets in time of distress?" — does the distress toward which this question points mysteriously — express the essence of art more profoundly, so that in such a presence art could no longer be anything, save its own absence? But what is the time of distress?

This expression is borrowed from the elegy *Bread and Wine* by Hölderlin:

> In these times, very often it seems to me
> Better to sleep than to be so without companions
> And to wait so; what is there to do in these times, what to say?
> I do not know; what use are poets in time of distress?[7]

What is this time during which, as René Char says as well, "the sole certainty which we possess of tomorrow's reality . . . the perfected form of the secret where we come to refresh ourselves, take precautions and sleep"? What is this time when poetry can only say: *what use are poets?* The elegy answers us with these other lines which precede a bit those we have just cited:

> From time to time man bears the divine plenitude.
> A dream of these times, that is what life is afterwards. But error
> Helps, like sleep, and distress makes us strong as does night.

It seems that art owes the strangest of torments and the very grave passion that animate it to the disappearance of the historical forms of the divine. Art was the language of the gods. The gods having disappeared, it became the language in which their disappearance was ex-

---

[7] *In dürftiger Zeit.* The German expression is tougher and drier than the French [*au temps de détresse*]. It announces that toughness, that rigor with which the late Hölderlin defends himself against his yearning for the gods who have withdrawn, and maintains the distinction between the spheres — the one above and the one here below. With this distinction, Hölderlin maintains the purity of the sacred realm left empty by the double infidelity of men and gods. For the sacred is this very void, the sheer void of the interval which must be kept pure and empty according to the ultimate requirement: "Preserve God with the purity of what distinguishes." (On this subject, which is central, see in the Appendixes the pages entitled *Hölderlin's Itinerary.*)

pressed, then the language in which this disappearance itself ceased to appear. This forgetfulness now speaks all alone. The deeper the forgetfulness, the more the deep speaks in this language, and the more the abyss of this deepness can become the hearing of the word.

Forgetting, error, the unhappiness of erring can be linked to an historical period: to the time of distress when the gods are absent twice over, because they are no longer there, because they are not there yet. This vacant time is that of error, where we do nothing but err because we lack the certitude of presence and the conditions of a true here. And nevertheless error helps us, "das Irrsal hilft." Elsewhere, in the variant of the poem *Dichterberuf,* Hölderlin says likewise that God's lack, his default helps us: "Gottes Fehl hilft." What does this mean?

The force, the risk proper to the poet is to dwell in God's default, the region where truth lacks. *The time of distress* designates the time which in all times is proper to art. But when historically the gods lack and the world of truth wavers, the time of distress emerges in the work as concern — the concern in which the work finds its preserve — threatening it: making it present and visible. The time of art is the time before time. The collective presence of the divine evokes this time by hiding it; history and the productive movement of history revoke it by denying it, and the work shows it, in the distress of the *What use?* as that which hides deep down in appearance, reappears in the heart of disappearance, comes to pass in the proximity and under the threat of a radical reversal, the reversal at work when "they die." Perpetuating being in the form of nothingness, this reversal changes light into fascination, the object into the image, and it makes us into the empty center of eternal repetition.

And yet "error helps us." It is the intimation in waiting, the deep of sleep keeping watch, the silent void of sacred memory. The poet is the intimacy of distress. He alone profoundly lives the empty time of absence, and in him error becomes straying's profundity, night becomes the *other* night. But what does this mean? When René Char writes, "May risk light your way"; when Georges Bataille, comparing fortune and poetry says, "The absence of poetry is misfortune"; when Hölderlin calls the empty, distressful present "bountiful suffering, bountiful happiness," what is seeking to express itself in these words? Why should our light come from risk? Why should the time of distress be the fortunate time? When Hölderlin speaks of poets who, like the priests of Bacchus, go wandering from country to country in the sacred night, is this perpetual departure, the *sorrow of straying* which has no place to arrive, to rest, also the *fecund migration*, the movement which mediates, that which makes of rivers a language and of language the dwelling, the power by which day abides and is our abode?

So then, is the work really the marvel of the beginning, in which error's indefiniteness would preserve us from inauthenticity's fraud? And is the nontrue an essential form of authenticity?[8] In that case, we do, then, have the work? We have art?

To this question there can be no response. The poem is the answer's absence. The poet is one who, through his sacrifice, keeps the question open in his work. At every time he lives the time of distress, and his time is always the empty time when what he must live is the double infidelity: that of men, that of the gods — and also the double absence of the gods who are no longer *and* who are not yet. The poem's space is entirely represented by this *and*, which indicates the double absence, the separation at its most tragic instant. But as for whether it is the *and* that unites and binds together, the pure word in which the void of the past and the void of the future become true presence, the "now" of dawn — this question is reserved in the work. It is that which reveals itself in the work by returning to concealment, to the distress of forgetting. That is why the poem is solitude's poverty. This solitude is a grasp of the future, but a powerless grasp: prophetic isolation which, before time, ever announces the beginning.

[8]To present this question in a context closer to historical actuality, one might say: the more the world is affirmed as the future and the broad daylight of truth, where everything will have value, bear meaning, where the whole will be achieved under the mastery of man and for his use, the more it seems that art must descend toward that point where nothing has meaning yet, the more it matters that art maintain the movement, the insecurity and the grief of that which escapes every grasp and all ends. The artist and the poet seem to have received this mission: to call us obstinately back to error, to turn us toward that space where everything we propose, everything we have acquired, everything we are, all that opens upon the earth and in the sky, returns to insignificance, and where what approaches is the nonserious and the nontrue, as if perhaps thence sprang the source of all authenticity.

Appendixes

The
Essential
Solitude and
Solitude in
the World

When I am alone, it is not I who am there, and it is not from you that I stay away, or from others, or from the world. I am not the subject to whom this impression of solitude would come — this awareness of my limits; it is not that I tire of being myself. When I am alone, I am not there. This is not a sign of some psychological state, indicating loss of consciousness, the disappearance of my right to feel what I feel from a center which I myself would be. What approaches me is not my being a little less myself, but rather something which there is "behind me," and which this "me" conceals in order to come into its own.

When I am on *the worldly plane*, which I share with things and beings, being is profoundly hidden. (It is the thought of this concealment that Heidegger urges us to welcome.) This dissimulation can become real action, negation. "I am" (in the world) tends to signify that I am only if I can separate myself from being. We negate being — or, to elucidate this by means of a particular example, we negate, we transform nature. In this negation which is action and which is time, beings are brought to fruition, and men stand forth erect in the liberty of the "I am." What makes me me is this decision to be by being separate from being — to be *without* being, to be that which owes nothing to being, whose power comes from the refusal to be. I decide to be absolutely "denatured," the absolutely separated: that is, the absolutely absolute.

However, the power with which I affirm myself by denying being, is real only in the all-encompassing community of men, the shared movement of projects actively undertaken and of time's progress. "I am" — the decision, that is, to be without being — has true meaning only because it is my decision based upon the whole of humanity, or because, in other words, this decision is taken within the movement which it makes possible and which makes it real. This reality is always historical. It is the world which is always the process of the world's own realization.

Yet it happens that this decision which causes me to be outside of being (which illuminates the refusal to be by concentrating it in that unique flash of lightning, the point at which "I am") — it happens that this masterful possibility to be free from being, separated *from* being, also becomes the separation *of* beings: the absoluteness of an "I am" that wants to affirm itself without reference to others. This is what is generally called solitude (as the world understands this term). It can be experienced as the pride of solitary mastery, the cultivation of differences, subjectivity breaking the dialectical tension through which it is realized. Or solitude may disclose the nothingness that founds the "I am." Then the solitary "I" sees that it is separated, but is no longer able to recognize in this separation the source of its power. It can no longer make of separation the means of action and productive undertakings, the expression and the truth which found all exterior communication.

No doubt this latter experience is the cause generally attributed to the anguish of the great upheaval. Man becomes aware of himself as separated, absent from being; he becomes conscious of the fact that he owes his essence to his not being. But however critical this may be, it still hides the essential. That I am nothing certainly implies that "I hold myself back within nothingness," and this is black and agonizing, but it also implies this marvel: that nothingness is my power, that I *can* not be. Hence man's liberty, his mastery, and his future.

I am he who is not, he who has seceded — the separated one, or as it is said, the one in whom being is brought into question. Men affirm themselves by means of the power not to be: thus do they act, speak, comprehend always other than they are, escaping being by defying it — by way of a risk, a struggle which continues even unto death, and which is history. This is what Hegel has shown. "The life of the mind begins with death." When death becomes power, then man begins, and this beginning rules that, in order for there to be a world, in order for there to be beings, being must lack.

What does this signify?

When being lacks, when nothingness becomes power, man is fully historical. But when being lacks, is there a lack of being? When being lacks, does this mean that this lack owes nothing to being? Or rather does it mean perhaps that the lack is the being that lies deep in the absence of being — that the lack is what still remains of being when there is nothing? When being lacks, it is still only profoundly concealed. He who approaches this lack — this lack which is present in the "essential solitude" — is approached by the being which the absence of being makes present. This is no longer concealed being, but the being *of this concealment*: dissimulation itself.

Here it certainly seems we have taken one more step toward what we seek. In the tranquility of ordinary life, dissimulation is hidden. In action, true action — the action which is history's laborious unfolding — concealment tends to become negation (the negative is our task, and this task is the task of truth). But in what we call the essential solitude, concealment tends to appear.

When beings lack, being appears as the depth of the concealment in which it becomes lack. When concealment appears, concealment, having become appearance, makes "everything disappear," but of this "everything has disappeared" it makes another appearance. It makes appearance from then on stem from "everything has disappeared." "Everything has disappeared" appears. This is exactly what we call an *apparition*. It is the "everything has disappeared" appearing in its turn. And the *apparition* says precisely that when everything has disappeared, there still is something: when everything lacks, lack makes the essence of being appear, and the essence of being is to be there still where it lacks, to be inasmuch as it is hidden . . .

The
Two Versions
of the Imaginary

But what is the image? When there is nothing, the image finds in this nothing its necessary condition, but there it disappears. The image needs the neutrality and the fading of the world; it wants everything to return to the indifferent deep where nothing is affirmed; it tends toward the intimacy of what still subsists in the void. This is its truth. But this truth exceeds it. What makes it possible is the limit where it ceases. Hence its critical aspect, the dramatic ambiguity it introduces and the brilliant lie for which it is reproached. It is surely a splendid power, Pascal says, which makes of eternity a nothing and of nothingness an eternity.

The image speaks to us, and seems to speak intimately to us of ourselves. But the term "intimately" does not suffice. Let us say rather that the image intimately designates the level where personal intimacy is destroyed and that it indicates in this movement the menacing proximity of a vague and empty outside, the deep, the sordid basis upon which it continues to affirm things in their disappearance. Thus it speaks to us, à propos of each thing, of less than this thing, but of us. And, speaking of us, it speaks to us of less than us, of that less than nothing that subsists when there is nothing.

The gratifying aspect of the image is that it constitutes a limit at the edge of the indefinite. This fine line does not hold us at a distance from things so much as it preserves us from the blind pressure of this distance. Thanks to the image, the remove is at our command. Because of the inflexibility of the reflection, we think ourselves masters of absence which has become interval, and the dense void itself seems to open onto the radiance of another day.

In this way the image fulfills one of its functions which is to quiet, to humanize the formless nothingness pressed upon us by the indelible residue of being. The image cleanses this residue — appropriates it, makes it pleasing and pure, and allows us to believe, dreaming the happy dream which art too often authorizes, that, separated from the real and immediately behind it, we find, as pure pleasure and superb satisfaction, the transparent eternity of the unreal.

"For in that sleep of death what dreams may come," says Hamlet, "when we have shuffled off this mortal coil . . ." The image, present behind each thing, and which is like the dissolution of this thing and its subsistence in its dissolution, also has behind it that heavy sleep of death in which dreams threaten. The image can, when it awakens or when we waken it, represent the object to us in a luminous *formal* aura; but it is nonetheless with *substance* that the image is allied — with the fundamental materiality, the still undetermined absence of form, the world oscillating between adjective and substantive before foundering in the formless prolixity of indetermination. Hence the passivity proper to the image — a passivity which makes us suffer the image even when we ourselves appeal to it, and makes its fugitive transparency stem from the obscurity of fate returned to its essence, which is to be a shade.

But when we are face to face with things themselves — if we fix upon a face, the corner of a wall — does it not also sometimes happen that we abandon ourselves to what we see? Bereft of power before this presence suddenly strangely mute and passive, are we not at its mercy? Indeed, this can happen, but it happens because the thing we stare at has foundered, sunk into its image, and the image has returned into that deep fund of impotence to which everything reverts. The "real" is defined by our relation to it which is always alive. The real always leaves us the initiative, addressing in us that power to begin, that free communication with the beginning which we are. And as long as we are in the day, day is still just dawning.

The image, according to the ordinary analysis, is secondary to the object. It is what follows. We see, then we imagine. After the object comes the image. "After" means that the thing must first take itself off a ways in order to be grasped. But this remove is not the simple displacement of a moveable object which would nevertheless remain the same. Here the distance is in the heart of the thing. The thing was there; we grasped it in the vital movement of a comprehensive action — and lo, having become image, instantly it has become that which no one can grasp, the unreal, the impossible. It is not the same thing at a distance but the thing as distance, present in its absence, graspable because ungraspable, appearing as disappeared. It is the return of what does not come back, the strange heart of remoteness as the life and the sole heart of the thing.

In the image, the object again grazes something which it had dominated in order to be an object — something counter to which it had defined and built itself up. Now that its value, its meaning is suspended, now that the world abandons it to idleness and lays it aside, the truth in it ebbs, and materiality, the elemental, reclaims it. This impoverishment, or enrichment, consecrates it as image.

However: does the reflection not always appear more refined than the object reflected? Isn't the image the ideal expression of the object, its presence liberated from existence? Isn't the image form without matter? And isn't the task of artists, who are exiled in the illusory realm of images, to idealize beings — to elevate them to their disembodied resemblance?

The Image, the Remains

The image does not, at first glance, resemble the corpse, but the cadaver's strangeness is perhaps also that of the image. What we call mortal remains escapes common categories. Something is there before us which is not really the living person, nor is it any reality at all. It is neither the same as the person who was alive, nor is it another person, nor is it anything else. What is there, with the absolute calm of something that has found its place, does not, however, succeed in being convincingly here. Death suspends the relation to place, even though the deceased rests heavily in his spot as if upon the only basis that is left him. To be precise, this basis lacks, the place is missing, the corpse is not in its place. Where is it? It is not here, and yet it is not anywhere else. Nowhere? But then nowhere is here. The cadaverous presence establishes a relation between here and nowhere. The quiet that must be preserved in the room where someone dies and around the deathbed gives a first indication of how fragile the position par excellence is. The corpse is here, but here in its turn becomes a corpse: it becomes "here below" in absolute terms, for there is not yet any "above" to be exalted. The place where someone dies is not some indifferent spot. It seems inappropriate to transport the body from one place to another. The deceased cleaves jealously to his place, joining it profoundly, in such a way that the indifference of this place, the fact that it is after all just a place among others, becomes the profundity of his presence as deceased —

becomes the basis of indifference, the gaping intimacy of an undifferentiable nowhere which must nevertheless be located here.

He who dies cannot tarry. The deceased, it is said, is no longer of this world; he has left it behind. But behind there is, precisely, this cadaver, which is not of the world either, even though it is here. Rather, it is behind the world. It is that which the living person (and not the deceased) left behind him and which now affirms, from here, the possibility of a world behind the world, of a regression, an indefinite subsistance, undetermined and indifferent, about which we only know that human reality, upon finishing, reconstitutes its presence and its proximity. This is an impression which could be said to be common. He who just died is at first extremely close to the condition of a thing—a familiar thing, which we approach and handle, which does not hold us at a distance and whose manageable passivity betrays only sad impotence. Certainly dying is an incomparable event, and he who dies "in your arms" is in a sense your brother forever. But now, he is dead. And as we know, certain tasks must be performed quickly, not so much because death's rigor will soon make these actions more difficult, but because human action will shortly be "displaced." Presently, there will be—immoveable, untouchable, riveted to here by the strangest embrace and yet drifting with it, drawing here under, bearing it lower—from behind there will be no longer an inanimate thing, but Someone: the unbearable image and figure of the unique becoming nothing in particular, no matter what.

The Cadaverous Resemblance

When this moment has come, the corpse appears in the strangeness of its solitude as that which has disdainfully withdrawn from us. Then the feeling of a relation between humans is destroyed, and our mourning, the care we take of the dead and all the prerogatives of our former passions, since they can no longer know their direction, fall back upon us, return toward us. It is striking that at this very moment, when the cadaverous presence is the presence of the unknown before us, the mourned deceased begins to *resemble himself.*

Himself: is this not an ill-chosen expression? Shouldn't we say: the deceased resembles the person he was when he was alive? "Resembles himself" is, however, correct. "Himself" designates the impersonal being, distant and inaccessible, which resemblance, that it might be someone's, draws toward the day. Yes, it is he, the dear living person, but all the same it is more than he. He is more beautiful, more imposing; he is already monumental and so absolutely himself that it is as if he were *doubled* by himself, joined to his solemn impersonality by resemblance and by the image. This magnified being, imposing and proud, which impresses the living as the appearance of the original never perceived until now — this sentence of the last judgment inscribed deep within being and triumphantly expressing itself with the aid of the remote — this grandeur, through its appearance of supreme authority, may well bring to mind the great images of classical art. If this connection is justified, the question of classical art's idealism will seem rather vain. And we might bear in mind the thought that idealism has, finally, no guarantee other than a corpse. For this indicates to what extent the apparent intellectual refinement, the pure virginity of the image is originally linked to the elemental strangeness and to the formless weight of being, present in absence.

Let us look again at this splendid being from which beauty streams: he is, I see this, perfectly like himself: he resembles *himself.* The cadaver is its own image. It no longer entertains any relation with this world, where it still appears, except that of an image, an obscure possibility, a shadow ever present behind the living form which now, far from separating itself from this form, transforms it entirely into shadow. The corpse is a reflection becoming master of the life it reflects — absorbing it, identifying substantively with it by moving it from its use value and from its truth value to something incredible — something neutral which there is no getting used to. And if the cadaver is so similar, it is because it is, at a certain moment, similarity par excellence: altogether similarity, and also nothing more. It is the likeness, like to an absolute degree, overwhelming and marvelous. But what is it like? Nothing.

That is why no man alive, in fact, bears any resemblance yet. In the rare instances when a living person shows similitude with himself, he only seems to us more remote, closer to a dangerous neutral region, *astray* in *himself* and like his own ghost already: he seems to return no longer having any but an echo life.

By analogy, we might also recall that a tool, when damaged, becomes its *image* (and sometimes an esthetic object like "those outmoded objects, fragmented, unusable, almost incomprehensible, perverse," which André Breton loved). In this case the tool, no longer disappearing into its use, *appears.* This appearance of the object is that of resemblance and reflection: the object's double, if you will. The category of art is linked to this possibility for objects to "appear," to surrender, that is, to the pure and simple resemblance behind which there is nothing — but being. Only that which is abandoned to the image appears, and everything that appears is, in this sense, imaginary.

The cadaverous resemblance haunts us. But its haunting presence is not the unreal visitation of the ideal. What haunts us is something inaccessible from which we cannot extricate ourselves. It is that which cannot be found and therefore cannot be avoided. What no one can grasp is the inescapable. The fixed image knows no repose, and this is above all because it poses nothing, establishes nothing. Its fixity, like that of the corpse, is the position of what stays with us because it has no place. (The idée fixe is not a point of departure, a position from which one could start off and progress, it is not a beginning, it begins again.) We dress the corpse, and we bring it as close as possible to a normal appearance by effacing the hurtful marks of sickness, but we know that in its ever so peaceful and secure immobility it does not rest. The place which it occupies is drawn down by it, sinks with it, and in this dissolution attacks the possibility of a *dwelling place* even for us who remain. We know that at "a certain moment" the power of death makes it keep no longer to the handsome spot assigned it. No matter how calmly the corpse has been laid out upon its bed for final viewing, it is also everywhere in the room, all over the house. At every instant it can be elsewhere than where it is. It is where we are apart from it, where there is nothing; it is an invading presence, an obscure and vain abundance. The belief that at a certain moment the deceased begins to wander, to stray from his place, must be understood as stemming from the premonition of the *error* which now he represents.

Eventually we have to put a term to the interminable. We do not cohabit with the dead for fear of seeing *here* collapse into the unfathomable *nowhere* — a fall the House of Usher illustrated. And so the dear departed is conveyed into another place. No doubt this site is only symbolically set apart; doubtless it is by no means really unsituatable. But it is nevertheless true that the here of the *here lies*, filled in by names, well-formed phrases and affirmations of identity, is the anonymous and impersonal place par excellence. And it is as though, within the limits which have been traced for it and in the vain guise of a will capable of surviving everything, the monotony of an infinite disintegration were at work to efface the living truth proper to every place and make it equivalent to the absolute neutrality of death.

(Perhaps this slow disappearance, this unending erosion of the end, sheds some light upon the remarkable passion of certain murderesses who kill with poison. Their joy is not to cause suffering, or even to kill slowly or surreptitiously, but, by poisoning time, by transforming it into an imperceptible consumption, to touch upon the indefinite which is death. Thus they graze the horror, they live furtively underneath everything living in a pure decomposition which nothing divulges, and the poison is the colorless substance of this eternity. Feuerbach recounts of one such murderess that the poison was a friend for her, a companion to whom she felt passionately drawn. When, after a poisoning that lasted several months, she was presented with a packet of arsenic which belonged to her, so that she would recognize it, she trembled with joy—she had a moment of ecstasy.)

The Image and Signification

Man is made in his image: this is what the strangeness of the cadaver's resemblance teaches us. But this formula must first be understood as follows: *man is unmade according to his image.* The image has nothing to do with signification or meaningfulness as they are implied by the world's existence, by effort that aims at truth, by law and the light of day. Not only is the *image* of an object not the *sense* of this object, and not only is it of no avail in understanding the object, it tends to withdraw the object from understanding by maintaining it in the immobility of a resemblance which has nothing to resemble.

Granted, we can always recapture the image and make it serve the world's truth. But in that case we reverse the relation which is proper to it. The image becomes the object's aftermath, that which comes later, which is left over and allows us still to have the object at our command when there is nothing left of it. This is a formidable resource, reason's fecund power. Practical life and the accomplishment of true tasks require this reversal. So too does classical art, at least in theory, for it stakes all its glory upon linking a figure to resemblance and the image to a body—upon reincorporating the image. The image, then, became life-giving negation, the ideal operation by which man, capable of negating nature, raises it to a higher meaning, either in order to know it or to enjoy it admiringly. Thus was art at once ideal and true, faithful to the figure and faithful to the truth which admits of no figure. Impersonality, ultimately, authenticated works. But impersonality was also the troubling intersection where the noble ideal concerned with values on the one hand, and on the other, anonymous, blind, impersonal resemblance changed places, each passing for the other, each one the other's dupe. "What vanity is painting which wins admiration for its resemblance to things we do not admire in the original!" What could be more striking than Pascal's strong distrust of resemblance, which he suspects delivers things to the sovereignty of the void and to the vainest persistence — to an eternity which, as he says, is nothingness, the nothingness which is eternal.

The Two Versions

Thus the image has two possibilities: there are two versions of the imaginary. And this duplicity comes from the intial double meaning which the power of the negative brings with it and from the fact that death is sometimes truth's elaboration in the world and sometimes the perpetuity of that which admits neither beginning nor end.

It is very true then, that as contemporary philosophies would have it, comprehension and knowing in man are linked to what we call finitude; but where is the finish? Granted, it is taken in or understood as the possibility which is death. But it is also "taken back" by this possibility inasmuch as in death the possibility which is death dies too. And it also seems — even though all of human history signifies the hope of overcoming this ambiguity — that to resolve or transcend it always involves the greatest dangers. It is as if the choice between death as understanding's possibility and death as the horror of impossibility had also to be the choice between sterile truth and the prolixity of the non-true. It is as if comprehension were linked to penury and horror to fecundity. Hence the fact that the ambiguity, although it alone makes choosing possible, always remains present in the choice itself.

But how then is the *ambiguity* manifested? What happens, for example, when one lives an event as an image?

To live an event as an image is not to remain uninvolved, to regard the event disinterestedly in the way that the esthetic version of the image and the serene ideal of classical art propose. But neither is it to take part freely and decisively. It is to be taken: to pass from the region of the real where we hold ourselves at a distance from things the better to order and use them into that other region where the distance holds us — the distance which then is the lifeless deep, an unmanageable, inappreciable remoteness which has become something like the sovereign power behind all things. This movement implies infinite degrees. Thus psychoanalysis maintains that the image, far from abstracting us and causing us to live in the mode of gratuitous fantasy, seems to deliver us profoundly to ourselves. The image is intimate. For it makes of our intimacy an exterior power which we suffer passively. Outside of us, in the ebb of the world which it causes, there trails, like glistening debris, the utmost depth of our passions.

Magic gets its power from this transformation. Its aim, through a methodical technique, is to arouse things as reflections and to thicken consciousness into a thing. From the moment we are outside ourselves — in that ectasy which is the image — the "real" enters an equivocal realm where there is no longer any limit or interval, where there are no more successive moments, and where each thing, absorbed in the void of its reflection, nears consciousness, while consciousness allows itself to become filled with an anonymous plenitude. Thus the universal unity seems to be reconstituted. Thus, behind things, the soul of each thing obeys charms which the ecstatic magician, having abandoned himself to "the universe," now controls. The paradox of magic is evident: it claims to be initiative and free domination, all the while accepting, in order to constitute itself, the reign of passivity, the realm where there are no ends. But its intention remains instructive: what it wants is to act upon the world (to maneuver it) from the standpoint of being that precedes the world — from the eternal before, where action is impossible. That is why it characteristically turns toward the cadaver's strangeness and why its only serious name is black magic.

To live an event as an image is not to see an image of this event, nor is it to attribute to the event the gratuitous character of the imaginary. The event really takes place — and yet does it "really" take place? The occurrence commands us, as we would command the image. That is, it releases us, from it and from ourselves. It keeps us outside; it makes of this outside a presence where "I" does not recognize "itself." This movement implies infinite degrees. We have spoken of two versions of the imaginary: the image can certainly help us to grasp the thing ideally, and in this perspective it is the life-giving negation of the thing; but at the level to which its particular weight drags us, it also threatens constantly to relegate us, not to the absent thing, but to its absence as presence, to the neutral double of the object in which all belonging to the world is dissipated. This duplicity, we must stress, is not such as to be mastered by the discernment of an either-or in it that could authorize a choice and lift from the choice the ambiguity that makes choosing possible. The duplicity itself refers us back to a still more primal double meaning.

The Levels of Ambiguity

If for a moment thought could maintain ambiguity, it would be tempted to state that there are three levels at which ambiguity is perceptible. On the worldly plane it is the possibility of give and take: meaning always escapes into another meaning; thus misunderstandings serve comprehension by expressing the truth of intelligibility which rules that we never come to an understanding once and for all.

Another level is expressed by the two versions of the imaginary. Here it is no longer a question of perpetual double meanings — of misunderstandings aiding or impeding agreement. Here what speaks in the name of the image "sometimes" still speaks of the world, and "sometimes" introduces us into the undetermined milieu of fascination. "Sometimes" it gives us the power to control things in their absence and through fiction, thus maintaining us in a domain rich with meaning; but "sometimes" it removes us to where things are perhaps present, but in their image, and where the image is passivity, where it has no value either significative or affective, but is the passion of indifference. However, what we distinguish by saying "sometimes, sometimes," ambiguity introduces by "always," at least to a certain extent, saying both one and the other. It still proposes the significant image from the center of fascination, but it already fascinates us with the clarity of the purest, the most formal image. Here *meaning* does not escape into another meaning, but into the *other* of all meaning. Because of ambiguity nothing has meaning, but everything *seems* infinitely meaningful. Meaning is no longer anything but semblance; semblance makes meaning become infinitely rich. It makes this infinitude of meaning have no need of development — it makes meaning immediate, which is also to say incapable of being developed, only immediately void.[1]

---

[1]Can we go further? Ambiguity defines being in terms of its dissimulation; it says that being is, inasmuch as it is concealed. In order for being to accomplish its work, it has to be hidden: it proceeds by hiding itself, it is always reserved and preserved by dissimulation, but also removed from it. Dissimulation tends, then, to become the purity of negation. But at the same time, when everything is hidden, ambiguity announces (and this announcement is ambiguity itself) that the whole of being *is* via dissimulation; that being is essentially its being at the heart of concealment.

Sleep,
Night

What happens at night? Generally we sleep. By means of sleep, day uses night to blot out the night. Sleep belongs to the world; it is a task. We sleep in accord with the general law which makes our daytime activity depend on our nightly repose. We call upon sleep and it comes. There is between sleep and us something like a pact, a treaty with no secret clauses, and according to this convention it is agreed that, far from being a dangerous, bewitching force, sleep will become domesticated and serve as the instrument of our power to act. We surrender to sleep, but in the way that the master entrusts himself to the slave who serves him. Sleeping is the clear action which promises us to the day. To sleep: admire this remarkable act of vigilance. Only deep sleep lets us escape what there is in the deep of sleep. Where is night? There is no longer any night.

Sleeping is an event which belongs to history, just as rest on the seventh day belongs to creation. Night, when men transform it into pure sleep, is not a nocturnal affirmation. I sleep. The sovereignty of the "I" dominates this absence which it grants itself and which is its doing. I sleep: it is I who sleep and none other — and men of action, the great men of history, are proud of their perfect sleep from which they

---

So ambiguity does not consist only in the incessant movement by which being returns to nothingness and nothingness refers back to being. Ambiguity is no longer the primordial Yes and No in which being and nothingness would be pure identity. The essential ambiguity would lie, rather, in this: that before the beginning, nothingness is not on equal standing with being, but is only the *appearance* of being's concealment, or again, that dissimulation is more "original" than negation. So, one could say: *ambiguity is all the more essential because dissimulation cannot quite be captured in negation.*

arise intact. This is why the sleep which in the normal pursuits of our life sometimes takes us by surprise is by no means a scandal. Our capacity to withdraw from everyday bustle, from daily concerns, from everything, from ourselves and even from the void is the sign of our mastery, an entirely human proof of our *sangfroid*. You must sleep: this is the watchword which consciousness assigns itself, and this commandment to renounce the day is one of day's first rules.

Sleep transforms night into possibility. Vigilance is sleep when night falls. Whoever does not sleep cannot stay awake. Vigilance consists in not always keeping watch, for it seeks *awakening* as its essence. Nocturnal wandering, the tendency to stray when the world is attenuated and grows distant, and even the honest professions which are necessarily practiced at night attract suspicions. To sleep with open eyes is an anomaly symbolically indicating something which the general consciousness does not approve of. People who sleep badly always appear more or less guilty. What do they do? They make night present.

Bergson said that sleep is disinterestedness. Perhaps sleep is inattention to the world, but this negation of the world conserves us for the world and affirms the world. Sleep is an act of fidelity and of union. I entrust myself to the great natural rhythms, to the laws, to the stability of order. My sleep is the realization of this trust, the affirmation of this faith. It is an attachment, in the affective sense of this term: I attach myself, not like Ulysses to the mast with bonds from which later I would like to free myself, but through an agreement expressed by the sensual accord of my head with the pillow, of my body with the peace and happiness of the bed. I retire from the world's immensity and its disquietude, but in order to give myself to the world, which is maintained, thanks to my "attachment," in the sure truth of a limited and firmly circumscribed place. Sleep is my absolute interest in assuring myself of the world. From this limit which sleep provides, I take hold of the world by its finite side; I grasp it firmly enough so that it stays, puts me in place, puts me to rest. To sleep badly is precisely to be unable to find one's position. The bad sleeper tosses and turns in search of that genuine place which he knows is unique. He knows that only in that spot will the world give up its errant immensity. The sleepwalker is suspect, for he is the man who does not find repose in sleep. Asleep, he is nevertheless without a place and, it may be said, without faith. He lacks fundamental sincerity, or, more precisely, his sincerity lacks a foundation. It lacks that position he seeks, which is also repose, where he would affirm himself in the stable fixity of his absence, which would be his support.

Bergson saw behind sleep the totality of conscious life minus the effort of concentration. On the contrary, sleep is intimacy with the center. I am, not dispersed, but entirely gathered together where I am, in this spot which is my position and where the world, because of the firmness of my attachment, localizes itself. Where I sleep, I fix myself and I fix the world. My person is there, prevented from erring, no longer unstable, scattered and distracted, but concentrated in the narrowness of this place where the world recollects itself, which I affirm and which affirms me. Here the place is present in me and I absent in it through an essentially ecstatic union. My person is not simply situated where I sleep; it is this very site, and my sleeping is the fact that now my abode is my being.[1]

It is true that in sleep I seem to close in upon myself, in an attitude which recalls the ignorant bliss of early childhood. This may be; and yet it is not to myself alone that I entrust myself. I do not find support in myself, but in the world which has become in me the narrowness and the limit of my repose. Sleep is not normally a moment of weakness; it is not that I despondently abandon my resolute point of view. Sleep signifies that at a certain moment, in order to act it is necessary to cease acting — that at a certain moment, lest I lose my way in aimless roving, I must stop and manfully transform the instability of myriad possibilities into a single stopping point upon which I establish and reestablish myself.

Vigilant existence does not dissipate in the sleeping body near which things remain; it withdraws from the remove which is its temptation. It returns from there to the primordial affirmation which is the authority of the body when the body is not separated but fully in agreement with the truth of place. To be surprised at finding everything still there in the morning is to forget that nothing is surer than sleep and that the meaning of sleep lies precisely in its being vigilant existence concentrating upon certitude, linking up all errant possibilities to the fixity of a principle and satiating itself with this certitude, so that the morning's newness can welcome it and a new day can begin.

The Dream

Night, the essence of night, does not let us sleep. In the night no refuge is to be found in sleep. And if you fail sleep, exhaustion finally sickens you, and this sickness prevents sleeping; it is expressed by insomnia,

[1]This is strongly expressed by Emmanuel Levinas (*From Existence to Existences*).

by the impossibility of making sleep a free zone, a clear and true resolution. In the night one cannot sleep.

One does not proceed from day to night. Whoever follows this route finds only sleep — sleep which ends the day but in order to make the next day possible; sleep which is the downward bending that verifies the rising curve; sleep which is, granted, a lack, a silence, but one imbued with intentions and through which duties, goals, and real action speak for us. In this sense the dream is closer than sleep to the nocturnal region. If day survives itself in the night, if it exceeds its term, if it becomes that which cannot be interrupted, then already it is no longer the day. It is the uninterrupted and the incessant. Notwithstanding events that seem to belong to time, and even though it is peopled with beings that seem to be those of the world, this interminable "day" is the approach of time's absence, the threat of the outside where the world lacks.

The dream is the reawakening of the interminable. It is an allusion at least, and something like a dangerous call — through the persistence of what cannot finish — to the neutrality that presses up behind the beginning. Hence the fact that the dream seems to bring up in each of us the being of earliest times — and not only the child, but still further back, the most remote, the mythic, the emptiness and vagueness of the anterior. He who dreams sleeps, but already he who dreams is he who sleeps no longer. He is not another, some other person, but the premonition of the other, of that which cannot say "I" any more, which recognizes itself neither in itself nor in others. Doubtless the force of vigilant existence and the fidelity of sleep, and still more the interpretation that gives meaning to a semblance of meaning, safeguard the outlines and forms of a personal reality: that which becomes other is reincarnated in another, the double is still somebody. The dreamer believes he knows that he is dreaming and that he is asleep, precisely at the moment when the schism between the two is effected. He dreams that he is dreaming. And this flight from the dream which plunges him back into the dream, into the dream which is an eternal fall into the same dream — this repetition whereby personal truth wanting to rescue itself loses itself more and more, and which is like the return of the same dreams or the unspeakable harassment of a reality which always escapes and which one cannot escape — all this is like *a dream of the night*, a dream where the form of the dream becomes its sole content. Perhaps one could say that the dream is all the more nocturnal in that it turns around itself, that it dreams itself, that it has for its content its possibility.

Perhaps there is no dream except of the dream. Valéry doubted the existence of dreams. The dream is like the reason for this doubt, and indeed its indubitable confirmation. The dream is that which cannot "really" be.

The dream touches the region where pure resemblance reigns. Everything there is similar; each figure is another one, is similar to another and to yet another, and this last to still another. One seeks the original model, wanting to be referred to a point of departure, an initial revelation, but there is none. The dream is the likeness that refers eternally to likeness.

Hölderlin's
Itinerary

The young Hölderlin, the author of *Hyperion*, yearns to take leave of his form, escape his limits, and be united with nature. "To be one with all that lives, and to return in blessed self-forgetfulness into the All of Nature — that is man's heaven." This aspiration to return into life's unity, into its eternal ardor, unreserved and immeasurable, seems to be the joyful movement which we are tempted to associate with inspiration. This movement is also desire for death. Diotima dies through the very impulse that makes her live in familiarity with all. But, she says, "we will part only to live more closely united, in a holier peace with all things, with ourselves."

Empedocles, in the tragedy which is the work of Hölderlin's first maturity, represents the will to burst into the world of the Invisible Ones by dying. The motifs of this unfinished work vary according to its different versions, but the wish remains the same: to be united with the fiery element, the sign and presence of inspiration, in order to attain the intimacy of the divine relation.

The great hymns no longer have the undisciplined or violent character of *Empedocles*. But the poet is still essentially the mediator. In *So on a festival day* (one of the best known of Hölderlin's hymns in France, through the various translations that have been made of it and Heidegger's commentaries), the poet stands before the god. He is as if in contact with the highest power, and thus he is exposed to the greatest danger — danger of being burned by the fire, of being destroyed by the upheaval. It is his task to tame this danger by silently, intimately welcoming it into himself so that in him glad words might be born which the sons of the earth can hear without peril. This task of mediation, to which we often attach Hölderlin's name, is perhaps never expressed so boldly by him as in this single passage.[1] The hymn probably dates from 1800, but the lines of this stanza may go back to an earlier period. In the same hymn, nature is again celebrated as the intimacy of the divine. Yet here nature is no longer the force to which one must surrender in an unrestrained movement of abandon. It "educates" the poet, but through his sleep, and in the calm time when the commotion is suspended, in the quiet that follows the storm (the fire). The hour that follows the storm: this is the favorable hour, the hour of grace and of inspiration.

"The Categorical Reversal"

And yet Hölderlin's experience, his meditation upon ancient Greece and his no less intense meditation upon European civilization, led him to conceive of an alternation in the life of peoples as well as in individual lives, between times when the gods are present and times when they are absent — periods of light, periods of darkness. At the end of the poem entitled *The Poet's Vocation*, he wrote initially:

> But when it is necessary man remains without fear
> Before God, simplicity protects him,
> And he needs neither arms nor guile
> As long as the God does not fail him.

But later, instead of the last line, he wrote, "Until God's default helps him." This is a strange revision. What does it mean?

After Hölderlin came back from his trip in the south of France — which ended with his first evident mental crisis — he lived several more years in semiretirement, writing his last hymns or fragments of hymns, the translations of *Antigone* and of *Oedipus*, and finally the theoretical considerations which comprise prefaces to these translations. It is in one of these texts that he formulates what he calls *die vaterländische Umkehr*, the native reversal: not simply a return toward the place of birth, toward the fatherland, but a movement accomplished according to what this place requires. What is this requirement? Hölderlin had answered this question a short time before his departure in a famous letter to his friend Boehlendorf in which he discreetly criticizes one of Boehlendorf's works, infused with too much enthusiasm. Hölderlin writes, "The clarity of representation is as naturally original to us as the

---

[3]And also in the poem, *Poet's Vocation*, cited below.

fire of the sky was to the Greeks." "Us" designates first the Germans, then the Hesperians, Western men. "The clarity of representation," which in the same letter he calls "lucidity or order, Junonian, Occidental measure," is the power to grasp and to define, the force of a firm ordering principle, in sum the will to distinguish well and to stay upon the earth. "The fire of the sky" is the sign of the gods, the storm, Empedocles' element. But Hölderlin adds right away that the instinct which forms and educates men has this effect: they only learn, they only really possess what is foreign to them. What is close to them is not near them. That is why the Greeks, strangers to clarity, acquired to an exceptional degree the power of sober moderation; Homer remains its finest example. That is why the Hesperians, and in particular the Germans, have become masters of the sacred pathos which was foreign to them. But now what they must learn is what is proper to them, and this is the most difficult: to learn measure, lucidity, and also how to subsist steadfastly in this world.

The kind of law Hölderlin formulates here still seems only as significant as a well defined precept advising the poets of his country—advising Hölderlin himself—not to give in unrestrainedly to the Empedoclean will, to the dizziness and the dazzling brilliance of the fire. At this point Hölderlin feels only too tempted by the sign of the gods and dangerously close to the foreign. In the same letter he says, "I will have to take care not to lose my head in France" (France represented for him the approach to the fire, the opening onto ancient Greece). Likewise he will say, when he has suffered the decisive blow, "We have almost lost our speech in a foreign land."

He goes, then, to a "foreign land," he submits to the decisive blow, he suffers it in some manner constantly, he lives under its threat, in its proximity. It is at this point that he elaborates in much grander terms upon the sort of reversal of which he had spoken to his friend.[2] Today, he says, we dwell under the law of a more authentic Zeus. This more authentic god "bends the course of nature—that course eternally hostile to man because it is directed toward the other world—back toward the earth." This formula is striking in itself and shows how far Hölderlin has moved away from Empedocles. Empedocles is the desire to go into the other world, and it is this desire which is now called inauthentic. It must be bent back toward the earth. And nature, so beloved,

[4]We refer here to Beda Allemann's study, *Hölderlin und Heidegger*, which seeks to elucidate the itinerary of the late Hölderlin.

so much sung, the educator par excellence, becomes "the eternal enemy of man" because it pulls him beyond this world.

Today's man must, then, turn back. He must turn away from the realm of the gods which is also the world of the dead — turn away from the call of the last god, Christ, who has disappeared and calls upon us to disappear. But how is this reversal possible? Is it an entirely human revolt? Is man urged to stand up against the superior forces which are hostile to him because they would turn him away from his terrestrial task? No, and it is here that Hölderlin's thought, though already veiled by madness, appears more reflective, less facile than that of humanism. If Western men are to bring about this decisive turning point, they must do so in the wake of the gods who themselves accomplish what Hölderlin calls "the categorical reversal." The gods today turn away; they are absent, unfaithful. And man must understand the sacred sense of this divine infidelity, not by opposing it, but by performing it himself. "In such a moment," Hölderlin says, " man forgets himself and forgets God; he turns back like a traitor, although in a holy manner." This reversal is a terrible act, it is treachery, but it is not impious. For through this infidelity whereby the separation of the worlds is affirmed, the purity of the gods' memory is also affirmed, in the separation, the firmly maintained distinction. Indeed, Hölderlin adds: "In order that the course of the world have no lacuna and that the memory of the Heavenly Ones not be lost, man and the god enter into communication in the form of infidelity where there is forgetting of everything. For infidelity is what can be contained the best."

These words are not easy to understand, but they become a little clearer if we bear in mind that they were written as commentary on the Oedipus tragedy. *Oedipus* is the tragedy of the god's departure. Oedipus is the hero who is constrained to live apart from the gods and from men. He must endure this double separation; he must keep this split pure, must fill it with no vain consolations. He must maintain there something like an in-between, an empty place opened by the double aversion, the double infidelity of gods and men. He must keep it pure and empty, in order that the distinction between the spheres be assured — the distinction which from now on is our task according to the rule expressed by Hölderlin when he is very close to the night: "Preserve God by the purity of what distinguishes."

The Poet and Double Infidelity

One might comment upon this idea of "reversal" from the point of view of Hölderlin and his personal destiny. It is a mysterious and moving idea. It is as if the desire formed at the time of *Hyperion* and of *Empedocles*—the desire to be united with nature and with the gods— had become an experience which entirely engages him and whose threatening excess he feels. What was formerly only a wish of the soul which he could safely express immoderately has been transformed into a real movement that exceeds him and makes him speak of an excess of favors under which he succumbs. And this excess is too intense a pressure, too strong a pull toward a world which is, not our world, but the world of divine immediacy. In the last hymns, in the fragments of hymns which have been discovered and which belong to this period (1801–1805) when the rupture has not yet occurred, the effort to master this irresistible call is ceaselessly felt—the effort to stay, to found stability and to remain on the earth. *"And as upon shoulders a burden of logs, there is much to contain. . . ." "And always toward the unlimited goes desire. But there is much to contain."*

The more Hölderlin's experience of "the fire of the sky" intensifies, the more he expresses the necessity not to surrender to it immoderately. This is in itself remarkable. But not only does he denounce the experience as dangerous; he denounces it as false, insofar at least as it claims to be immediate communication with the immediate. "The immediate," he says,

> is in a strict sense impossible for mortals and for the immortals. The god must distinguish the different worlds, in conformity with his nature, for the celestial goodness, in consideration for itself, must remain sacred, unalloyed. Man too, as the power of knowing, must distinguish the different worlds, because the opposition of contraries alone allows knowledge.

There is an energetic lucidity in this statement, an energetic affirmation of the limits of the experience to which everything must have been pressing him to surrender without restraint. This experience must not turn us toward the immediate, for not only is there the risk of perishing in the fire's blaze, but the experience cannot so turn us. The immediate is impossible.

As for inspiration, there results from the "reversal" a richer conception of it, one more foreign to simple desire. Inspiration no longer consists in receiving the sacred ray and softening it so that it not burn men. And the poet's task is no longer restricted to the overly simple mediation which required of him that he stand before God. It is before the absence of God that he must stand. He must become the guardian of this absence, losing neither it nor himself in it. What he must contain and preserve is the divine infidelity. For it is "in the form of infidelity where there is forgetting of everything" that he enters into communication with the god who turns away.

This is a task closer to the goals of man as these are known to us today. But it is more tragic than the task which promised to Empedocles and guaranteed to the Greeks union with the gods. Today the poet no longer has to stand between gods and men as their intermediary. Rather, he has to stand between the double infidelity; he must keep to the intersection of this double — this divine and human — reversal. This double and reciprocal movement opens a hiatus, a void which must henceforth constitute the essential relation of the two worlds. The poet, then, must resist the pull of the gods (notably Christ) who disappear and draw him toward them in their disappearance. He must resist pure and simple subsistence on the earth which poets do not found. He must accomplish the double reversal, take upon himself the weight of the double infidelity and thus keep the two spheres distinct, by living the separation purely, by being the pure life of the separation itself. For this empty and pure place which distinguishes between the spheres is *the sacred*, the intimacy of the breach which is the sacred.

The Mystery of the God's Departure

This requirement, the native reversal — "the extreme limit of suffering," as Hölderlin says — has, then, nothing in common with the sweet call of childhood familiarity, the desire to return to the mother which hasty erudition and certain psychiatrists attribute to Hölderlin. Still less does it signify a glorification of the earthly fatherland or of patriotic sentiment or a simple return to the duties of this world, an apology for the happy medium, prosaic sobriety, and everyday naïveté. The idea or vision of the categorical reversal, of that very demanding moment when time somehow turns back, answers to what Jean-Paul had called — and announces what later Nietzsche, louder will call — "The Death of God." Hölderlin lives this same event but with a broader understanding, more foreign to the simplifications which even Nietzsche seems to authorize. He helps us, at any rate, to reject these simplifications. And when today Georges Bataille gives to a part of his work the title *Atheological Summa*,[3] he invites us not to read these words in the tranquility of their manifest sense.

We are at a turning point. Hölderlin felt in himself the force of this reversal. The poet is he in whom time turns back essentially and for whom in this time the god always turns and turns away. But Hölderlin also conceives profoundly that this absence of the gods is not a purely negative form of relation. That is why it is terrible. It is terrible not only because it deprives us of the gods' benevolent presence, of the inspired word's familiarity — not only because it casts us back upon ourselves in the bare distress of an empty time — but because it substitutes for the measured favor of divine forms as represented by the Greeks (gods of light, gods of the initial naïveté) a relation which threatens ceaselessly to tear and disorient us, with that which is higher than the gods, with the sacred itself or with its perverted essence.

This is the mystery of the night of the gods' departure. By day, the gods have the form of day. They enlighten, they care for man, they educate him and cultivate nature in the guise of slaves. But in the nighttime the divine becomes the spirit of time turning back, carrying everything away. "Then it cares not for men, it is the spirit of unexpressed and eternally living savagery, the spirit of the realm of the dead." Hence the temptation of the inordinate, the measureless; hence the desire that drags the poet immoderately toward that which has no attachments. But hence also his greater duty to contain himself, to maintain the will to distinguish correctly in order to preserve the distinction between the spheres and thus to safeguard, pure and empty, the place of the breach which the eternal reversal of the gods and of men causes to appear and which is the pure space of the sacred, the place that is all interval, the time of intervening time. In the very late fragment *Mnemosyne*, Hölderlin says:

> They cannot do everything,
> The Heavenly Ones. Mortals touch
> the abyss. Thus with them
> Is the reversal accomplished.

The abyss is reserved for mortals. But it is not only the empty abyss; it is the savage and eternally living deep from which the gods are preserved. They preserve us from it, but they do not reach it as we do. And so it is rather in the heart of man, symbol of crystalline purity, that the truth of the reversal can be fulfilled. It is man's heart that must become the

[3] *L'Expérience intérieure.*

place where light tests itself most severely, the intimacy where the echo of the empty deep becomes speech. But this does not happen through one easy metamorphosis. As early as 1804, in the hymn *Germania*, in lines that have a splendid rigor, Hölderlin had formulated the task of poetic language, which belongs neither to the day nor to the night but always is spoken between night and day and one single time speaks the truth and leaves it unspoken:

> But if more abundantly than the pure sources
> God shines and when in heaven the color darkens,
> It is necessary that between day and night
> A truth appear once.
> In a triple metamorphosis transcribe it,
> Yet always unexpressed, and it is,
> Innocent, as it must remain.

When madness had completely obscured Hölderlin's mind, his poetry too reversed itself. All the toughness, all the concentration there had been, and the almost unbearable tension in his last hymns became repose, tranquility, and appeased power. Why? We do not know. Alleman suggests that it is as if he had been broken by the effort of resisting the impulse which dragged him away toward the boundlessness of the All—as if he had been worn out by the effort of withstanding the threat of nocturnal savagery—but as if he had also vanquished this threat, accomplished the reversal. It is as if, between day and night, the sky and the earth, there opened henceforth, pure and naïve, a region where he could see things in their transparency: the sky in its empty clarity and in this manifest void the face of God's remoteness. "Is God," he says, in one of the poems of this period, "unknown? Is he open like the sky? I rather believe so." Or: "What is God? Unknown, yet rich with particularities is the view which the sky offers of him." And when we read these words gleaming with madness: "Would I like to be a comet? Yes. For they have the speed of birds, they flourish in fire and are as children in purity," we sense how the desire to be united with the fire and with the light of day may have been realized for the poet in the purity which his exemplary rectitude assured him. And we are not surprised by this metamorphosis which, with the silent speed of a bird's flight, bears him henceforth through the sky, a flower of light, a star that burns but that unfurls innocently into a flower.